Christ the sacrament
of the encounter with God

Christ the sacrament

of the encounter with God

EDWARD SCHILLEBEECKX, O P

Sheed and Ward · London

CONTENTS

ABBREVIATIONS

AAM	*Antonianum*
AAS	*Acta Apostolicae Sedis*
BJ	*Bijdragen*
DB	Denzinger-Bannwart, *Enchiridion Symbolorum*
DTC	*Dictionnaire de théologie catholique*
FS	*Franciscan Studies*
GL	*Geist und Leben*
GM	*Gregorianum*
MC	Mansi, *Sacrorum Conciliorum Nova et Amplissima Collectio*
MST	*Medieval Studies*
NRT	*Nouvelle revue théologique*
PG	Migne, *Patrologia Graeca*
PL	Migne, *Patrologia Latina*
PO	*Patrologia Orientalis*
RTAM	*Recherches de théologie ancienne et mediévale*
SC	*Studia Catholica*
SCG	St. Thomas Aquinas, *Summa Contra Gentiles*
SH	E. Schillebeeckx, O.P., *De Sacramentele Heilseconomie*, Antwerp and Bilthoven (1952)
SK	*Scholastik*
ST	St. Thomas Aquinas, *Summa Theologiae*

FOREWORD

The author of this book, Fr. E. Schillebeeckx, O.P., was born at Antwerp in 1914, and after many years of teaching at Louvain, both in the Dominican *studium* there and in the University, is now Professor of Dogmatic Theology at the University of Nijmegen. A bibliography of his books and articles would include over a hundred items; it is hoped that some of these will be published in English translation in the near future. His chief book so far is *De sacramentele Heilseconomie*,[1] published in 1952 as Part 1 of a projected book in two parts, though it now appears that the author intends to publish in a single volume a revised version of the matter of Part 1 together with the matter originally intended for separate publication. The work here presented in English translation (it has already appeared in German and French) may be regarded as a non-technical summary of the projected single volume of *De sacramentele Heilseconomie*.

Under the conditions prevailing in the world of publishers and readers today, especially in "religious publishing," and especially in England, it is not easy to acquire a very fine sense of discrimination, of standards of theological depth and excellence. Such large claims are so frequently made for minor figures that it becomes difficult to give due credit to the authors who really deserve our respect. I shall merely say here, then, that of the many writers who have contributed to the renewal of Catholic theology in our day, Fr. Schillebeeckx and Fr. Karl Rahner, in their different ways, stand in a class by themselves.

[1] A useful account of this work may be found in Dom J. Gaillard, "Chronique de liturgie," *Revue Thomiste*, 57 (1957), pp. 510–51.

Writing of the French translation of the present work, Fr. B. D. Dupuy speaks of the way in which Fr. Schillebeeckx "rediscovers, as it were from within, the notions forged by scholastic theology, and thus restores to us a theology of the sacraments rooted in the biblical and patristic soil from which it first sprang."[2] The reader of this work, who may catch only occasional glimpses of the enormous work of detailed and creative examination of biblical, patristic and liturgical sources embodied in *De sacramentele Heilseconomie,* needs perhaps to be assured that while Fr. Schillebeeckx's summary manifestly possesses the unity of a single vision, it is not merely as a personal vision that it commends itself to the reader, but as the obedience of a trained sensibility to revelation in the Church. It is this insight into the profound intentions of scholastic theology, of what it was trying to "fix" theologically, which allows him to disclose its genetic and original sense, and indeed to modify it and enlarge its scope. For it is difficult to conceive of someone truly original in theology, as anywhere else, who lacks sympathetic insight into the originality of his predecessors.

One important way in which Fr. Schillebeeckx displays this originality which is appreciative of earlier creative endeavours is to be found in his "anthropological" insight into the sacraments. "Anthropology" in its ordinary English usage refers to those investigations which, whether they are regarded as belonging to the natural or the moral sciences, at any rate depend on field studies, usually of primitive societies. On the Continent the term is frequently used to mean in general a "doctrine of man," especially a metaphysical or phenomenological one. It is in this latter sense that the word is used here, for Fr. Schillebeeckx has found theologically fruitful the work of such writers on phenomenological anthropology as Merleau-Ponty, Buytendijk and Binswanger.[3] To say that he has found

---

[2] *Revue des sciences philosophiques et théologiques,* 47 (1963), p. 297.

[3] The English reader now has at his disposal some of the classics of phenomenology: M. Heidegger, *Being and Time;* M. Scheler, *The Nature of Sympathy* and *On the Eternal in Man;* M. Merleau-Ponty, *The Phenomenology of Perception* (and indeed Husserl's *Ideas*). The Eranos-Jahrbuch paper by F. J. J. Buytendijk (referred to by Fr. Schillebeeckx in

them theologically fruitful is not to suggest that he used them merely as a source for ready-made categories of explanation; it is rather that through these studies it is possible to enlarge our understanding of the properly human already given in our experience, and, in a theological context, to allow this enlarged understanding to be taken up into our human experience as Christians.

The point may be made by referring briefly to the word which occurs in the title of this book, "encounter." What seems to be true of all pre-phenomenological philosophy, including scholastic epistemology, is that it conceives of all knowledge on the model of our knowledge of things, physical realities. In their very different ways, philosophy in England since Wittgenstein, and phenomenology, have abandoned this model. It would be a mistake to suppose that phenomenological philosophy is always a *personalism,* simply substituting personal relationships for the knowledge of things or facts; perhaps the nearest approach to this oversimplification is to be found in the writings of Marcel. However, it is true to say that the personal existent and the structure of his existence engage philosophical interest centrally in phenomenology, so much so that "knowledge of things" is seen as derivative from a fundamental being-in-the-world. Now, "encounter" is a fundamental mode of existence of the human existent, a structural possibility inherent in it. We may treat each other as physical objects or mechanisms, but that is to choose to mistreat each other; the misuse, the deficiency, throws light on that preordained openness to our fellows which releases our being into the fellowship of a *we.* It may be noted further that our *bodily* presence to each other is essential to encounter;

his essay, "The Sacraments: an Encounter with God," in *Christianity Divided,* edited by Callahan, Obermann and O'Hanlon) is available in French, *Phénoménologie de la rencontre,* Paris (1952). The only writings of Binswanger I know of in English are to be found in the collective volume, *Existence: A New Dimension in Psychiatry and Psychology,* edited by May, Angel and Ellenberger, New York (1958). The opening sections of the book by Heidegger and Merleau-Ponty are particularly useful for what is meant by "phenomenology"; Buytendijk's study of "encounter" is obviously important for the present book.

we may smile at each other or make our faces into masks, give ourselves to each other or withhold ourselves. Again, just as there are conventions in any given culture which shape the styles of this bodily encounter, so there is a ritual idiom, continuous with the ceremonial of secular life, which shapes the styles of our liturgical encounter with God—e.g., kneeling.

However inadequate these brief remarks may be to give a fair idea of what phenomenological investigation has revealed of the structure of human encounter, it will, I hope, be plain firstly that "encounter" in Fr. Schillebeeckx's writings is not simply a "mode-word" but represents a concept which has been the subject of a good deal of careful analysis; and secondly, that its theological application would seem to be preordained in a religion where God's personal gift of himself to man has been consummated in the Incarnation, God addressing man as a man amongst men.[4]

The value of this concept in theology, then, is the generality of its scope, its power to unify. The account of the sacraments offered here is very far from those narrowly conceived treatises, whether technical or popular, where the sacraments are treated of in isolation from the rest of Christian and human experience, either as matter for specialists or as the object of a purely liturgical enthusiasm. Once the Christian religion is seen as an encounter of God and man in Christ the "primordial sacrament," the sacraments themselves can be seen as inseparable from a whole economy of revelation in word and reality, a revelation of God in Trinity, of Incarnation, grace, the Church and indeed of man and his destiny, for it is within this economy of sacramental encounter that we as men achieve the fullness of our personal being. In fact, what is

---

[4] Fr. Schillebeeckx himself, acknowledging that "encounter" has become a *modewoord*, an "existential slogan," goes on to point out that it is simply a modern word for a reality always recognized in religious life: "the *theological*, personal relationship to God in virtue of grace"—"De zin van het mens-zijn van Jesus, de Christus," *Tijdschrift voor Theologie*, 2 (1962), p. 128. This is a good example of his re-creation of the *original* sense of a scholastic theological concept ("theologal"; see chapter 1, note 14) by way of a grasp of the reality it was intended to "fix," the grasp itself trained by exercise in non-scholastic, phenomenological analysis.

offered here is not simply an account of the sacraments but of the Christian religion, the *religio Christianae vitae* in St. Thomas's fine phrase, and through it of non-Christian religion and life. Once again the reader must be warned not to be misled by the condensed expression of Fr. Schillebeeckx's views in this book. Many of the topics briefly raised here have been dealt with at length elsewhere, in *De sacramentele Heilseconomie* and in substantial articles.

There is one last point I should like to make about this book, and indeed about all Fr. Schillebeeckx's writings, though it is not easy to do so without embarrassing the author. Professional theologians, like all other professionals, tend to lose contact with the living realities with which they are concerned; the mystery tends to disappear behind the problem to which it gave birth. This is not a reproach which can be made against the author of this book. There is manifest throughout a pressure and an urgency which only come from living contact with the mystery of Christ, and explain in part some of the density of the author's language. Theologians ought to bear inscribed on their hearts the wonderful words of St. Augustine:

> And what shall we say, O my God, my life, my holy, dear delight, or what can any man say when he speaketh of thee? And woe be to them that are silent in thy praise, when even they who speak most thereof may be accounted to be but dumb. (*Confessions,* 1, 4.)

The present translation has been made from the third, revised edition of *Christus, Sacrament van de Godsontmoeting* (earlier editions bore the title *De Christusontmoeting als Sacrament van de Godsontmoeting*), with some modifications and additions made by the author. While the basic work of translation was done by Fr. Paul Barrett, O.P., the English text was revised by Fr. Mark Schoof, O.P. (Fr. Schillebeeckx's assistant) and by Fr. Laurence Bright, O.P. The publishers, both Dutch and English, should be publicly thanked for the exemplary patience they have shown throughout the long process of successive revisions.

CORNELIUS ERNST, O.P.

Christ the Sacrament
of the Encounter
with God

INTRODUCTION
PERSONAL ENCOUNTER WITH GOD

One cannot help remarking that the theology of the manuals does not always make a careful distinction between that unique manner of existence which is peculiar to man, and the mode of being, mere objective "being there," which is proper to the things of nature. The absence of this distinction, particularly in treating of grace or of the sacraments, occasionally obscures the simple fact of encounter with God. The intimateness of God's personal approach to man is often lost in a too severely objective examination of that which forms the living core and centre of religion, the personal communion with the God who gives himself to men.

In the study of the sacraments, the consequence of this tendency towards a purely impersonal, almost mechanical approach was that they were considered chiefly in terms of physical categories. The inclination was to look upon the sacraments as but one more application, although in a special manner, of the general laws of cause and effect. Inevitably, the result of this view was that we appeared to be merely passive recipients of sacramental grace, which seemed to be "put into us" automatically. We do not, however, want to divert ourselves with the defects of the theological works of the last two centuries, but positively and constructively to take up the study of the Church's sacraments, with the concept of human, personal encounter as the basis of our consideration.

Religion is above all a saving dialogue between man and the living God. Although man can reach God through creation, he cannot, through his creaturely powers alone, establish any immediate and personal contact with God. The simple reason for this is that by means of his natural faculties alone (and these faculties are no fiction), man reaches God only in and through creation, actually as something belonging to creation; that is to say, as the absolute principle of its being. In our human way, then, we reach God, but not as a *person* in and for himself. But since we nonetheless affirm, although by way of creation, that God is a personal absolute in whom is found the reason for our existence, and therefore that he is the being who gives ultimate meaning to our lives, we are able—and this is the supreme possibility of our life in this world—to *desire* a personal relationship with God. However, on account of the fact that of ourselves we are able to reach God only by way of creatures, this desire is by its nature powerless; it is essentially a nostalgia for religion or for a personal relationship with God. Left to ourselves, we cannot really bring this desire to fulfilment. Depending on our own efforts, we find ourselves returning continually to our point of departure; to the world in which we live, and its principle. Religion is beyond all our human capabilities. Only by grace, and not in virtue of our own merits, can we truly serve God as person to person. Personal communion with God is possible only in and through God's own generous initiative in coming to meet us in grace.

But this means that religion is therefore essentially a personal relation of man to God, of person to person; a personal encounter or a personal communing with God. It is precisely in this that the essential condition for a life truly centred on God consists. It is because God lovingly takes the initiative and comes down to meet man in grace that man lives in a condition of active and immediate communication with the one who, in this relationship, becomes the "living God." The act itself of this encounter of God and man, which on earth can take place only in faith, is what we call salvation. On God's part this encounter involves a disclosure of himself by revelation, and on the part of man it involves devotion to God's service—that is religion. This encounter itself, seen from man's side, is the reality of what is called sanctifying grace,[1] which in consequence cannot be separated in our understanding from either God's personal love for man or from man's response to this divine advance.[2] Where philosophy speaks of a divine presence which is the enduring creative act of God maintaining man in being, and which is therefore fully real only in man's awareness of his own creatureliness,[3] Scripture speaks, much more profoundly, of the "indwelling of God." "Indwelling" refers to the familiar living together of God the three persons and man. It is only on this level that we can speak of a personal communion between God and man. Only in grace does God's presence in man blossom forth into an intimate and living communion.

Revelation and religion, i.e., man's created and time-circumscribed encounter with the uncreated God, of their nature "create history"; they impinge upon the course of history as evident facts belonging to history itself. For God through his revelation personally intervenes on behalf of mankind, not merely as the Creator who guides history in creative transcendence, but as someone who himself takes part in the unfolding play of history and comes to take his place at our side. Because grace is a personal encounter with God, it "makes history," and precisely for this reason it is also "sacramental." For every supernatural reality which is realized historically in our lives is sacramental. That which God intends for man, he brings about in the course of human history, and this he does in such a fashion that his saving acts become visible precisely

[1] With all the consequences which this involves for man, who being a creature is unable of himself to encounter God as God, and so only in this encounter begins to live in virtue of a new inner vitality ("created grace") which cannot be explained in merely human terms.

[2] In the fullest sense of the word, this is true only of grace as it concerns adults. We shall later have occasion to deal expressly with the case of those who have not yet reached the age of reason. In any event one would not construct a treatise on grace based on infancy as the normal human state.

[3] This awareness of being a creature, with all its consequences, could be termed "religion," but in a wide analogical sense. (Cf. "Godsdienst en Sacrament," in SC, 34 [1959], pp. 267–83.)

as divine. God's saving activity "makes history" by revealing itself, and it reveals itself by becoming history.

In this book we are directing our attention to sacramentality in religion in order to arrive eventually at the insight that the sacraments are the properly human mode of encounter with God.

1

CHRIST, SACRAMENT OF GOD

1. HUMANITY IN SEARCH OF THE SACRAMENT OF GOD

St. Augustine explains in a masterly manner how that service of
God which we know and practise in the Church is as old as the
world. He has divided the gradual coming into being of the Church
in the course of human history into three great phases: the
"Church" of the devout heathen; the pre-Christian phase of the
Christian Church in the form of the chosen race of Israel; and finally the emergence of the mature Church, the "Church of the first-
born." (Heb. 12.23.) This development already gives us a first
insight into the meaning of a sacramentality of the Church.

1. Sacrament in Pagan Religion

In a nebulous but nonetheless discernible fashion the sacramental Church is already present in the life of the whole of mankind.[1] All humanity receives that inward word of God calling men
to a communion in grace with himself. This obscure call causes
those among the heathen who listen to it in uprightness of heart
dimly to suspect that there is a redeeming God who is occupying
himself personally with their salvation. Such an inward religious
experience produced by grace does not yet encounter the visible
embodiment of that grace, the fact of which remains unknown, hidden in the depths of the human heart.

Nevertheless, life in this created world gains a new and deeper

[1] St. Augustine: see *PL*, 44, cols. 161, 315 and 974; *PL*, 43, cols. 609–10.

meaning when man lives in the world as one who has received this call from God in his inmost being. The world of creation then becomes an actual part of the inner yet still anonymous dialogue with God. If the God who wants to enter into a bond of personal relationship with us is the creator of heaven and earth, it implies that our being confronted with the world, existence in this world, is going to teach us more about the living God than the world alone can teach us, more than merely that God is the creator of all things. Life itself in the world then belongs to the very content of God's inner word to us. It interprets dimly at least something of that which God personally, by the attraction of his grace, is whispering in our hearts. However vaguely, life itself becomes a truly supernatural and external revelation, in which creation begins to speak to us the language of salvation, in which creation becomes a sign of higher realities. The course of nature, human life in the world and with the world, tells us more because of God speaking within us than ever it could of itself. All is seen to have an extraordinary, indeed a personal, purpose; a purpose which lies beyond the possibilities of nature and of earthly life. Thus in paganism, too, the inward grace achieves a certain visible manifestation.

Heathen religion itself was striving to give outward shape to its inner expectations.[2] Man cannot sever himself from God, because

[2] In this connection St. Thomas, in keeping with a long-standing tradition, speaks of the "sacraments of nature," in which he recognizes a truly supernatural element. The author refers the reader to *SH*, Antwerp-Bilthoven (1952), 1, pp. 52–9, where the positive data for a satisfactory study of this question are gathered and analysed. The basic premise of the argument is that the present universal order of human existence is a supernatural order: man is created for Christ (εἰς αὐτον, cf. Col. 1.16); no fully human personal moral orientation is possible without immediately being implicitly an orientation for or against the *Deus Salutaris*. A religion founded purely on philosophical insight, "natural religion" based on that which the unaided human spirit can achieve of itself, is a fiction, metaphysically impossible in fact, because the *eidos* of religion, as phenomenologically established in the analysis of the universally human fact of religion, necessarily implies personal relations between God and man, and these clearly cannot be achieved by the created powers of man alone. In the concrete all religion presupposes an at least anonymous supernatural revelation and faith. There is thus, anterior

God will not let him go. As an outcome of the quest for some manner of expressing the deeply hidden but authentic religious urge, there has arisen among pagan peoples a motley collection of religious forms and aspirations which in its queries and in its beliefs, and through all its diversity, can still be traced back to a few particular fundamental religious motives. It is not easy for the human mind correctly to disentangle these motives, to tell what is genuine in all this, and what on the other hand is false. Precisely because they did not have the support of a special, a visible divine revelation, they became a mixture of true devotedness to God, of elements of an all-too-fallible humanity, of dogmatic distortion, moral confusion and finally even of diabolical influence; yet in all of this there was a spark of real holiness which now and again managed to shine forth. Only in their fulfilment in the Old Testament, and eventually in the New, does it become clear to us that God was showing us his active concern for the heathen too. His revelation has enabled us to appreciate the motives behind the pagan reaction to his concern: Man exists in an I-Thou relationship, in a situation of dialogue with God. Man had lost his living contact with God, the attitude of child to father, and of himself he could not regain it. Life in this world made this quite clear to him. But it is only in its

---

to any Judaeo-Christian religion, an *instinctus divinus* arising from the deepest foundations of human religious psychology as influenced by the attraction of divine grace. Thus it is that the development of rites or of "sacramentality," as an expression of, and a field of experience for, the fundamental human need to approach God, can at the same time and in the measure of the authenticity of the religious experience underlying it, be the manifestation of an anonymous but nonetheless effective operation of grace. Hence the "sacraments of nature": "Sacramenta legis naturae . . . ex voto celebrabatur quod unicuique dictabat sua mens, ut fidem suam aliis exteriori signo profiteretur ad honorem Dei, secundum quod habitus caritatis inclinabat ad exteriores actus." (St. Thomas, *In IV Sent.*, d.1, q.2, a.6, sol.3.) The same principle explains the ready assimilability of not a few of the symbols of the "nature religions" into the rites and sacraments of the Church. As foreshadowing of the Christian mystery of worship, the nature sacraments and the Jewish sacraments are the indicated source from which Christ and his Church were to draw, not the essentials indeed of the Christian sacraments, but the natural forms and rites in which they are embodied. (Tr.)

visible fulfilment, first in the holy ones of Israel, and then definitively in the man Jesus, that we see the substance of truth which
lay hidden in the tortuous myths of heathen religion. For that
which was given distorted shape in these myths—projections of
human experience in which grace was nevertheless obscurely active
—at the same time faintly foreshadowed what was to come. It was
in the visible form of something tangibly holy (Israel and Christ)
that it received its true shape. Pagan religious society, frequently
revitalized by great religious leaders, which supported the heathen
in his religious life and upon which that life was nourished, was the
first providential sketch of the true Church of Christ which was
to come. Thus this "Church," as the visible presence of grace, is a
world-wide reality. More than this: as even the Fathers suggested,
it is a fragment of unconscious Christianity.[3] For every grace in the
order in which we live is a grace that comes from the one mediator,
Christ Jesus. In general we can therefore say that there is no religion if there is no Church. Grace never comes just interiorly; it
confronts us in visible shape as well. To separate religion from
Church is ultimately to destroy the life of religion. If one is to serve
God, to be religious, one must also live by Church and sacrament.

2. *Israel as Sacrament of God*

It is seen from the foregoing that in the life of all mankind
open to the inward call of salvation, God caused that to be foreshadowed which he was to bring to fulfilment in Israel and later in
Christ. But grace, in the visible manifestation of its presence in the
pagan world, remained strictly anonymous (this is equally true
today concerning such religion as is to be found in "modern
pagans"). The clear shape of this life-giving grace became explicit
only in special divine revelation, and this occurred first of all in
Israel.

A group of Bedouin of various ethnological origins, whose fore-

[3] This is the reason why St. Thomas says that in the "sacraments of
nature" there is even a concealed indication of Christ himself. (*ST*, I–II,
q.103, a.1.)

fathers had been enticed into the region by the fertile abundance of the Nile Delta, wearied beyond endurance by the forced labour which Egypt imposed, formed themselves into the caravans of the Exodus. Out of the different clans thrown together in this way, each of which seems to have had its own religion, there grew one people which united itself in the desert under the name of the God Yahweh who had appeared to Moses. This was the birth of Israel, the people of God. As the Bible sets it forth, the account of God's appearing to Moses is evidently intended to show that this people had become a unity through the personal intervention of Yahweh the living God. When Israel had taken possession of their new land Canaan, prepared by God for the new nation, Joshua reminded the people of the strange god they had served "beyond the river [referring to Abraham in Mesopotamia] and in Egypt."[4] Yahweh alone made the nation to be what it was. In blunt but moving terms the prophet Ezekiel describes the metamorphosis of a crowd of nomad Bedouin into the Church of God: "Thus saith the Lord God to Jerusalem: Thy root and thy nativity is of the land of Canaan. Thy father was an Amorrhite and thy mother a Cethite [which is to say, they were heathen]. And when thou wast born, in the day of thy nativity thy navel was not cut, neither wast thou washed with water for thy health nor salted with salt [an ancient method of purification and disinfecting], nor swaddled with cloths. No eye had pity on thee to do any of these things for thee, out of compassion to thee; but thou wast cast out upon the face of the earth in the abjection of thy soul [i.e., because you were found worthless], in the day that thou wast born. And passing by thee I [Yahweh] saw that thou wast trodden under foot in thy own blood. And I said to thee when thou wast in thy blood: Live . . . And I washed thee with water and cleansed away thy blood from thee, and I anointed thee with oil . . . And I clothed thee with fine garments. And thou wast adorned . . . and advanced to be a queen."[5] Israel, the first phase of the Church, is the fruit of God's merciful intervention, a foreshadowing of that which St. Paul would

---

[4] Joshua 24.14. See also Judith 5.7; Exod. 20.6–9.
[5] Ezek. 16.3–13.

say of the Church of Christ: ". . . Christ loved the Church, and delivered himself up for it, that he might sanctify it, cleansing it by the laver of water . . . that he might present it to himself, a glorious Church, not having spot or wrinkle or any such thing, but that it should be holy and without blemish."[6] Israel's visible religion, its faithful people, its cult, sacraments, sacrifices and priesthood, was the first phase of the great Church.[7]

This Church was already a visible presence of grace, a sign of saving grace which at the same time bestowed grace, not on account of a kind of anticipated effect of the mystery of Christ yet to come (such an anticipation is not easy to understand), but rather because Israel itself was already a partial realization of the mystery of Christ, it was the "Christ-event" in process of coming to be. The Church of the Old Testament was a sign and cause of grace insofar as in it the Christian age had really begun. Since it was as yet an incomplete presence of the mystery of Christ, the Church in Israel could not bestow the fullness of grace, but only the grace of a perfectly open readiness for the awaited Messiah; a saving Advent-grace of messianic expectation, a religion of the "God who is to come."[8] The quintessence of divine revelation in the Old Testament is expressed in various places thus: "I will be your God, and you will be my people."[9] For Israel's good, God would remain faithful to the Covenant, together with and at times even in opposition to Israel. But Israel in its turn had to keep faith with the Covenant; it had to live as God's true people. Such is the commission of the Church.

The whole of the Old Testament revelation is simply the historical process arising out of God's fidelity and the often repeated infidelity of the Jewish people. In the development of this situation,

[6] Ephes. 5.25–7.

[7] St. Augustine: see *PL,* 44, cols. 973–4; *PL,* 33, col. 281; 523 and 845–6; *PL,* 42, col. 356.

[8] It is in this light that we are to understand the teaching of the Council of Florence, that the Jewish sacraments did not confer grace. (*DB,* 695.)

[9] Exod. 6.7; Lev. 26.12; Deut. 26.17–18:29.12–13; Jer. 7.23:11.4:24.7:-31.33, Ezek. 11.20:14.11:37.27; Osee 1.9.

revelation was gradually perfected. God's ultimate purpose was to call a faithful people into life. Broadly speaking, there would be continual failure, until God himself raised up a man in whom was concentrated the entirety of mankind's vocation to faithfulness, and who would himself keep faith with the Covenant in the perfection of his fidelity. This man was Jesus. In him there was a visible realization of both sides of faith in the Covenant. In the dialogue between God and man, so often breaking down, there was found at last a perfect human respondent; in the same person there was achieved the perfection both of the divine invitation and of the human response in faith from the man who by his resurrection is the Christ. The Covenant, sealed in his blood, found definitive success in his person. In him grace became fully visible; he is the embodiment of the grace of final victory, who appeared in person to the Apostles. Christ himself is the Church, an invisible communion in grace with the living God (the Son made man with the Father) manifested in visible human form. For this is what he is as the "first-born" and Head of all creation. Consequently the whole of humanity is already, in its Head, "assembled" into communion with God (in Hebrew "Church" is *qahel,* the great assembly).

We have first to analyse this visible presence of grace which Christ is personally, in order to work from it towards an insight into the sacramentality of the Church.

2. CHRIST THE PRIMORDIAL SACRAMENT

1. *Encounter with the Earthly Christ as Sacrament of the Encounter with God*

The dogmatic definition of Chalcedon, according to which Christ is "one person in two natures," implies that one and the same person, the Son of God, also took on a visible human form. Even in his humanity Christ is the Son of God. The second person of the most holy Trinity is personally man; and this man is personally God.[10] Therefore Christ is God in a human way, and man in a divine way. As a man he acts out his divine life in and according to his human existence. Everything he does as man is an act of the Son of God, a divine act in human form; an interpretation and transposition of a divine activity into a human activity. His human love is the human embodiment of the redeeming love of God.

The humanity of Jesus is concretely intended by God as the fulfilment of his promise of salvation; it is a messianic reality. This messianic and redemptive purpose of the incarnation implies that the encounter between Jesus and his contemporaries was always on his part an offering of grace in a human form. For the love of the man Jesus is the human incarnation of the redeeming love of God: an advent of God's love in visible form. Precisely because these human deeds of Jesus are divine deeds, personal acts of the Son of God, divine acts in visible human form, they possess of their nature a divine saving power, and consequently they bring salvation; they are "the cause of grace." Although this is true of every specifically human act of Christ[11] it is nevertheless especially true of those actions which, though enacted in human form, are according to their nature exclusively acts of God: the miracles and the redemption. Considered against the background of the whole earthly life of Jesus, this truth is realized in a most particular way in the great mysteries of his life: his passion, death, resurrection and exaltation to the side of the Father.[12]

[10] St. Thomas expresses himself strongly. "Ipsum Verbum . . . personaliter . . . est homo"—the Word himself is personally man—(*De Unione Verbi Incarnati*, q.un., a. 1); and more strongly yet: "In quo [Christo] humana natura assumpta est ad hoc quod sit persona filii Dei"—in whom (Christ) human nature was assumed in order that it might be the person of the Son of God. (*ST*, III, q. 2, a. 10.) Unjustifiably, the Leonine edition "corrects" the manuscripts, which all, with one exception, have *persona* and not *personae* as the Leonine would have it. This latter weakens the text, where St. Thomas wishes to say that the humanity of Jesus is in reality a manner of being of God the Son himself.

[11] See, for example, St. Thomas, *ST*, III, q.48, a.6; q.8, a.1, ad 1; q. 78, a. 4. Here St. Thomas is relying above all on Greek patrology.

[12] Cf. *ST*, III, q. 48, a.6; q. 50, a. 6; q. 56, a. 1 ad 3; q.57, a. 6, ad 1.

That is not all. Because the saving acts of the man Jesus are performed by a divine person, they have a divine power to save, but because this divine power to save appears to us in visible form, the saving activity of Jesus is *sacramental*. For a sacrament is a divine bestowal of salvation in an outwardly perceptible form which makes the bestowal manifest; a bestowal of salvation in historical visibility. The Son of God really did become true man—become, that is to say, a human spirit which through its own proper bodiliness dwelt visibly in our world. The incarnation of the divine life therefore involves bodily aspects. Together with this we must remember that every human exchange, or the intercourse of men one with another, proceeds in and through man's bodiliness. When a man exerts spiritual influence on another, encounters through the body are necessarily involved. The inward man manifests itself as a reality that is in this world through the body. It is in his body and through his body that man is open to the "outside," and that he makes himself present to his fellow men. Human encounter proceeds through the visible obviousness of the body, which is a sign that reveals and at the same time veils the human interiority.

Consequently if the human love and all the human acts of Jesus possess a divine saving power, then the realization in human shape of this saving power necessarily includes as one of its aspects the manifestation of salvation: includes, in other words, sacramentality. The man Jesus, as the personal visible realization of the divine grace of redemption, is *the* sacrament, the primordial sacrament, because this man, the Son of God himself, is intended by the Father to be in his humanity the only way to the actuality of redemption. "For there is one God, and one mediator of God and men, the man Christ Jesus."[13] Personally to be approached by the man Jesus was, for his contemporaries, an invitation to a personal encounter with the life-giving God, because personally that man was the Son of God. Human encounter with Jesus is therefore the sacrament of the encounter with God, or of the religious life as a theologal atti-

[13] 1 Tim. 2.5.

tude of existence towards God.[14] Jesus' human redeeming acts are therefore a "sign and cause of grace."[15] "Sign" and "cause" of salvation are not brought together here as two elements fortuitously conjoined. Human bodiliness is human interiority itself in visible form.

Now because the inward power of Jesus' will to redeem and of

[14] By "theologal attitude of existence" we mean a vital human activity of which God himself is the object and the motive, and in the perfecting of which God is coactive: namely, the life of grace in faith, hope and love, the only virtues which of their nature bring about a personal relationship with God.

(Need we make an apology for resurrecting the word "theologal" in this work? Current today in its Dutch, French and German equivalents, and indicating existential God-centredness as distinct from the abstract-analytic nuance of "theological," it was employed in this same sense in English in the sixteenth and seventeenth centuries, but has since fallen into disuse. Cf. the *Oxford English Dictionary.* Tr.)

[15] In *SH* (see pp. 158–60) the author remarks that "efficiunt quod significant," as a synthetic formulation of the determinable and the mysterious aspects of the seven sacraments, is primarily and fundamentally true of the "mysteria carnis Christi" which are pre-eminently the "signum efficax gratiae." St. Thomas, following a universal patristic tradition, emphasizes this point, both implicitly and explicitly. He stresses it implicitly in that, like the Latin Fathers, translations of the Scriptures, and the earlier scholastics, St. Thomas uses *sacramentum* and *mysterium* as synonymous and interchangeable terms. Compare, for example, *III Sent.,* d. 25, q. 2, a. 2, sol. 1, ad 5—"Mysterium redemptionis"—with *III Sent.,* sol. 2, "sacramentum redemptionis"; or *ST,* III, prologue: ". . . de ipso Incarnationis *mysterio*" with *ST,* q. 30, a. 1: ". . . testis huius [i.e., Incarnationis] *sacramenti.*" The emphasis is explicit in that St. Thomas nevertheless prefers the term *mysterium* for the *significatum,* the *res sacra,* and makes *sacramentum* a technical term for the Church's ritual (significant and effective) action: "In hoc *sacramento,* totum *mysterium* nostrae salutis comprehenditur." (*ST,* III, q. 83, a. 4 etc.). But in spite of this differentiation of the terms, it is precisely in the "mysterium gratiae," in the "res sacra," that St. Thomas sees the prime analogate of the term "sacrament": only in virtue of its significative and causal relation to the "res sacra" can the representative ritual action be called a sacrament in the Christian sense. Thus Christian sacramentality in its full sense is predicated primarily of the "mysteria carnis Christi," which are thus the primordial sacraments, the fundamental *causes* and *signs* of salvation. "Caro eius et mysteria in ea perpetrata operantur instrumentaliter [cause] . . . et per quandam exemplaritatem [sign]." (*ST,* q. 62, a. 5, ad 1. Cf. also the *corpus articuli,* and q. 56, a. 1, ad 3.) (Tr.)

his human love is God's own saving power realized in human form, the human saving acts of Jesus are the divine bestowal of grace itself realized in visible form; that is to say they cause what they signify[16]; they are sacraments.

2. The Actions of Jesus' Life as Manifestations of Divine Love for Man and Human Love for God: Bestowal of Grace and Religious Worship

"As the Father has sent me, I also send you. When he had said this, he breathed on them and he said to them: Receive the Holy Spirit; whose sins you shall forgive, they are forgiven them."[17] Thus it is as a revelation of God's merciful redeeming love that we are to understand the sending of the Son on earth. By the incarnation of the Son God intended to divinize man by redeeming him; by being saved from sin man is brought into a personal communion of grace and love with God. This implies two things. First, the fullness of grace which properly belongs to the man Jesus in virtue of his existence as God was intended by God to be a source of grace for others; from him all were to receive. Christ's love for man thus manifests God's love for men by actually bestowing it; it is the redeeming mercy of God himself coming to meet us from a human heart. But as well as this movement down from above, coming to us from God's love by way of Jesus' human heart, there is in the man Jesus also a movement up from below, from the human heart of Jesus, the Son, to the Father.

The human actions of Jesus' life as they come from above show us their character as acts of redemption of his fellow men; these acts, in the mode of a human love, are the merciful redeeming love of God himself. As coming from below they show their character

[16] We shall have occasion later to make a closer analysis of this relationship between sign and power to save.
[17] John 20.21–3.

as acts of worship; these acts are a true adoration and acknowledge-ment of God's divine existence; they are a service of praise or cult, religion, prayer—in a word, they are the man Jesus' love of God. Thus Jesus is not only the revelation of the redeeming God; he is also the supreme worshipper of the Father, the supreme realization of all religion. Jesus became the Redeemer in actual fact by freely living his human life in religious worship of and attachment to the Father. In Christ not only were God and his love for men revealed, but God also showed us in him what it is for a man to commit him-self unconditionally to God the invisible Father. In this way God revealed to us the embodiment of religion, the countenance of a truly religious man. The living and personal relation of Jesus to the Father reveals to us what is meant by the majesty and mercy of God. In and through the religious service of Jesus, God has re-vealed himself.

If we now consider that this humanity of Jesus represents us all, then it also becomes clear that the movement up from below is a movement to the Father ascending, by way of Jesus' humanity, from the whole of mankind. Therefore Jesus is not only the offer of divine love to man made visible but, at the same time, as prototype (or primordial model) he is the supreme realization of the response of human love to this divine offer: "in our place" and "in the name of us all," as Scripture repeatedly says. Whatever Christ does as a free man is not only a realization in human form of God's activity for our salvation; it is also at the same time the positive human acceptance, representative for all of us, of this redeeming offer from God. The man Jesus is personally a dialogue with God the Father; the supreme realization and therefore the norm and the source of every encounter with God. As a reality religion can only be under-stood in the context of the incarnation of God the Son. For since redeemed existence means that through the intervention of God mankind itself is once more turned towards God in close com-munion of life with him, then the whole of mankind is already truly redeemed objectively in the man Jesus, as in its Head.

The foundation of all this is the incarnation. But this incarnation of God the Son is a reality which grows. It is not complete in a matter of a moment; for example, at Jesus' conception in Mary's womb or at his birth. The incarnation is not merely a Christmas event. To be man is a process of becoming man; Jesus' manhood grew throughout his earthly life, finding its completion in the supreme moment of the incarnation, his death, resurrection and exaltation. Only then is the incarnation fulfilled to the very end. And so we must say that the incarnation in the Son itself redeems us. This mystery of Christ or of redemption we can call, in its totality, a mystery of saving worship; a mystery of praise (the upward movement) and of salvation (the downward movement).

This ascending and descending dynamism pervades the whole human life of Jesus. For although Jesus in his earthly life was always the humiliated "Servant of God," he remained even in his humiliation the Son of God, the grace-abounding revelation of God.[18] And although in his glorification Christ can bestow grace in full measure, there too he remains a man who, in religious and filial[19] service, adores and honours the Father from whom he must receive all. Nonetheless we can trace a development in the course of the saving history of the mystery of Christ. By the fact that he became man, the Son of God is fundamentally already the Christ. But we must also realize that it was only upon his rising from the dead that, because of the love and obedience of his life, the Father *established* him absolutely as the Christ. We must look closely into this growth towards the fullness of redemption, for in it we are confronted with the mystery of Christ's life, which is this: The man Jesus, as "Servant of God," by his life of obedience and love on earth, even unto death, earned for us that grace of salvation which he, in glory with the Father, can himself as Lord and Christ, bestow

[18] Therefore St. Thomas says repeatedly: ". . . thus by the power of his divinity his [Jesus'] actions bring salvation for us, seeing that they cause grace in us, both by merit and by a certain efficient causality." (*ST*, III, q. 8, a. 1, ad 2.)

[19] There is no exact English translation of the word *Kinderlijk*, which for this author sums up what he has said of Christ's relation to his Father in his risen humanity, with all this implies. (Tr.)

upon us in abundance. This saving reality calls for the closest consideration, for in it we find the key to the sense of the sacramentality of the Church in its relation to the *Kyrios,* the risen and glorified Lord, and so also to the Holy Spirit.

3. Jesus' Humiliation in the Service of God and His Heavenly Exaltation: The Redemptive Mystery of Christ

"It was God who reconciled us to himself in Christ."[20] This must underlie every consideration of our redemption. The living God himself, Father, Son and Holy Ghost, is our redeemer. But he brought about the redemption in the human nature of the second person, the Son of God, who in union with the Father and together with him is the source of the life of the Holy Spirit. It is this in its human embodiment—from Jesus' conception in Mary's womb, in and beyond his death, to his "establishment in power" as the risen Christ—which constitutes his redemptive mystery. We can distinguish four phases in this redemption:

First: The initiative of the Father through the Son in the Holy Spirit. This initiative is the trinitarian background within the Godhead which, though veiled, can be discerned through the temporal order of salvation in the incarnate Son, "who through the eternal Spirit offered himself without blemish to the Father."[21]

Second: The human response of Christ's life to the Father's initiative in sending him: ". . . becoming obedient unto death, even to the death of the cross"[22]—in other words, the religious obedience of the "Holy One of Yahweh" or of the "Servant of God."

Third: The divine response to Jesus' obedience in the humiliation of his life. "For which cause also God [i.e., the Father] has exalted him exceedingly, and given him a name which is above all names,"[23] that is, given him might above all powers: Jesus has be-

[20] Cf. 2 Cor. 5.18. [21] Heb. 9.14.
[22] Phil. 2.8. [23] Phil. 2.9

come the Lord, the *Kyrios,* meaning "the Mighty," he who exercises lordship—"God has made him *Kyrios.*"[24]

Fourth: The sending of the Holy Spirit upon the world of men by the glorified *Kyrios* or Lord. Christ, "having reached the consummation [only now] became . . . the source of eternal salvation" for us.[25] The force of the redemption came fully into operation only when Jesus was exalted at God's right hand. "And I, when I am lifted up . . . will draw all things to myself."[26] The last phase of the mystery of Christ, between the ascension and the *parousia,* is therefore the mystery of the sending of the Holy Spirit by Christ as the climax of his work of salvation.

We must consider the whole of this in detail. First of all we shall enquire what Scripture teaches about the Passover, the Ascension, and Pentecost, as a foundation for our further analysis.

(a) *Passover, Ascension and Pentecost*

At the Last Supper, Christ clearly gave his death the significance of a sacrifice of himself to God for all.[27] This gift of himself to God was essentially an act of love. But this was realized and embodied in the death he suffered at the hands of sinful humanity. He offered himself sacrificially for us to the Father, and the particular way in which this came to completion was by his laying down his life. The words of interpretation which Scripture uses in connection with the bread and wine show us Christ's approaching death as a true sacrifice of reconciliation that reinstates the covenant with God. The body of Christ, the "Servant of God," is given in a death of vicarious reconciliation. "The blood of Christ" is a theme that is truly central in the primitive Church, as Scripture shows it to us. This death sanctifies mankind, reconciles, establishes peace, redeems,

[24] Acts 2.36. [25] Heb. 5.9
[26] John 12.32. This gospel sees the exaltation on the Cross in the perspective of the exaltation of Jesus at the right of the Father (though there are certain exegetes—C. H. Dodd, for example—who do not admit this).
[27] Heb. 9.14; Ephes. 5.2.

constitutes the Church, and therefore unites man in communion with God and his fellow men.[28] We are redeemed *in sanguine,* through the blood of Christ—this we find on almost every page of Scripture. It is impossible therefore to "spiritualize" Christ's sacrifice, to make of it merely an internal act of love. There was indeed the act of love, but it was embodied in the sacrifice of blood. Because of Jesus' free acceptance of it, death has an essential part to play in the redemptive event. For the incarnation through which we are redeemed is not, as we have seen, something that was complete all in one instant. It embraces the whole human life of Christ, including his death. And in this human life, and thus also in this death, Christ lives his sonship of the Father in fidelity and loving attachment to the Father.

At the same time this death is the utmost effort of Satan and sinful man to stamp out everything godly in the world. But no sooner had sin put Christ to death than God called him back to life. Such is God's victory over man's sin. The resurrection therefore enters into the essence of the redemption. But God the Father not only raised Christ to life: he also made him Lord or *Kyrios.* "Let all the house of Israel know most certainly that God has made both Lord and Christ this same Jesus whom you have crucified."[29] In this text we find a fundamental *credo* of the primitive Church: we have killed Jesus of Nazareth, but God has raised him to life again. The Passover is thus our actual redemption, the expression of the "Ego vici mundum," "I have overcome the world."[30] In and through Christ's rising from the dead, God himself has called "the new earth" into being in this world.[31]

In the resurrection, then, as the eternally enduring act of salvation, there is also included Christ's ascension and establishment as Lord, the sending of the Holy Spirit which is Christ's actual exercise of lordship, and to a certain extent the *parousia* as well. In their essential core all these together form the single enduring mystery

---

[28] Ephes. 1.7:2.13; Rom. 3.25:5.9; Col. 1.20; Heb. 9.12ff.: 10.19, 29:13.12; 1 Pet. 1.18–19; 1 John 1.7:2.2; Apoc. 1.5:5.9; Acts 20.28.

[29] Acts 2.36.   [30] John 16.33.

[31] Cf. 2 Cor. 5.17; Gal. 6.15.

of salvation: the person of the humiliated and glorified Christ who is the saving reality. However, as they are shown forth in being given to us, the riches of this mystery enter one by one into the sequence of saving history. It is precisely for this reason that the New Testament indicates separate phases of the redemption which, included as they all are in the resurrection from the dead, nevertheless possess distinct meanings for salvation and manifest themselves in time in different ways.[32] Thus we may state the dogmatic content of the Passover, the Ascension and Pentecost as follows:

(1) The Passover is the mystery of Jesus' loving attachment to the Father unto death itself; it is the fidelity to the Father of the Son made man despite the condition proper to fallen humanity in which he had found himself because of our sinfulness. But at the same time it is the mystery of the divine response to this loving fidelity; the answer of divine mercy to the sacrifice of love, and the nullifying or the destruction of the power of sin: the resurrection.

(2) The Ascension is: (a) the investiture of Christ risen from the dead as universal Lord and King,[33] with which is connected (b) the glorification of Christ[34] which constitutes him definitively and fully the Messiah[35] and the eschatological "Son of Man."[36] The Ascension is the change from *exinanitio* to *glorificatio,* from humiliation to exaltation[37]; it is the eternally enduring goal of the incarnation of the Son of God. We may say the Ascension is the incarna-

---

[32] Cf. "Ascension and Pentecost," in *Worship*, 35–6 (1961), pp. 336–63, where an attempt has been made to set this out at greater length.

[33] In Luke: Acts 5.31:2.34–6:3.13. In Mark: 8.38:13.26:14.62. In Paul: Gal. 4.4; Phil. 2.9,11; 1 Cor. 12.3; Rom. 14.9:15.43; Col. 1.4; Ephes. 1.2,3, 15,17:2.21; 4.1,17:5.8, etc. In Heb.: 1.8,13:2.9. In John: 12.23:13.31; 17.1,5; Apoc.: 3.21:17.14.

[34] Implicit in the above texts, expressly stated in the following: Matt. 24.30; Mark 8.38:13.26; Luke: Acts 3.13; Paul: 1 Cor. 15.43; Col. 3.1–4; John: the texts already cited; Heb. 2.9; Apoc., the apotheosis of the Lamb (5.12–14).

[35] "This same Jesus whom you have crucified, God has made both Lord and 'the Anointed.' " (Acts 2.36.)

[36] Presupposed in Mark 14.62 ". . . you shall see the Son of Man sitting at the right hand of the power of God and coming in the clouds of heaven."

[37] Cf. the texts cited in notes 21–27; expressly stated in Phil. 2.6–11; Acts 3:13; Heb. 2:9.

tion itself in its completion, which precisely is the redemption. (c) Thus the Ascension is the prelude to the giving of the Spirit[38] and the termination of Jesus' earthly mission.[39] All these divine prerogatives of the man Jesus come to him through the fact that by the Ascension he is "with the Father,"[40] taken up in the cloud of the divine presence[41] which "makes all things new"; this Jesus of Nazareth is the king of the universe, the *Christus Victor*. It is clear that according to Scripture Christ had to *become* king. But this does not exclude the fact that the foundation of it all was given in the incarnation itself. St. John, especially, emphasizes this point.[42] But the incarnation of Christ is not something static. Christ's redeeming action, though a single reality, grows and develops so that, in the context of his whole human life, we can distinguish in it three principal elements: (a) his death and descent into hell; (b) the resurrection from the dead; (c) his glorification or his being established by the Father as Lord and thus sender of the Holy Spirit. St. John sees this progressive action as all one process of *glorification*.

Since all this came to completion in Christ as the first-born and precursor of all mankind,[43] in his ascension we too are already in principle "with the Father."[44]

(3) Pentecost is the eternally continuing actuation or application of this mystery in and through the Holy Spirit who now realizes and perfects *in us* that which was completed in Christ. Only through the Spirit whom Christ sends us does what is a reality in Christ—that in him all the faithful sit at the right hand of the Father —become actual in ourselves. The Spirit makes actual in us that

[38] In Luke: Acts 2.33; in Mark (typologically):1.10; in Matthew (typological too, but less certainly): 3:16; in Paul: Gal. 4.4–6; in John: 7.39: 14.16:15.26.

[39] Heb. 1.3 and the underlying theme throughout Luke.

[40] Especially in St. John; ascension into heaven is "going hence to the Father," or is at least one phase of this progressively realized reality. (14.12, 28:16–28, etc.)

[41] Especially in the theology of St. Luke (cf. the account in Acts).

[42] See W. Grossouw, "La Glorification du Christ dans le quatrième évangile," *Recherches bibliques, L'Evangile de Jean,* Bruges (1958), pp. 131–45.

[43] Heb. 6.20.   [44] Especially in St. Paul, Ephes. 2.6.

which Christ achieved for us once and for all. Thus the action of the Spirit, after the earthly activity of Jesus, is truly proper to him as third person of the Trinity. But all that he does he draws out of Christ's work of redemption; Christ said, "He shall receive of mine. . . ."[45] Christ is therefore not idle in heaven. For as well as praying and interceding for us,[46] it is he who out of his love for the Father sends the Holy Spirit upon us. And it is the Father who remains the ultimate source of the saving activity of both Christ and the Holy Spirit, for "it was God [viz., the Father] who reconciled us to himself in Christ."[47]

(b) The Significance of the Saving Mysteries of Jesus, the Christ

"I came forth from the Father and am come into the world; again I leave the world and I go to the Father." (John 16.28.)

(1) The Mystery of the Earthly Adoration of God the Father by God the Son Incarnate

The incarnation is the whole life of Christ, from his conception in the womb, through all his further life of action, completed finally in his death, resurrection and being established as Lord and sender of the Paraclete; it is prolonged everlastingly in his uninterrupted sending of the Holy Spirit. In this incarnation there is outwardly realized that mystery which St. John has expressed in the words "If I go not, the Holy Spirit will not come to you."[48] Christ can send us the Spirit only "from the Father," only when he is "with the Father."[49] There is a sense in which the earthly Christ is not "with the Father," no matter how closely he, as man too, may be

---

45 John 16.14–15.   46 Heb. 7.25–7; Rom. 8.34.
47 2 Cor. 5.18. See also John 16.15.
48 John 16.7. See also 14.16:15.26 and 20.22. Also John 7.37–9: Acts 2.32–3 and 5.31–2. Gal. 4.4–6 seems to recognize this theme as well.
49 John 15.26.

united to the Father in loving attachment. This is not a question of
some kind of local separation that supposedly would be involved in
Christ's being on earth while the Father is "in heaven." But still
it does mean some kind of "absence from home" or "estrangement"
from God. For "while we are at home in the body [the actual
meaning is, "while we are men existing in the fallen state"] we are
away from the Lord."[50] And Christ really did become thoroughly
sarx; the Word, says St. John, was made flesh (*sarx*); that is, he
became man not merely in the sense of "human being," but man in
the existential condition of the children of Adam. Becoming man,
God the Son entered into a humanity that had made its history one
of condemnation, and that was branded with the sign of disobedience and alienation from God: death. By the concrete reality of his
incarnation, St. Paul says in his own blunt way, God has "made
Christ to be sin."[51] Although personally sinless, the earthly Christ
lived in a situation of "estrangement from God," not so much personally on his own account, but rather because, as our representative, he personally took the place of sinful mankind before the
Father.

This was no mere "acting as if. . . ." Although we cannot plumb
the depths of this saving reality with our human minds, for Christ
it must have been a vivid and fearful experience, reaching its climax
in the Garden of Olives and on the Cross. In the human core of his
personal existence, Jesus is truly he who is laden with our sins; it
is thus that he confronts his heavenly Father. "We all have sinned
and lack the glory of God,"[52] that is, we do not have the Spirit of
God. Thus too the glory of God was wanting in Jesus' humanity
here on earth, and so, shortly before his death, he could pray to the
Father with urgent insistence: "Father . . . glorify thy Son,"[53]
which is to say "give thy glory to this man Jesus." During Jesus'
earthly life, St. John says, "the Spirit was not given, because Jesus
was not yet glorified."[54] If indeed there is strife between the spirit
and the flesh, the *pneuma* and the *sarx*,[55] it means that the Spirit

[50] 2 Cor. 5.6.
[52] Rom. 3.23.
[54] John 7.39.

[51] 2 Cor. 5.21.
[53] John 17.1
[55] Gal. 5.17.

has first to overcome the unsaved state of humanity of Jesus, its condition as *sarx,* and has to deify and to renew the whole of his humanity through and through, including its very bodiliness. Only when this is done can the man Jesus, who is God, give the Spirit of God to us, too, in a sovereign way: "Now that he is exalted at the right hand of God, and having received of the Father the promise of the Holy Spirit, he has poured forth this which you see and hear."[56]

In his earthly life Jesus, as Messiah or representative of sinful mankind, did truly go forth from the Father. So truly, in fact, that he can pray with us, "Out of the depths have I cried to thee, Lord" —not in a local but in a qualitative sense: "Out of the depths of the miserable state of fallen mankind, I call upon you, my God." This cry echoes above all from the Cross. It is the outburst of a man who, even though knowing himself personally bound to the Father in love from the depths of his human heart, was nevertheless living in utter truth, through to the very end, the experience of the estrangement from God belonging to *our* sinfulness, identifying himself with everything there ever was, or will be of sin-spawned alienation from God in this world. He had to pass through the helplessness of this alienation from God to receive the glory the Father would give him. In dispossessing himself of himself, Jesus hallowed himself to the Father in whom he finds his exaltation and glory. And behind all this there lies a mystery of unfathomable depth.

In Jewish family life "to go out from the father" is a technical term denoting that the son is sent on some mission by the father who is in charge in the home. The mission we are considering is the *redemptive* incarnation. But then the going forth from the Father implies at the same time the Son's entry into sinful humanity. The Father, it is true, continues to love the Son[57]; the Son himself is never forsaken by the Father, not even on the Cross (as some have mistakenly suggested); he is never alone.[58] But neither is he merely "himself"; he is also "all of us"; he takes our place in the most

---

[56] Acts 2.33. See also Heb. 5.9.   [57] John 3.35.
[58] John 8.16.

real sense of the phrase. And we are sinners. In this connection, the meaning Jewish tradition gives to the term "to go out from the father" is that family relations are ruptured (compare the parable of the Prodigal Son). According to this second meaning, the Son's going out from the Father into this world at enmity with God because of its sins is a commission given to Jesus, that he should bear witness in estranged, ungodly humanity to mankind's dependence on the Father, right up to the bitter end.

Here our prospects open upon God himself. For within the life of the Trinity, the Son is pure self-giving to the Father. Within God, this self-giving does not involve any giving-up, any self-dispossession. But on the level of the incarnation, Christ's self-giving to the Father does become a giving-up; it becomes the sacrificial offering of his life. Only a creature can sacrifice, because to be a creature is to be dependent. The Epistle to the Hebrews discloses to us a perspective in mystery that opens out upon the unfathomable mystery of the life of God itself: ". . . and whereas indeed he was the Son of God, he learned obedience by the things which he suffered."[59] In his sacrifice Christ consecrated himself entirely to the Father. The result of this is that "being made perfect, he became to all that obey him the cause of eternal salvation."[60] Christ's obedience and his attachment to the Father are therefore the essential precondition for the sending of the Spirit of Sanctification. In this the most profound significance of the incarnation is revealed; in Jesus' earthly humanity there is made known to us, in the first instance, that Christ is the Son of God through and through, even in his humanity, filial and obedient in all things to the Father. This is the interpretation in human reality of what he is in the heart of the Trinity: "from the Father." And only when he has lived his sonship through to the very end in his human life, and lived his life in utter obedience to the Father even to death itself, is his divine sonship fully realized and fully revealed on the level of the incarnation. Let us examine this in greater detail.

[59] Heb. 5.8.   [60] Heb. 5.9.

As God, Christ is equal in all things to the Father; in such a way, however, that it is through the Father that he is *himself*. Receiving all from the Father, he is in accord with the Father in all. Nonetheless there is no genuine dependence of the Son on the Father in the strict meaning of the word.[61] The truth of the matter is this: Between the Father and the Son there is an intimacy of life. Within the equality of the persons and the divine unity the Father is the origin of this life, in such a way that the Son, although equal to the Father, is beholden to him in all things by a perfect active receptivity.

The human existence of Jesus, as the humanness of the divine Son, is the revelation of these relations in the life of God; their transposition and interpretation into human forms—incarnation. Hence in the incarnate Son, the Son's intimacy of life with the Father enters into the sphere of creation and therefore of true dependence. For indeed to be man is to be a creature. This also means that the man Jesus' intimacy of life with the Father becomes, in Christ, truly a loving obedience. Dependence now enters the relation of love. As the revelation of this reality-within-God, the human life of Christ is the expression of adoration of God. As man, Christ *is* supreme worship of the Father. Christ was to live this worship of God in a human way, in the world of fellow men and things. The whole of the earthly life of Christ is loving obedience to the Father, lived in all the common situations of the life of man. In its actual content his human life becomes the religious expression of his abiding submission to the holy will of the Father, in spite of everything, in spite of death itself. This is the *whole* content of his human life; not something outside it or over and above it. Among all the acts of the life of this man, his death is the supreme expression of his religious surrender to the Father. Christ as man realizes his divine sonship in this living human form.

He does this as the Messiah, in our name and in the place of all

---

[61] "In this Trinity none is before or after another; none is greater, or less than another; but the whole three Persons are co-eternal together, and co-equal." (Pseudo-Athanasian Creed, B.C.P. translation.)

of us, as a prototype. The supreme moment in his life, the death to which he freely assents, is a messianic death; a death thus for the good of the people. As an act of messianic adoration of God, this is "liturgical." For in Christ our head and representative the sacrifice of the Cross, as that in which Jesus' inward adoration of God becomes an external reality and constitutes itself a real sacrificial cult, is an "act of the community" (*leiton ergon:* an act of the people), not yet performed by the people itself, but offered by the representative of the whole family of man and thus in the name of all and to the advantage of all. The sacrifice of the Cross itself is the great *liturgical mystery of worship,* through which Christ pleads with the Father for the grace of redemption for every man. It is in this way that Christ, in our name and in our place, makes reparation to the Father for our disobedience and for our irreligion.

The fact that he makes reparation to God means that in his human life, prototype of our lives, he makes God truly *God;* by his surrender he certifies God's infinite superiority to man ("oblation"): "The Father is greater than I,"[62] and in this he perfects his renunciation of self as the greatest of all values ("immolation"): "He offered himself without blemish to the Father."[63] This self-giving, in the manner of self-dispossession, is the essence of all religious life, life in the service of God.[64] Along with this it should be

---

[62] John 14.28.   [63] Heb. 9.14.

[64] The reader is referred to *SH,* pp. 515–18, where the author argues the following *in extenso:* Inseparable from the creaturely status of man, oblation and immolation are fundamental aspects of all theological life; they are not reparation, except in the sense of giving full recognition to, realizing God in, our lives. The immolation aspect is not only a consequence of sin, but essential prior to sin; the fact of sin has only added the character of suffering, painful self-denial, to the necessary immolation; because man's existence is essentially a bodily one this implies an element of sacrifice; outward symbol of the total inward surrender of all our being to the Creator and Saviour. In the present supernatural economy of salvation, man of himself cannot achieve this oblation and immolation apart from a divine initiative; the principle of all actual religion, charity, is lacking in man because of sin. Moreover, sin calls forth the *ira Dei,* the external reality of which is man's condition as fallen sinner. But in spite of sin the mercy of God continues to enact God's saving will; this takes the form of a renewal in

remembered that the Son of God became man precisely in order to be able to give himself in this sacrificial, self-dispossessing way. For however much the Son as God is pure self-giving to the Father, on the divine level it is nevertheless not possible for this to be in the mode of a giving-up, a dispossession of self or a sacrifice, as certain Russian Orthodox theologians (Bulgakov, Lossky) have wanted to suggest. Only in his human existence can the Son's eternal giving of himself to the Father be realized in the true form of a sacrifice and of self-dispossession. This is the reason why the Son, entering into the fallen world of mankind, has taken to himself precisely the *sarx;* a human existence which is branded with the sign of sin, condemned to suffering and to death. This he has done to make the curse itself, the sign of condemnation, into a sign of supreme adoration of God.[65] Thus his death becomes a death to sin.[66] As the earthly Messiah or head of *fallen* mankind, whose sinfulness he takes upon himself,[67] he had to win mankind to himself by that adoration of the Father which formed his whole human life, so making of mankind a redeemed messianic People of God. Thus Christ, by the religious service of his human life culminating in the sacrifice of the Cross, *becomes* the head of redeemed mankind.

---

earthly humanity of the fundamentally necessary oblation and immolation of which humanity had become radically incapable. In Christ the redemptive love of God has become an historical reality; Christ's sufferings are due to sin; the redemptive nature of his life is pure gratuitous grace on the divine initiative. And through the Hypostatic Union—Jesus' humanity assumed in a divine person which thus becomes the ultimate goal of all humanity—Christ is not merely morally representative of all mankind. Christ's death is the supreme realization, representative for us all, of theological life, of that adoration of God for which we exist. Therefore in the present order of life, religion can have meaning only insofar as it is a personal communion in, and identification with, the objective, representative oblation and immolation of Christ. The consummated incarnation of God the Son *is* redemption; there is no other way to God than through Christ, in whom God's initiative has broken through the barrier of the Fall and reunited humanity to himself. (Tr.)

[65] Cf. "The Death of a Christian," in *The Life of the Spirit,* 16 (1962), pp. 270–9 and 335–45.

[66] Rom. 6.10.

[67] 2. Cor. 5.21; Rom. 6.6, etc.

"Christ . . . loved the Church [the messianic People of God] and delivered himself up for it, that he might sanctify it . . . that he might present it to himself, a glorious Church, not having spot or wrinkle or any such thing, but that it should be holy and without blemish."[68]

In and through the liturgical mystery of worship that is his sacrifice on the Cross, against the background of the whole of his life in God's service, the being of the Son of God as "from the Father" and "to the Father" is fully revealed and given reality on the human plane of his sonship. The divine procession of the Son from the Father and his eternal return are completely revealed and made human reality in the man Jesus in the supreme moment of his life: "Father, into thy hands I commend my spirit"—into thy hands I lay down my life.[69] "I came forth from the Father and am come into the world; again I leave the world and I go to the Father."[70] In and through his death for love, as the human interpretation of his divine attachment to the Father, in a messianic, redeeming act of love, to the very end Jesus sacrificially uttered his human love to the Father.

(2) The Father's Response to the Son's Life of Worship on Earth: The Resurrection and Glorification of Jesus and His Establishment as Lord and Sender of the Holy Spirit

The divine acceptance of the sacrifice belongs to the essence of this sacrificial offering up of life. The Father's acceptance of Jesus' sacrifice is the resurrection of Christ. The resurrection is the sacrifice of the Cross heard and answered by the Father. And answered precisely as a messianic sacrifice; as the sacrifice, therefore, of all mankind. Only in this response does the "objective redemption" be-

[68] Ephes. 5.25–7.　　　　　　[69] Luke 23.46.
[70] John 16.28.

come a reality; only then are we all already redeemed in principle (*in principe*), i.e., in Christ our Head. The Father exalted Christ as a result of his sacrifice—"Sit at my right hand"[71]—this is Christ's enthronement by the Father as *Kyrios*. "The government is upon his shoulder."[72] Only in his resurrection and exaltation with the Father does Christ become unconditionally Messiah: he is then, *in* his humanity, "the Son of God in power."[73] Through this acceptance by the Father of the whole life of Jesus lived as the expression of his adoration of God, the entire cycle of mutual love between the Father and the Son is fully incorporated in the sphere of Christ's humanity. Only in this does Jesus reach his consummation.[74] Thus, in virtue of Jesus' sacrificial love for the Father, the Father, through the resurrection, calls a "new creation" into being in the *sarx* of Christ: humanity in glory. Only in this is the redemption of humanity a reality.

(3) *The Christ of Heaven, Sender of the Spirit of Sanctification*

"When the Paraclete cometh, whom I will send you from the Father." (John 15.26.)

According to the insight the New Testament affords us, Christ can send forth the Spirit upon us only after his exaltation. This fact can be appreciated now in its most profound trinitarian significance. As God, the second person of the Trinity is not only the Son of the Father, but as Son in union with the Father he is at the same time the principle of the Holy Spirit: ". . . qui procedit a Patre per Filium." Within the triune God, the Father and the Son are pure giving and re-giving, and the life of these two persons in their giving and returning is so intense that, within the one divinity, it goes forth from their own persons and in a receptive returning is the

[71] Ps. 109 (110), repeatedly applied to the glorified Christ in the New Testament (see above).

[72] Isa. 9.6.   [73] Rom. 1.3–4.

[74] Heb. 5.9.

fount of life of the Holy Spirit. The third divine person is thus conceivable only in terms of the reciprocal love of Father and Son.

Within the Trinity it is in his infinitely perfect belonging to the Father that the Son himself is the principle of life of the Holy Spirit; and therefore on the plane of the incarnation—as man—he can give us the Holy Spirit only when his sonship is consummated in his humanity too, which is only when he has freely and humanly given himself in love to the Father, who responds to this gift by the resurrection. The cycle of mutual love of Father and Son, as the origin of the Holy Spirit, is translated in the man Jesus by his sending the Spirit upon us. Only in the perfecting of the religious obedience of the man Jesus to his Father, who accepts this sacrifice of life out of love for his Son, out of love indeed for his Son as the representative of all mankind (as Messiah)—only in this can the man Jesus, "established in power," also be a co-principle of the sending of the Holy Spirit upon us. The *Kyrios* in his *humanity* is the sender of the Spirit. For this reason Pentecost can be understood only in terms of the Passover as a "passage from death to life." In its essence Pentecost is an Easter event. This is how St. John sees it; he does not speak of the pentecostal event peculiar to Luke on the fiftieth day after Easter. According to St. John, the first sending of the Holy Spirit took place on Easter Day itself, after the Easter-Ascension. After Christ had said to Mary Magdalen that he was about to go to the Father, and that she must tell this to the Apostles, he appeared to them. His first act as the risen and glorified Christ is, then, immediately to send the Holy Spirit upon the Apostles: "As the Father has sent me, I also send you. When he had said this he breathed on them; and he said to them, Receive the Holy Spirit."[75] We can call this quite simply the Johannine Pentecost motif, in which it appears just as clearly as in Luke that the Ascension is the immediate condition for the sending of the Holy Spirit. The essential Christian Pentecost is an Easter event.

[75] John 20.21 St. John says explicitly that this happened "at that same day," i.e., Easter Day.

But with this first bestowal of the Spirit the manifestation of the Lord established in power is not at an end. Pentecost is a continuing event. Nevertheless, among the various unceasing bestowals of the Holy Spirit upon the primitive Church, we can point to several that stand out from the rest. This is already done in the New Testament itself. The first sending of the Holy Spirit, on Easter Day, is the one St. John emphasizes. St. Luke, on the contrary, places the pentecostal event on the fiftieth day after Easter,[76] stressing the sending of the Holy Spirit upon the community of the first Church, the Church of Jerusalem. This is the inauguration of the christianizing of the Jewish people, and through this "christened" people (or some of them), of the whole world. We may call this the Lucan Pentecost motif. Finally, it is also possible to indicate a Pauline Pentecost motif,[77] in the passage where the sending of the Holy Spirit upon the Church of Ephesus is seen by the same St. Luke as the starting-point of the christianizing of the pagan world. The account is clearly built up on the same lines as the account of the sending of the Spirit upon the Church of Jerusalem. This already indicates that to a certain extent there is something arbitrary in the promotion of the fiftieth day after Easter to the feast of Pentecost, or the feast of the sending forth of the Holy Spirit. It is obviously a case of thematic presentation (based on historical fact, and in the present instance also in connection with the Jewish Pentecost). Pentecost remains essentially an Easter reality; through his establishment as *Kyrios* (the Ascension motif, at least logically distinct from the Resurrection understood precisely as arising from the dead), Christ is the sender of the Holy Spirit. For this reason too, the givings of the Holy Spirit begin from Easter Day. Nonetheless, certain historical gifts of the Spirit are placed thematically at the origin of the founding of the Church and of particular Church communities.

As far as the Liturgy is concerned, the Lucan Pentecost motif has prevailed over the others. The reason for this is quite under-

---

[76] Acts 2.1–14.   [77] Cf. Acts 19.1–7.

standable, for the establishment in power of the Mother Church of Jerusalem does indeed definitely introduce the Church's period of salvation, the history of the Church as the saving community of the risen Lord, who through his apostolic college and through his Spirit extends the Church in space and time.

Conclusion

In this brief analysis we can see sufficiently clearly that the mysteries of the Passover (death, resurrection and exaltation) and of Pentecost are the representation in human form, realized in the mystery of Christ, of the mystery of the redeeming Trinity. Passover and Pentecost are the interpretation on the human plane of the divine relations of Son to Father, and of the Son in unity with the Father to the Holy Spirit. For within the life of the Godhead, that the Son should be the principle of the Holy Spirit is something which he receives from the Father. In the sphere of the incarnation this gift of the Father is represented in the commission of the man Jesus to be Christ, to be the *Kyrios* and the sender of the Holy Spirit upon the world of men.

(4) The Mystery of Christ's Love for the Father as the Foundation of His Unfailing Gift of Grace

The mystery of Christ, seen in this way, is the mystery of Christmas that reaches its fulfilment, by way of the whole human life of Jesus, in a mystery of Passover and Pentecost. This whole forms for us the revelation of the redemptive mystery of the Trinity, being progressively realized in human form. Through the earthly mystery of worship in his life Christ "merited"[78] or obtained for us from the

[78] This merit will later be explained Christologically. In general we can already say that to have merited the grace of redemption or of the Holy Spirit indicates that the man Jesus was filled with grace even in his free

Father the grace of redemption which now, as the *Kyrios,* he can in fact give us to the full. All the Lord's activity in heaven is still a filial intercession with and adoration of the Father,[79] but it is also a continual sending out of the Holy Spirit upon mankind. We must appreciate the order in which this takes place. The salvation of humanity is brought about in Christ's life of service as the Father's Son incarnate. For in his divine union with and total orientation towards the Father, the Son is the principle of the Holy Spirit. This relationship within God is exhibited in the plane of Christ's glorified messianic humanity in the following manner: because of his love for the Father, on the Father's initiative, the Lord sends us the Spirit of sonship. Hence the mystery of worship, which is Christ, is at the same time our salvation: a mystery of saving worship.[80]

As we have said, these are two inseparable aspects of all the activity of Christ's life, both in his humiliation and in his glory, although in his humiliation we see his redemptive worship of the Father more plainly, while in his glorification it is rather his gift of grace that strikes us. This implies no contradiction, for though Christ be-

---

human acts. Consequently grace from the Father through the Son in the power of the Holy Spirit includes the man Jesus, too (includes him as our representative), and pervades his humanity even in the free human actions done by him in our name, thus raising him throughout his human life towards glorification for our sake. Merit is the gratuity of grace in human freedom. It is clear then that it is precisely God who redeems us, though in and through Christ's humanity.

[79] ". . . always living to make intercession for us." (Heb. 7.25.) See also Rom. 8.34.

[80] "Mystery of worship" is not to be understood in the narrow sense of worship as cult. Not only Jesus' prayer, not only his entire moral and religious attitude of life, but also all his apostolic activity is worship of the Father. The complete notion of worship includes all these expressions, and all are at the same time an apostolate. The same must be said of the term "liturgical mystery of worship." "Liturgical" means for and in the name of the community; this qualification applies to all the actions of Christ in their character both of worship and of apostolate. The importance of a right understanding of this matter is clearly seen in the two apparently irreconcilable contentions with regard to the sacrament of confirmation; as cult in the narrow sense and as apostolate.

fore his glorification had still to realize actual redemption, and was not yet in reality a sender of the Holy Spirit, even in his humiliation, he was nevertheless the Son always beloved of the Father. In this we see how encounter with the earthly Jesus was already a grace. For in his heart Jesus already bore his sacrifice, with which, in anticipation, the Father was well pleased: "Thou art my beloved son. In thee I am well pleased."[81] But this does not eliminate the fact that the great "pouring forth" of grace could take place only after the resurrection from the dead. So therefore we say that, on the foundation of his earthly mystery of worship, the Lord himself does in fact bestow the grace of redemption on us, at the same time not forgetting that his earthly mystery of worship had already touched hearts with grace and that the heavenly sending of the Spirit is founded upon the heavenly liturgy of Christ, who in his worship of the Father "is always living to make intercession for us."

Thus Christ is and remains the "high priest for ever." In our name and in the place of all of us he is ever praying the Father for grace for us, and then in actual fact giving us the grace for which he has prayed. For his prayer is unfailingly heard, because even in his humanity he is the well-beloved Son. He is unfailingly heard,[82] it used to be said, because of his "meritorious" work of redemption on earth. But what this means is that he is heard because of his existence as Son, the existence which through his earthly activity he lived freely and faithfully to the end. The so-called "merit" is his service; is the free realization in human form of Jesus' divine love as the Son. Thus Christ's earthly and heavenly mystery of worship (i.e., the human religious shape of his sonship) is the foundation of the Lord's unfailing gift of grace. It is the expression in human form of the mystery of divine love; a mystery which in the Godhead manifests itself as mutual gift within the unity of love.

Thus, when we speak of Christ's mystery of saving worship or about his work of salvation-through-worship, we must not lose sight of the fact that Jesus' human adoration of the Father is itself

81 Luke 3.21–2. Matt. 17–5.   82 John 11.42.

the revelation of the divinity which he receives from the Father.[83] Jesus' human love is the translation of divine love itself into human form. And this love from the human heart of God the Son drove him to the redeeming adoration of his death on the Cross. This adoration arises therefore from God's own love. For the man Jesus this means that even his adoration itself is a pure gift and grace from the Father without whom he can do nothing.[84] Our salvation through Jesus' adoration is thus intelligible only in virtue of the fact that Jesus as man was himself sanctified by the Spirit of God; the redeeming activity of love of the man Jesus is a personal worship-through-salvation, and so, in our regard, salvation-through-worship. Thus even in Christ, the Lord, the mystery of the Trinity retains its absolute priority with regard to our Christological redemption through the man Jesus. That absolute generosity which the Trinity simply *is* remains the universally dominant background of the mystery of saving worship in Christ.

The result of the redeeming incarnation, as an enduring heavenly reality, is that we are children of the Father in Christ. By the incarnation of his divine life of love, Christ earned for us that his Father should also be our Father; and by the same incarnation, but now through its fulfilment in glory, Christ in actual fact bestows upon us the Spirit which makes us children of the Father,[85] so that we, too, truly are children of the Father. Thus we become by grace what Christ is by nature: Son of God. As *filii in Filio* we are thus caught up into the special providential relationships which hold between the Father and the incarnate Son, and the Father proves himself, in his Son's continual sending of the Holy Spirit, truly our Father all our life long. That which was brought to realization under the providence of the Father in the exemplar or prototype, the man Jesus, by the way which led from his humiliation to his glory, must now be renewed in the reproduction or antitype, the messianic family of the Church. But how in actual fact will this come about?

[83] St. Thomas, *De Potentia,* q.3, a. 15, ad 17.
[84] John 5.30.   [85] "Spiritus adoptionis": Rom. 8.15.

3. THE NECESSITY FOR THE EXTENSION TO EARTH OF THE GLORIFIED CHRIST, THE PRIMORDIAL SACRAMENT

1. Our Need to Encounter the Christ of Heaven

In the preceding pages we have been clarifying the meaning of the saving reality which is Christ, the one and only saving primordial sacrament. But it is precisely this, proper to Christ as the one and only "Sacrament of God," that confronts us with a problem from the moment that Jesus by his resurrection and glorification disappeared from the visible horizon of our life. For on the foundation of God's economy of salvation the gift of grace, or the encounter with God, remains bound up with our personal encounter with the man Jesus who is our only way to the Father. Now how can we encounter the glorified Lord, who has withdrawn himself from our sight? For Jesus' bodiliness, as the means of immediate communication, has vanished from our earthly life. The difficulty is even accentuated by Christ's words: "It is the Spirit that gives life; the flesh profits nothing."[86] Still more pointedly, in flagrant contradiction of all that has been said so far, it would seem that bodily mediation in our encounter with Christ is meaningless, since Jesus himself has said, "It is good for you that I go."[87] It would seem that it is rather Christ's bodily absence that is conducive to actual encounter with him.

It is true that Christ had to go away to where we are not able as yet to follow him. He has risen and thus disappeared from all our visible walks of life. But it was not his disappearance in itself that was "best for us," but rather his glorification at the Father's side, which of course implied that he had to disappear from those who are still not glorified. But at the same time this means that being in body together with the Lord in glory, which will happen at the *parousia,* is the eternally enduring and supreme realization of

[86] John 6.64.　　　　　　　　　　[87] John 16.7.

Christian living. Christ's incarnation is, as it were, some paces ahead of our deification, so that for a time he has passed out of sight beyond the visible horizon; but from there he is preparing the perfect reunion in bodily life and remoulding us from within, so that when our hearts are pure enough we, ourselves glorified, may see him face to face in the bodily encounter of the *parousia*. It is precisely for this reason that Christianity, as life between Passover and *parousia,* is so markedly eschatological. In part we have indeed to manage now without encountering Christ in the body. Precisely on this account Christian life is an Advent. We must be on the lookout, waiting for the encounter which has yet to come. Christianity is the religion of the *Maranatha:* "Come, Lord Jesus."

But in this we do not have the whole picture. For it is not possible to understand this expectation of the ultimate perfect encounter except in virtue of the fact that we have already in some way encountered the glorified Lord, not in the mere commemoration of something that happened ages ago in Palestine, nor even simply by our faith in him as now living, glorified and invisibly active in our lives. This is not all: Christ makes his presence among us actively visible and tangible too, not directly through his own bodiliness, but by extending among us on earth in visible form the function of his bodily reality which is in heaven. This precisely is what the sacraments are: the earthly extension of the "body of the Lord." This is the Church.[88] But before we go on to study the character as Church of the earthly "body of the Lord" we must have a clear insight into the general meaning of an earthly prolongation of Christ's glorified humanity.

For why in fact this sacramental extension? Without it one of the profoundly human qualities of the incarnation of God would be lost to us. Now God has always remained faithful to his own methods of teaching us salvation. Because God loves man and has a sovereign respect for our earthbound humanity—for our reality as persons who in their own bodiliness live in a world of people and of things,

[88] Ephes. 1.23:4.12, etc.

and thereby grow to spiritual maturity—God always offers us the kingdom of heaven in an earthly guise. So he did in the Old Testament. So it was in the *ephapax:* the appearance once and for all of God the Redeemer in human shape. So, too, finally, does he continue to teach us in the sacramental Church which is the visible organ on earth of the living Lord. We shall now try to bring out the inner significance of this fact.

2. *The Real Possibility of This Encounter from Christ's Side*

Mutual human availability is possible only in and through man's bodiliness. Therefore men who are dead and not yet risen again can exercise no direct influence upon us by mutual human contact. If the dead are holy and already with the Lord, they can influence us only through their prayerful intercession with God, and not directly from man to man. This already makes it clear that on the side of Christ the man it is the resurrection which makes it possible for him precisely *as man* to influence us by grace. This is of capital importance. For we are ever inclined to pass cursorily over the human life of Christ, to overlook his existence as man and consider only his existence as God. But it is as *man* that the Son is the mediator of grace; he is mediator in his humanity, according to the ways of humanity. His human mediation of grace therefore presupposes his corporeality, ". . . la face de l'âme qui est tournée vers les autres âmes." (Jean Guitton.) Redemption turns its face towards us in Christ's glorified bodiliness. Thus in the risen Christ the mystery of saving worship truly remains an active offer of grace for us. For the glorious body of Christ gives his soul the outward openness he as man must have if he is really to exercise influence upon us.

So even from considerations of what man is, the Greek patristic affirmation St. Thomas has taken over is seen clearly to be right; on the one hand "grace in us derives from Christ . . . only through the personal action of Christ himself,"[89] and on the other hand, "the whole of Christ's humanity, that is to say both body and soul, exercises an influence on men."[90]

3. The Necessity for Earthly Sacraments so that the Encounter between the Glorified Christ and Men on Earth Might Take Place in Terms of Mutual Human Availability

On Christ's side, the possibility of a human encounter is positively established. Human encounter, however, calls for mutual availability. Now it is certainly true that because of his glorified corporeality the Christ of heaven can, full of grace, reach us and influence us whoever or wherever we may be. But we, earthly men, cannot encounter him in the living body (*in propria carne*) because his glorification has made him invisible to us. From this it follows that if Christ did not make his heavenly bodiliness visible in some way in our earthly sphere, his redemption would after all no longer be for us; redemption would no longer turn its face towards us. Then the human mediation of Christ would be meaningless. Once he had completed the work of redemption, there would no longer be any reason for the existence of Christ's humanity. The logical consequence would be the position taken by Julian of Halicarnassus, that once the work of redemption had been completed the incarnation ceased to exist.

But on the other hand it follows from the dogma of the perpetuity of the incarnation, and of Christ's human mediation of grace, that if Christ does not show himself to us in his own flesh, then he can make himself visibly present to and for us earthbound men only by taking up earthly non-glorified realities into his glorified saving activity. This earthly element replaces for us the invisibility of his bodily life in heaven. This is precisely what the sacraments are: the face of redemption turned visibly towards us, so that in

[89] *ST*, III, q. 8, a. 5, ad 1.   [90] *ST*, III, q. 8, a. 2.

them we are truly able to encounter the living Christ. The heavenly saving activity, invisible to us, becomes visible in the sacraments.

We do not propose to study the historical revelation of the sacraments here. Taking it for granted, and seeking an understanding of the inner significance of this reality of saving history, we must hold that the sacraments are intrinsically required, since the mediation of grace by the *man* Jesus is a permanent reality.[91] From the moment that, by his ascension, the "primordial sacrament" leaves the world, the economy of the "separated sacraments" becomes operat. *e* in consequence of the incarnation and as its prolongation. From Scripture we learn that while none of the twelve Apostles who enjoyed immediate contact with the "primordial sacrament" himself was baptized, St. Paul, the "thirteenth Apostle," who had not encountered the earthly Christ in faith, was in fact baptized.[92] Sacramentality thus bridges the gap and solves the disproportion between the Christ of heaven and unglorified humanity, and makes possible a reciprocal human encounter of Christ and men even after the ascension, though in a special manner. A permanent sacramentality is thus an intrinsic requirement of the Christian religion.

From this account of the sacraments as the earthly prolongation of Christ's glorified bodiliness, it follows immediately that the Church's sacraments are not things but encounters of men on earth with the glorified man Jesus by way of a visible form. On the plane of history they are the visible and tangible embodiment of the heavenly saving action of Christ. They are this saving action itself in its availability to us; a personal act of the Lord in earthly visibility and open availability.[93]

[91] In the first section of this chapter we considered briefly how, and to what extent, religion is still possible among men where there is no explicit connection with Christ, the only mediator of grace.

[92] Acts 9.18.

[93] St. Thomas says very neatly in this connection: Christ himself administers all the sacraments; it is he who baptizes; he forgives sins; he is the true priest who offered himself on the Cross and by whose power his body is daily consecrated on the altar. But because he was not going to remain

Here the first and most fundamental definition of sacramentality is made evident. In an earthly embodiment which we can see and touch, the heavenly Christ sacramentalizes[94] both his continual intercession for us and his active gift of grace. Therefore the sacraments are the visible realization on earth of Christ's mystery of saving worship. "What was visible in Christ has now passed over into the sacraments of the Church."[95]

The fact which we must now begin to analyse in detail is therefore this: Through the sacraments we are placed in living contact with the mystery of Christ the High Priest's saving worship. In them we encounter Christ in his mystery of Passover and Pentecost. The sacraments *are* this saving mystery in earthly guise. This visible manifestation is the visible Church. This will be the first point to analyse.

---

bodily present to all his brethren ("quia corporaliter non cum omnibus fratribus praesentialiter erat futurus"), he chose out ministers (for his Church). (*SCG*, IV, 76.)

[94] "Sacramentalizes" indicates the personal act of Christ who through his Church gives visible shape to his invisible saving activity or gift of grace, and thereby makes himself present to us.

[95] St. Leo the Great, "Quod conspicuum erat in Christo transivit in Ecclesiae sacramenta." (*Sermo LXXIV*, 2 [*PL*, 54, col. 398].)

2

THE CHURCH,
SACRAMENT OF THE RISEN CHRIST

1. THE MYSTERY OF THE CHURCH, THE EARTHLY "BODY OF THE LORD"

1. The Church, Earthly Sacrament of Christ in Heaven

We have said that Jesus as man and Messiah is unthinkable without his redemptive community. Established by God precisely in his vocation as representative of fallen mankind, Jesus had by his human life to win this community to himself and make of it a redeemed people of God. This means that Jesus the Messiah, through his death which the Father accepts, becomes in fact the head of the People of God, the Church assembled in his death. It is thus that he wins the Church to himself, by his messianic life as the Servant of God, as the fruit of the sufferings of his messianic sacrifice: "Christ dies that the Church might be born."[1] In his messianic sacrifice, which the Father accepts, Christ in his glorified body is himself the eschatological redemptive community of the Church. In his own self the glorified Christ is simultaneously both "Head and members."

The earthly Church is the visible realization of this saving reality in history. The Church is a visible communion in grace. This communion itself, consisting of members and a hierarchical leadership,

[1] "Moritur Christus ut fiat Ecclesia." (St. Augustine, *In Evangelium Johannis*, tract 9, 10 [*PL*, 35, col. 1463].)

is the earthly sign of the triumphant redeeming grace of Christ. The fact must be emphasized that not only the hierarchical Church but also the community of the faithful belong to this grace-giving sign that is the Church. As much in its hierarchy as in the laity the community of the Church is the realization in historical form of the victory achieved by Christ. The inward communion in grace with God in Christ becomes visible in and is realized through the outward social sign. Thus the essence of the Church consists in this, that the final goal of grace achieved by Christ becomes visibly present in the *whole* Church as a visible society.

It was the custom in the past to distinguish between the soul of the Church (this would be the inward communion in grace with Christ) and the body of the Church (the visible society with its members and its authority). Only too rightly, this view has been abandoned. It was even, in a sense, condemned by Pope Pius XII. The visible Church itself is the Lord's mystical body. The Church is the visible expression of Christ's grace and redemption, realized in the form of a society which is a sign (*societas signum*). Any attempt to introduce a dualism here is the work of evil—as if one could play off the inward communion in grace with Christ against the juridical society of the Church, or vice versa. The Church therefore is not merely a means of salvation. It is Christ's salvation itself, this salvation as visibly realized in this world. Thus it is, by a kind of identity, the body of the Lord.

We remarked that this visibility of grace defines the whole Church; not the hierarchical Church only, but also the community of the faithful. The whole Church, the People of God led by a priestly hierarchy, is "the sign raised up among the nations."[2] The activity, as much of the faithful as of their leaders, is thus an ecclesial activity.[3] This means that not only the hierarchy but also

---

[2] Thus the Vatican Council. (*DB*, no. 1794.)

[3] It is necessary for a clear presentation of the argument to adopt this form of the adjective. In everyday usage "ecclesiastical" has become so closely linked with all that concerns the hierarchical element in the Church; this currently more common word would therefore be misleading here and in the pages to follow, and circumlocution would not only prove cumber-

the believing people belong essentially to the primordial sacrament which is the earthly expression of this reality. As the sacramental Christ, the Church too is mystically both Head and members. When the twofold function of Christ becomes visible in the sign of the Christian community, it produces the distinction between hierarchy and faithful—a distinction of offices and of those who hold them. Even though the hierarchy, on the one hand, are themselves part of the believing Church, and the faithful, on the other hand, share in the lordship of Christ and to some extent give it visibility, the sacramental functions of hierarchy and faithful differ within the Church and show the distinction.

2. The Ecclesial Character of the Office of Hierarchy and Laity

How are we to understand this distinction in office? The sacramental manifestation of the Lord in his role as head of the People of God is realized formally and functionally in the apostolic office, the ecclesiastical hierarchy. In this respect the hierarchical Church is sovereign with regard to the community of the faithful. On the other hand, the whole community of the faithful, or the People of God, is the sacramental realization on earth of the Lord as representatively the People of God. In this aspect the faithful themselves are the Church. In its entirety—apostolic office and community of the faithful—the Church is the sacramental or mystical Christ. And in its entirety it is at the same time both community of the redeemed and redeeming institution. In and through the visible activity of the Church—that is, of the apostolic office and of the faithful who are signed with the Christian character—the Lord brings to fulfilment the work of redemption for which he laid the foundation as the historical Messiah. The Church on earth is the visible presence of

---

some but also obscure the already compact text. "Ecclesial" is used to signify all that is proper to the Church in its entirety, a synthesis of hierarchical and lay elements. (Tr.)

the work of fulfilment in which Christ is now engaged in his glorified body and so also in his Spirit. This visible presence of grace
and consequent bestowal of grace in the Church is achieved in a
twofold manner: through the apostolic office in virtue of the
character of the priesthood, and through the faithful in virtue of
their character of baptism and confirmation.[4] What Christ is doing
invisibly in this world through his Spirit, he is at the same time
doing visibly through the mission of his apostles and of the
members of the Church community. These two missions (of the
Spirit and of the Church) are organically connected. What the
hierarchy does in virtue of its apostolic office, and the faithful do in
virtue of their baptismal and confirmational mission, each in the
sphere of the objective visible life of the Church, the Spirit of Christ
does inwardly in this visible activity and in the hearts of men.

In his article on the Church in the Epistle to the Ephesians H.
Schlier says that according to St. Paul the glorified body of Christ is
the Church of heaven, which comes on earth through the Spirit and
becomes the earthly Church.[5] We have come to the same conclusion
by a different route. The body of Christ in heaven is also the
enduring sign of the messianic redemption or of the mystery of
saving worship which Christ is; a sign that contains what it signifies,
for it is this messianic act of redemption itself in visible form. But
for the time being, until the *parousia,* this sign remains invisible to
us earthly men. Therefore the Lord gave this external sign of the
redemption a visible prolongation on earth: the visible Church.
Through this visible prolongation the redemption is revealed in this
world in which we live as something that is for us, and thus it is
precisely through this that the redemption is offered to us.

[4] We do no more than mention this point here. At a later stage in this
work the significance of the character of baptism and confirmation, and in
contrast to them of the priesthood, will be analysed. It has been found
necessary to anticipate this analysis to a certain extent, for otherwise the
present exposition might be incorrectly interpreted, as reactions to earlier
editions have shown.

[5] "Die Kirche nach dem Briefe an die Epheser," in *Die Zeit der Kirche,*
Freiburg (1956), pp. 159–85.

3. Office and Charism in the Church

The Church in its entirety is not only a saving institution; as such it is also a saving and sanctifying community. As the earthly representation of the sign of salvation in heaven, the Church in its entirety is itself a sign already containing the redemptive reality of Christ. The Church's own inward invisible communion in grace with God in Christ becomes visible in its saving activity. This earthly body of the Lord, the Church, is at the same time the Lord's *pleroma;* being filled with Christ, it in turn fills the faithful. For this reason the sacramental Church, in the hierarchy and in the community of the faithful signed with the sacramental character, is not only the earthly visible form of the activity of Christ as High Priest, but at the same time is a sign that in its sacramental or visible saving activity it is itself filled with the reality to which it is giving form. This means that the Church in its institutional existence as a society manifests not only Christ in himself but also its own communion of grace and life with Christ. As earthly representative of Christ, the Church too is the "child of the Father"; being supreme worship of the Father, and also the one who at Pentecost was "established in power," the Church bestows the Spirit whom it has itself received in prayer from Christ. Therefore in the Church too there is the twofold movement we have already discovered in Christ: the movement down from above and up from below.

Thus the Church in its own proper activity is a historical manifestation of God's own love for men in Christ (bestowal of grace) and, at the same time, of its own love and adoration of God in the same Lord (worship). Because the Church, as the bride Christ won to himself, is itself "full of grace" it is an offer of grace to those who approach it, and the bestowal of grace upon those who open themselves to it. In this way the Church is a community of salvation and of worship.

Thus the grace of redemption becomes visible in the Church in a twofold manner: through office and through charism. The grace of redemption becomes visible, in other words:

(1) *Through office, or institutionally:* both through the priestly activity of the hierarchy (that is, through the administration of the sacraments, through the administration of the word, ecclesiastical preaching or authority to teach, and through pastoral government or the care of souls), and through the ecclesial office proper to the laity, that is, through their activity in virtue of the characters of baptism and confirmation (cf. below).

(2) *Through charism:* that is, through the activity of both hierarchy and laity, in so far as this activity is an outward manifestation of inward communion in grace with God.

Both the institutional and the charismatic elements are genuinely ecclesial. We must not lose sight of the fact that the Church is a mystery, a sign bearing within itself the reality of inward union with God in Christ. The consequence of this is that both hierarchy and laity must carry out the functions of their office in virtue of the charism associated with it. Office and charism could never be dissociated within the Church as a whole, but they are dissociated at times in individual members of the hierarchy or laity, creating a distorted situation in which the Church is deprived of something proper to herself. This will emerge more clearly through the analysis of particular factors during the course of this essay.

4. A Sacrament: Official Act of the Church as Redemptive Institution

We are now in a position to draw up a definition of the sacramental action of the Church. A sacrament, that is an act of the primordial sacrament which is the Church, is a visible action proceeding from the Church as redemptive institution, an official ecclesial act performed in virtue either of the character of the priesthood or of the characters of baptism and confirmation. Hence in this sense a sacrament is actually something more than that which we usually understand under the term "seven sacraments," but it is also something more limited than that which we have just called "general visibility," meaning sacramentality as an outward manifestation not of office, but directly of inward communion in grace (i.e., the outwardly visible holiness of the life of the faithful in the Church). It is, however, necessary to assess the seven sacraments in their proper place within the wider sacramental context of the entire Church. A sacrament is primarily and fundamentally a personal act of Christ himself, which reaches and involves us in the form of an institutional act performed by a person in the Church who, in virtue of a sacramental character, is empowered to do so by Christ himself: an act *ex officio*.

We do not now intend to embark upon an exhaustive study of the Church, but rather to speak of the ecclesial significance of the reality referred to by the term "the seven sacraments."[6] To this end we shall confine our attention for the time being to what is called the proper sacramental activity of the Church. At a later stage, when we come to consider the characters of baptism and confirmation (lay office in the Church) and the life of grace of the faithful (charism), we shall have occasion to examine the specifically sacramental function, both institutional and charismatic, of the community of the faithful as itself a sign. At present we are concerned with the seven official constitutive sacraments (not omitting those particular cases in which a sacrament is administered by laymen—i.e., marriage and, in the case of necessity, baptism).

It follows from all we have said that these seven sacraments— before this or that particular one is specified—are all fundamentally and primarily a visible, official act of the Church.[7] Thus from the

---

[6] In contrast to the sacramentality of the whole Church, St. Thomas calls these sacraments "quae ad cultum pertinent."

[7] It is not possible to set out every element implicit in our analysis. But it should be clear enough from all the subsequent discussion that the seven sacraments, although primarily an official action of the hierarchical Church (through the minister), are not this alone, but also an official action of the recipient who, in virtue of his baptism, by the intention he expresses in the

definition of the Church as the primordial sacrament, we come already to a first and general definition of the seven sacraments: Each sacrament is the personal saving act of the risen Christ himself, but realized in the visible form of an official act of the Church. In other words, a sacrament is the saving action of Christ in the visible form of an ecclesial action. The validity of a sacrament is therefore simply its authenticity as an act of the Church as such. The essential reality that in one or other of seven possible ways is outwardly expressed in the reception of each of the sacraments is consequently the entry into living contact with the visible Church as the earthly mystery of Christ in heaven. To receive the sacraments of the Church in faith is therefore the same thing as to encounter Christ himself. In this light the sacramentality of the seven sacraments is the same as the sacramentality of the whole Church. This pervading "structure" of sacramentality is manifested by each of the seven sacraments in its own proper way. All that follows is simply the gradual clarification of this point.

2. THE SACRAMENTS AS ECCLESIAL CELEBRATION-IN-MYSTERY OF THE MYSTERIES OF CHRIST'S LIFE

1. The Presence of the Mystery of Christ in the Sacraments

When we see that the seven sacraments are Christ's heavenly activity itself in ecclesial-institutional form, our attention is at once called to this problem: how, precisely, is the heavenly mystery of grace present in the sacraments? Ever since the appearance of O.

---

actual reception of the sacrament truly and coessentially contributes to the validity, the fully ecclesial realization, of the sacrament. This does not eliminate the differences specific to each individual sacrament (e.g., the special instances of the Eucharist, of matrimony, and of that sacrament which is the first to be received, baptism).

Casel's publications[8] it has been the custom to refer to this as the problem of the *Mysteriengegenwart* or "presence in mystery." Leaving aside any objection we may have to Casel's solution, we intend now simply to clarify the insight we have so far gained.

(a) Christ's Mystery of Redemption as Eternally Actual

Expressed in terms of time, the incarnation of God is the personal entry of the Eternal into the boundaries of time; Eternity itself in temporal form. And this happens in such a way that the historical actions of the man Jesus are personal actions of the eternal Son of God. Eternal divine act is realized in historical human form. This divine-human reality therefore covers two dimensions which are neither separate nor merely contiguous.

There are two aspects to Jesus' redemptive acts; they take place in history, yet have a perennial character. First, time itself is irreversible. Whatever is historically past cannot now, in any way at all, be made once more actually present, not even by God himself, not even "in mystery." Whatever has already happened in history is irrevocably past and done.[9] A fact historically past cannot therefore be actualized anew mystically or in the sacrament. If Casel agrees with what I have said, then it seems to me that a contradiction is

---

[8] Cf. *SH*, pp. 215–19 for a brief account of Casel's theory, and for bibliographical data. Casel (and the lively controversy around his works) gave perhaps the greatest single impetus to the general movement in theology and spirituality away from the individualistic, sometimes excessively objectivised approach characteristic of the post-Renaissance period up till the last decades of the nineteenth century. The development of the critical study of Scripture and the Fathers led inevitably to a renewed appreciation and awareness of the community character of the Church as Mystical Body, and of the essentially sacramental character of salvation.

[9] Certainly the past influences the present and has, especially in the human person, some form of actuality still. But this actuality is not the historical actuality of an event as it occurs now. So this aspect cannot be fundamental to a true "presence in mystery."

inherent in his thesis. For if God truly became man, then necessarily the sacrifice of the Cross in its historical manifestation is a reality belonging to the past and cannot be actualized anew in a sacrament. The historicity of the man Jesus and of his human acts of redemption shares inevitably in the irrevocability of temporal events. Should we wish to maintain the contrary, we would support a new form of Docetism[10]; we should deny the genuine historicity of Jesus' existence as man. The omnipresence of God the Son takes on a human form in the man Jesus; a form which through his physical reality is historically situated. God's omnipresence in the man Jesus becomes the presence of a man to his fellow men. Because this human mode of being present is conditioned by bodily qualification, it remains limited and cannot be equated with omnipresence.

But if in the sacraments there is nevertheless a certain presence in mystery, this is possible only if, in Christ's historical redemptive acts, there already was an element of something perennial; an enduring trans-historical element which now becomes sacramentalized in an earthly event of our own time in a visible act of the Church. And indeed, in keeping with sound Christology, we must hold that this trans-historical element is unquestionably present in the acts of Christ's life. This brings us to the second aspect of the redemptive acts of Jesus.

In the man Jesus God the Son is personally present. His human existence itself is wholly and entirely a presence of God among us. But it is in the activity of Jesus' life alone that this personal presence of God the Son is fully realized. The historical redemptive acts of Christ, which as historical are irrevocably past, are personal acts of God the Son, although performed in a human mode. They are acts in time which are the personal acts of the eternal God the Son. Consider now that the man Jesus is not first a man and then God as

[10] Docetism is a heresy that in the early days of Christianity denied the genuineness of Jesus' humanity. Jesus, it is said, took on only the appearance (*dokesis*) of being a man.

well; he is God-man; not a mixture, but God existing *in* human form. In virtue of the Hypostatic Union we are confronted with a divine way of being man and a human way of being God. The man Jesus is the existence of God himself (the Son) according to and in the mode of humanity. For person and nature are never extrinsic elements separate from one another. The God-man is one person.[11] Since the sacrifice of the Cross and all the mysteries of the life of Christ are personal acts of God, they are eternally actual and enduring. God the Son himself is therefore present in these human acts in a manner that transcends time. For of course we cannot conceive of the presence of a mere act; presence in this kind of context is always the presence of the person who acts; a personal presence which renders itself actual here and now, and active in and through an act. Jesus' human act, being the act of the Son of God in his humanity, cannot, therefore, be expressed merely in terms of time, as though the person who is man were something quite extrinsic to the humanity of Christ. Precisely because the human acts of Christ are acts of God they share, in and according to humanity, in the mystery of God. Being radically the act of the eternal God, Jesus' human act of redemption, in spite of its true historicity, cannot be merely something of the historical past. His human presence to his fellow men is permeated with his divine mode of being and of being present.

In the first chapter we were considering the redemptive mystery of Christ as the revelation of the redeeming Trinity made real in the man Jesus. In the light of that discussion we should grasp the essential significance of the perennially enduring character of the redemption. The resurrection and the exaltation of the Servant of God were seen to be the Father's response to the sacrifice of the Cross; by this the cycle of love between Father and Son is perfected on the human plane, so that this man is established by the Father

---

[11] St. Thomas says, "persona humanae naturae." Note that his phrase is not "persona humana": "Persona . . . Filii Dei est persona . . . humanae naturae in Christo." (*Compendium Theologiae*, c. 211.)

as the principle of the sending of the Holy Spirit upon us. The exalted Christ is the sacrifice of the Cross in glory, and therefore the sacrifice of the Cross in its power as source of the Spirit. And this exalted Christ is "the same yesterday and today and for ever."[12] Christ's glorified humanity is the enduring reality in which we first see the love within God of the Son for the Father transposed into the form of the sacrifice of the Cross, which the Father accepts; and in which we also see in full human reality one of the Two from whom the Holy Spirit proceeds. In the mode of glory, the sacrifice of the Cross, the relationship of loving obedience between the Son incarnate and the Father is an enduring reality. The perennial element in Christ's historical acts is thus identical with the enduring character of the incarnation. It was for this reason that the Greek Fathers reacted spontaneously against Julian of Halicarnassus, who held that upon completion of the work of redemption on earth there was no longer any sense in the continued existence of the humanity of Christ. Considering that Christ's entire human life on earth was the living out of that relationship in which, within God, he stands to the Father—so that it was his very sonship realized in human form—we must conclude that all the mysteries of the human life of Christ[13] endure for ever in the mode of glory. Passover and Pentecost are an eternal mystery of which the glorified body of Christ is the permanent sign, established for ever.

For this reason the Epistle to the Hebrews could speak of a "heavenly altar" and an "eternal sacrifice," and on the same account the early Christians were deeply convinced of the "once for all" character of the redemption, of its being *ephapax*. As the realization in human form of the redeeming Trinity, the historical mysteries of Christ's life, which were personal acts of the God-man, are a permanent, enduring reality in the mode of the Lord's existence in glory. The mystery of saving worship, or Christ's act

[12] Heb. 13.8.

[13] In the very apt phrase of the Greek Fathers and the great scholastics, the *mysteria carnis Christi*.

of redemption is, in the mode of glory, an eternally actual reality, as the Epistle to the Hebrews repeatedly stresses.[14]

(b) The Sacramental Presence of the Enduring Mystery of Redemption

In an earlier part of this work we argued that the personal activity of the risen Christ—which is his eternally actual mystery of worship—is able to reach us and influence us all, whoever and wherever we may be, through the medium of his glorified body. In this way the man Jesus is present among us in his grace-giving activity. But on the other hand we saw that without assuming earthly form, Christ's heavenly activity cannot become visibly present to us and for us, because of our unglorified state. The man Jesus is the presence of the redeeming God among us, though in the mode of a human presence bodying that presence forth to us. Precisely for this reason the plan of the incarnation requires, from the moment of Christ's ascension, a prolongation of his bodily mediation in time. We know already that this sacramental body of the Lord is the Church. We called the sacraments the specific activity of this ecclesial reality and sign. Just as Christ through his risen body acts invisibly in the world, he acts visibly in and through his earthly body, the Church, in such a way that the sacraments are the personal saving acts of Christ realized as institutional acts in the Church.

[14] It will be noted that in explaining this perennial element in Christ's action we make no appeal to the so-called "visio beata viatorica" of the man Jesus, in which there would be a "participated eternity." Even if this were admitted, it would still not be the principle of the element in question. Nor do we base our argument, at least not directly, on the basic saving human will of Christ; for although this will is a stable fundamental will, it cannot, at least not directly, be the principle of the "presence in mystery." We find the essential principle in the fact that Jesus' human acts are personal acts of God, so that the permanence is a quality of both the spiritual and corporeal aspect of the sacrifice of the Cross; in its bodily-spiritual mode the act itself of this sacrifice is permanently present in Christ. And this act is operative in the sacraments.

When all this is considered together with what we have just been saying about the perennial character of the redemption, it becomes clear that it is precisely the eternally actual mystery of worship, Christ himself, who becomes present to us and is active for our benefit in the sacraments. This is the authentic and essential factor of the "presence in mystery." The "presence in mystery" rests, therefore, on the fact that the sacraments are personal acts of Christ—as, for example, Pope Pius XII, in keeping with tradition, says in his encyclical *Mystici Corporis:* "Christ baptizes . . . absolves, offers sacrifice."[15] Although this presence in mystery is at its greatest in the Eucharist, because there Christ, personally and really present, is both priest and victim under sacramental forms, every sacrament is a personal presence of Christ, though in the other six sacraments the principle of his presence is the eternally actual *act* of redemption alone. In both cases we have a personal presence of Christ himself, but the principle of the presence differs; in the Eucharist Christ himself is present by the power of transubstantiation; in the other sacraments Christ is present only in virtue of his redemptive *act* sacramentally embodied. The chief merit of Dom Casel's work, striking in its visionary approach, is that it did lead the way to an appreciation of this fact, even though it took its course through a somewhat nonchalant exegesis of Scripture and the Fathers, and the doctrinal exposition was theologically not wholly sound. The sacraments are mysteries, or celebrations in mystery, of the redemption by Christ.

(c) The Eternally Enduring Actuality of the Redemption and the Historical Perspective of Salvation in the Sacraments

The essence of sacramental saving efficacy is the eternally actual redemptive act of the mystery of Christ. This means that sacramental efficacy is identical with the historical sacrifice of the Cross in its character as mystery; and consequently it is identical with the

---

[15] *AAS,* 25 (1943), p. 218.

actual saving activity of the risen Lord too. St. Thomas is therefore not contradicting himself when, after saying that the power of the sacraments derives from the "suffering of Christ," he then says that the heavenly Christ is working in the sacraments[16]; these two expressions refer to one and the same saving activity according to its eternally enduring reality. From this also it is clear that, while maintaining the doctrine of sacramental efficacy, we do not contradict or deny the *ephapax* or the "once-and-for-all" character of the sacrifice of the Cross; for the sacraments are that very sacrifice made visible.

Even so the sacraments are a celebration in mystery of the past historical acts of the life of Christ, too.[17] The sacraments always include a reference to the historical event, because it was upon the

[16] In *SH,* pp. 161–74, the author has undertaken a brief study of St. Thomas's theory of the "presence in mystery" with particular attention to the presence and real efficient causality today of Christ's past historical acts of redemption. In recognizing such a causality in the past acts of Christ, St. Thomas was entirely alone in the Middle Ages. John of St. Thomas, Sylvius, Suarez and other commentators (and more recent manuals depending on them) have held that St. Thomas was not really attributing present efficient causality to historical acts of the past, on the principle that the past cannot affect the present *in linea efficientiae.* "Passio et mors et resurrectio Christi, licet iam transierint in actu et in ratione motus aut actionis, manent tamen virtute in effectu suo, videlicet in humanitate quae affecta fuit passione. . . ." (John of St. Thomas, *Cursus Theol., De Sacram.,* disp. 25, a. 1, db. 9.) This, however, is merely a weak dilution of St. Thomas's thought, and cannot be presented as historical Thomism. From a critical reading of the texts, St. Thomas' doctrine is clearly that not the *Christus passus* only (Christ who had died, had been buried, risen; thus the *Christus gloriosus*), but also the actual *passio* (*ST,* III, q. 48, a. 6), the death (III, q. 50, a. 6), the burial (q. 51, a. 1, ad 2), the resurrection (q. 56, a. 1, ad 3), etc., exercise a real efficiency in Christ's work of salvation now. The principal argument is that "humana natura in Christo assumpta est ut instrumentaliter operetur ea quae sunt operationes propriae solius Dei" (*SCG,* IV, 41.) Implicit in the mystery of the incarnation itself, St. Thomas clearly recognizes a perennial actuality (which therefore transcends the historical moment) in the acts of Jesus' life on earth. St. Thomas is referring to the historical act of Christ (not a new act) not precisely in its historicity, for as such it is past, but as eternally actual because properly divine.

[17] The *acta-et-passa-Christi* repetition makes the term almost stereotyped in St. Thomas.

historical Cross, and there alone at that moment of history, that God really sacrificed his human life for us. Might we not call it typical that the Epistle to the Hebrews repeatedly asserts that Christ, in virtue of the sacrifice of his blood, entered the Holy of Holies as High Priest? In its human realization the eternally actual redemptive act itself retains this relation to the historical sacrifice of the Cross. In the sacraments the redemptive act is therefore made visible with this relation to the event of history.

From all this we see that the sacraments, as "mediation" between Christ and ourselves, must be situated not immediately between the historical sacrifice of the Cross and our twentieth-century situation, but rather between the Christ who is living now and our earthly world. More precisely, what takes place in the sacraments is the immediate encounter in mutual availability between the living *Kyrios* and ourselves. The sacraments are this encounter. And it is this immediate encounter with Christ that explains the threefold historical orientation of the sacraments. For they are first of all an *anamnesis* or a commemoration of the past sacrifice of the Cross[18] because of the relation of the eternally actual redemptive act, present in the sacrament, to the historical moment in which Christ shed his blood. Secondly, they are a visible affirmation and bestowal of the actual gift of grace[19] inasmuch as the recipient becomes concerned in the enduring redemptive act by which the *Kyrios* is reaching out to him here and now. In the third place, they are a pledge of eschatological salvation and a herald of the *parousia*,[20] because the sacraments are the sacramental presence of Christ the *Eschaton,* either because of a real transubstantiation (in the case of the Eucharist), or because of the sacramentalizing of his eternally actual redemptive act (in the case of the remaining six sacraments). Hence a visible intervention in our time of the *Eschaton* himself takes place in the sacraments. Sacramental encounter with the living Christ in the Church is therefore, in virtue of the historical

---

18 "Signum rememorativum." (*ST*, III, q. 60, a. 3.)
19 "Signum demonstrativum." (*ST*, III, q. 60, a. 3.)
20 "Signum prognosticum." (*ST*, III, q. 60, a. 3.)

mysteries of Christ's life, the actual beginning of eschatological salvation on earth.

To say that the Church in her sacraments is a prolongation of
the earthly life of Christ appears therefore to be an elliptical or insufficient statement of the case. Certainly the Church in her visibility prolongs the function of the earthly visibility which Christ
once enjoyed. But the Passover brought about a change of emphasis; the Christ *lives* now, at this moment. His glorious body continues to fulfil the function it had during his earthly life. But because
this sign of Jesus' life-giving redemptive act has become invisible
to us, this body of the Lord is prolonged in a form which is visible
on earth—in the sacramental Church. In this sense, the Church
is a prolongation primarily of the heavenly Christ, and therefore it
prolongs the function of the earthly body of Jesus. In many a
treatise on the Church this point is out of perspective, and consequently one is inclined to forget that Jesus' "sitting at the right
hand of the Father" was the centre of primitive Christian faith,
which was more a confession of the Christ who lives now than of
what he had achieved for us in the past, although the latter was the
foundation of the former, and in this sense fundamental. Precisely
because of this awareness of the presence of the living Christ, the
first Christians longed for the fullness of his presence, the *parousia*.
"Christ is the Lord, sitting at God's right hand," is the fundamental
confession of faith in both past and future *parousia*. And all of this
we rediscover in the sacraments.

2. The Sacraments as Ecclesial Manifestation of Christ's Divine Love for Men (Bestowal of Grace) and of His Human Love for God (Worship)

The second aspect brought out in the signification of the sacraments is, as we have said, the fact that not only are they the visibility of Christ's redemptive act, but also of the inner worship and

holiness of the ecclesial community itself. We must now examine this aspect more closely.

(a) Ritual Activity in General

Though this discussion calls for a developed analysis, we shall keep it brief. What is the explanation of sacramental ritual worship by the whole of religious mankind? The fact itself is incontrovertible and finds its immediate explanation in the material limitation of the human person. The world of matter is, as it were, the field of experience within which man finds and comes to himself as a spirit-in-the-world. Bodiliness is thus caught up into a specifically human, free and purposeful activity. For in virtue of the primordial datum of his own bodiliness, it is within the material world, and in a certain sense by means of it, that man fulfils himself as a person, and consequently it is in the material world that man expresses his developing personality. That man's existence is *de facto* a bodily one thus provides the principle of the human tendency to create symbols. In this sense corporeality, caught up into human life, is a sign and a symbol. It is no more than a sign of the inner life of man's spirit, though belonging to it as part of his "sign-making" activity; it can be no more because it veils and alienates that life even while providing it with the means of expression. For indeed it is only in an element borrowed from the world that the human spirit can express itself.[21]

In religious life especially, that is in personal relationship with God, symbolism will play an important role, because inner religious experiences are upon a plane that we are not able to cover in our own proper terms. The religious man, then, gropes for the things of daily life and makes of them the field in which he expresses his higher experiences. And not merely the field of expression, for such symbolizing at the same time creates the possibility of grasping

[21] Cf. D. M. de Petter, "De oorsprong van de zijnskennis volgens de H. Thomas van Aquino," in *Tijdschrift voor philosophie*, 17 (1955), pp. 199-254, for an appreciation of the foundation of this view in the philosophy of the human person.

what has been experienced; it makes it possible to intensify his religious experience. So the "external cult" becomes the manifestation of the "inner worship of God" and at the same time makes it possible to live that inner worship to the full. The external cult, St. Thomas already has noted, is a "confession of faith" made externally visible, "a certain confession of faith through outward signs."[22] If now this symbolic expression is made communal—that is, if it becomes, by means of communal symbols, the normal expression of the faith of a confessional community, then we actually call these ritual confessions of faith "sacraments" or "sacramental cult," as St. Augustine[23] and St. Thomas[24] have already said. Considered in a human-religious context, sacraments are therefore symbolic acts of worship arising from the faith of a particular religious social group. Therefore the symbolic forms in which religion is expressed are, according to their fundamental structure, more or less the same in all religions. C. G. Jung names them the "primitive human archetypes" of symbol-making religious activity. These are the "sacraments of nature" of which St. Thomas so frequently speaks.[25]

(b) Sacramental Symbolic Action of the Church: Ecclesial Worship and Salvation

The ecclesial acts in which Christ, through his eternally actual redemptive act, makes himself here present are, in their human religious form, precisely this kind of act of ritual symbolism performed by the religious community which is the Church. Because they are the Church's activity in worship through symbols, St. Thomas calls the sacraments the *insignes* of the Church[26]; the typical proper activity of this religious community by which one is able to identify it. The fact that this ecclesial symbolic action is at the

---

[22] *ST*, III, q. 63, a. 4, ad 3.
[23] *Contra Faustum*, 19. (*PL*, 42, col. 355.)
[24] *ST*, III, q. 61, a. 1.
[25] E.g., *ST*, III, q. 61, a. 2 and 3c and ad 2; q. 70, a. 4, ad 2.
[26] *In Ad Ephesios*, 4, lect. 2.

same time able to be the personal action of Christ himself naturally presupposes the institution of the sacraments by Christ himself. We shall study this point later. At the moment we are concerned with the fact that the sacraments, as the sacramental realization of Christ's mystery of saving worship, are, by reason of the fact that they are ecclesial symbolic actions, at the same time the manifestation of the inner worship and of the holiness of the ecclesial community itself. The Church itself in its sacramental visibility is no empty sign. As the holy Church, it is itself already a communion in grace, the *pleroma* of Christ; it is itself filled with Christ's holiness. In its symbolic action the Church gives expression to what it is in itself; the redeemed People of God bound in faith, hope and love to its leader, the *Kyrios*. Thus in the Church's sacraments the ecclesial communion in grace with God in Christ receives its sacred manifestation. And the same ecclesial grace-abounding visibility is simultaneously the personal saving act of the living Christ. A sacrament is the visibility of Christ's divine love for men (bestowal of grace) and equally of his human love for God (worship).

All of this simply means that a sacrament, as a visible symbolic action of the Church, is not only the rendering here present on earth of Christ's mystery of saving worship, but also the Church's inward identification of itself in faith, hope and love with this mystery of worship. The ecclesial life of grace adds nothing to the fullness of Christ's grace, but is a sharing in that grace. The sacraments are therefore acts of the whole mystical body, of Christ and of his Church. And indeed in this sense they are acts of Christ in and through his Church. Christ acts in the sacraments together with the People of God already realized and existing in this world.

In this way we arrive at a more determinate definition of the sacraments. They are ecclesial acts of worship, in which the Church in communion of grace with its heavenly Head (i.e., together with Christ) pleads with the Father for the bestowal of grace on the recipient of the sacrament, and in which at the same time the Church itself, as saving community in holy union with Christ, performs a saving act.

In manifesting sacramentally its own holiness, the Church makes holy. Thus in the strength of its own being filled with the fullness of Christ—to which the Church gives ritual expression in the sacraments—the Church in its sacraments acts as a saving community. As in Christ himself, we have here salvation-through-worship, in which the worship itself is a pure result of grace. Only in this sense can the sacraments, as symbolic action of Christ in and through the Church, be fully understood. That which Christ alone did in the objective redemption, although in our name and in the place of us all, he does now in the sacraments (for the recipient of the sacraments, or, in the case of the Eucharist, for all men) together with the holy and ecclesial People of God whom he has won to himself. Christ's worship and that of his Church, present in the other sacraments, appears in the Eucharist in a special manner; in the other six sacraments it is not present in the manner and under the aspect of sacrifice. For this reason St. Thomas says that the holiness, faith and *devotio* or prayerful deliberateness of the whole Church as well is operative in the sacraments.[27] Hence every sacrament is a ritual prayer of the whole Church, which thus infallibly confers on the religiously disposed recipient the grace prayed for. For the recipient this means that to receive a sacrament fruitfully is to enter upon (in the case of baptism) or become more intimately caught up in (in the case of the other sacraments) the Church's communion of life with Christ and with his eternal mystery of Passover and Pentecost. This means that as time goes on the Church is moving more and more towards its essential realization in its sacramental activity.

One practical conclusion is this: that the administration of a sacrament, being an ecclesial action, though it concerns the recipient personally never concerns him alone. All the faithful are concerned in a sacramental act of faith of the Church as a public confession of their own faith. Not only the Eucharist (to which still other considerations apply) but also, for example, the baptism of an infant is a liturgical act for the whole community of the faithful; each is a specific communal act of the People of God who must have a concern for the salvation of the one who is receiving the sacrament.

[27] *ST*, III, q. 39, a. 5.

The holiness of the Church, which together with the holiness of Christ is here sacramentalized, is not the holiness of some abstract entity, but rather of all those who belong in grace to this Church. It is therefore also fitting, and is indeed required by the essence of the sacrament itself, that on behalf of the recipient the faithful community should unite in prayer with the sacramental ritual prayer of the Church—of the Church which is here uniting itself sacramentally with Christ's heavenly mystery of saving worship. That which Christ as *Kyrios* is doing invisibly through his glorified body in heaven for all men on earth, he does visibly for the same men through his earthly body the Church, which is thus the one who "is always praying and interceding for us" and the "holy Saviour." Even in the sacrament of penance, where we have most lost the awareness of the communal character of the action, the grace of forgiveness of sins is assured to the penitent sinner because the Church, together with Christ, is praying for him. In former times penitential practice threw this fact into sharp relief. Today its obscure but nevertheless still true expression is found in the prayers that precede the absolution (*Misereatur, Indulgentiam, Dominus . . . te absolvat*). The Church is busy on the penitent's behalf long before he kneels down in the confessional. Sins are forgiven because Christ, together with his Church, prayed for their forgiveness. Christ and his Church are always ahead of us. In the sacrament this ecclesial prayer is sacramentally identified with the prayer of the Son of God which is always heard. And this brings us to the infallible working of grace in the sacraments.

(c) The Infallible Working of Grace in the Sacraments: the Sacramental Mystery of Passover and Pentecost

We mentioned above that the mystery of worship which is Christ himself infallibly bestows the grace for which it prays. The sonship of Christ is the principle of the infallible connection between this mystery of worship and the bestowal of grace through his sending of the Holy Spirit. On the plane of the sacramental realization of this saving mystery of worship of Christ in the Church, the infallible connection is given ecclesial incarnation. Traditionally this connection is indicated by the somewhat threadbare phrase, "The sacraments confer grace *ex opere operato*."[28] Not infrequently this was taken, especially among the Reformers, as an indication of "magic." We must therefore examine the notion carefully. The Council of Trent, in reaction to the Protestant teaching that faith alone saves, defined that given the required dispositions in the recipient,[29] the sacraments confer grace *ex opere operato*.[30] Reformers opposed this point of faith because they thought, unjustifiably, that in such a view the sacraments would lay an obligation on God, and that this would endanger our appreciation of the free mercy of God, who bestows grace as he wills. However, this is a fundamental misinterpretation of what the Catholic sacrament is intended to be—though it must be granted that in Luther's day in some popular notions a true and satisfactory insight into the sacraments of the Church was not very much in evidence. But one does not judge the faith and ideology of a Church by some misinterpretations current among those unqualified to speak on the subject. In any case, in the much-maligned Middle Ages the profound Christological significance of sacramental *ex opere operato* efficacy was abundantly evident. St. Thomas, who in his *Summa* did not even consider it necessary to use this term, nevertheless accepted it in his earlier works, and in them we are able to see how foreign the phrase was to any magical interpretation of the sacraments or to any imposition on the grace of God. Put negatively, the significance of sacramental efficacy *ex opere operato* is that the bestowal of grace is not dependent upon the sanctity of the minister, nor does the faith of the recipient put any obligation on grace; Christ remains free, sovereign and inde-

---

[28] Literally, this means "by the fact that the sacramental rite is [validly] performed"; thus, "by the power of rite." What it actually signifies will become clear as our investigation proceeds.

[29] *DB*, no. 849.   [30] *DB*, nos. 851 and 894.

pendent with regard to any human merit whatsoever. Put positively, *ex opere operato* efficacy means that this act is Christ's act. *Ex opere operato* and "in the power of the mystery of Christ" mean the same thing.[31]

The genuine Catholic interpretation of the saving power of the sacraments may be brought out more clearly still if we recall what was said in a previous section of this work. The sacraments are the saving mystery of the worship of Christ himself in ecclesial visibility; the mystery of his worship, to which the infallible response is the effective bestowal of grace. This infallible connection is now present in the sacraments, expressed by the term *ex opere operato,* or "by the power of the rite." For what reason? For a double reason. In the Church's ritual symbolic act, not only are Christ's prayer and worship really present in visible and sacramental form, but really present also is the infallible response to this prayer, the effective bestowal of grace. In all of this we are confronted simply with the ritual making real of the saving mystery of Christ, and therefore with the embodiment—thus the concrete offering—of the gratuitous saving will of God in Christ.

To maintain that the sacraments lay an obligation on grace, grace thereby losing its gratuitousness, is to turn the whole matter upside down. The untrammelled freedom of God's mercy remains unhindered in the Catholic sacraments. For in the concrete a sacrament is simply the outwardly perceivable glance of God's generosity towards a particular man; the sacrament is the divine generosity. Needless to say, this Catholic view presupposes belief in the mystery of the Church itself, and therefore presupposes too the institution of the sacraments by Christ; for an ecclesial act could never be the visibility of a personal glance of love from Christ, in the sense of an effective bestowal of grace; a human act on purely human initiative could lay no claim to grace. But granted the mystery of the Church instituted by Christ (and the Reformation is coming more and more to see this as a biblical fact), any accusation

---

[31] See Appendix, pp. 82 ff., for a fuller account of this view.

alleging a human attempt to force the giving of grace is seen to be unfounded. Consequently, because the sacraments are, in ecclesial embodiment, the mystery of the worship of Christ to which the Father always responds, they themselves also infallibly bestow grace,[32] i.e., *ex opere operato:* by the power of Christ the Lord.

Therefore the *ex opere operato* thesis, which gave rise to many objections against the Catholic sacramental doctrine, is as a matter of fact the doctrine's most essential mystery—the sacramental reality of the mystery of the redeeming Trinity in Christ. The mystery of saving worship of the Church is (under a special aspect indicated by the outward sign) the sacramental mystery of Passover and Pentecost as personally directed through the Church to the recipient of the sacrament. As the mystery of worship which *ex opere operato* pleads for and brings the grace of redemption to the recipient, a sacrament stands in relationship to Christ as Son of his Father. As the mystery of grace that *ex opere operato* actually bestows the grace for which it prays upon the recipient, the sacrament stands in relationship to Christ as the co-principle of the Holy Spirit.

The Church, as the earthly body of the Lord whose heavenly body is the established sign of the mystery of Passover and Pentecost, is itself the earthly sign of this same mystery. Therefore it also follows that in virtue of the mystery of Christ, both the Son and the Holy Spirit, in their distinctness and within the unity of the Trinity, have their own proper active share in the sacraments, and that this whole is dominated by the all-embracing initiative of the Father: to him, in union with Christ, the Church addresses its sacramental prayer; from him, in and through the Son, the eternal emission of the Holy Spirit proceeds. It is in the man Jesus, the

[32] This should not be forgotten. Our emphasis on the ritual efficacy (all too long neglected in sacramental doctrine) does not imply that we now have to lay emphasis on instrumental saving causality of the sacraments. Both of these are authentic aspects. At the same time, note that the ritual efficacy which we also acknowledge in the sacraments is something quite different from the so-called "moral causality" which Franzelin attributes to the sacraments on account of their "intrinsic worth."

central person of the Trinity, that these divine relationships are revealed and made real for us. The heavenly sign of this mystery, expressed in terms of human redemption, is the glorified body of Jesus. The Church, as the earthly body of the Lord, mediates the earthly visibility of this heavenly sign among us, until the Lord comes visibly again at the *parousia*.

Now all this must not be taken to mean that, as worship, the sacraments are the work of God the Son only and not of the Holy Spirit; for we cannot even call on Christ in faith unless by the power of the Spirit in us crying "Father." Nor, on the other hand, is it to be taken to mean that the sacraments as salvation are the work of the Holy Spirit only, for whatever the Spirit does he receives from the Father through the Son. Nevertheless within the unity of this sacramental activity the three persons, within their unity and in their diversity, fulfil a work which is also one and diverse. From this it will later become clear that, in Christ, sacramental grace is trinitarian.

This twofold aspect of the sacraments (first Christ's own ritual prayer for grace, in which the Church prayerfully joins and with it gives ritual expression to her prayer, and second the effective bestowal of the prayed-for grace) helps us the better to grasp that the substance of a sacrament always includes a twofold element: an *epiclesis* in the form of a request (*in forma deprecativa*) that is to say, a prayer in which we plead with the Father by the power of the Spirit and together with Christ; and a definitive bestowal (*in forma indicativa*). Both elements are always present, even when they no longer appear, as was formerly the case, in two separate ritual moments in the Liturgy. Moreover the one essential moment (whether it be an expression in the form of an *epiclesis* or an exclusively indicative formula) has in any case the twofold significance. In the contraction of the essential sacrament to the one moment in the whole of the richly developed liturgical rite, we have unfortunately all too often lost sight of this double significance. There seems then to be reason to regret the fact that, at least in the Western liturgy, the form of ritual realization has nearly always concentrated on an "indicative formula" as the essentially sacramental moment, while the *epiclesis,* the request or deprecatory formula, sometimes obscured but still always really present within the liturgical whole, is mostly relegated to the level of a merely ceremonial adjunct. This is a fact that easily (though unjustifiably) might be taken as confirming a juridical interpretation of the sacraments. Thus when a theologian states that, upon the correct performance of the external sacramental rite, this rite effects grace of itself or *ex opere operato,* we must above all not forget the profound Christological and trinitarian mystery these words imply. For this is what they mean: When the human prayer of the glorified Son of God is sacramentally realized among us in a truly ecclesial religious act, through the sending of the Spirit by Christ, grace is really bestowed upon us in the same sacrament by the Father of Mercies.

(d) The Ecclesial Visibility of Grace: "The Sacraments Confer the Grace They Signify"

The preceding investigation makes immediately clear the connection between the value of the sacraments as signs and their saving power; or in the terminology of a more recent tradition, it makes clear that a sacrament is a *signum efficax gratiae,* a sign which really and actually bestows the grace it signifies.[33] Just as the established sign of salvation which is the risen body of Christ also actually gives that which it signifies, through the Lord's incarnate saving activity,[34] so also the earthly body of the Lord, the Church, actually gives the grace it signifies in its sacraments, since this body is sacramentally identical with the heavenly body of Christ. It is true that we are not now considering the primordial sacrament per-

[33] "[Sacramentum] continet gratiam quam significat, et [eam] non ponentibus obicem . . . confert," in the words of the Council of Trent. (*DB,* no. 849.)

[34] Thus St. Thomas names the "mysteria carnis Christi" a sign and cause of salvation: e.g., *Compendium Theologiae,* c. 239; cc. 227–8; *ST,* III, q. 56, a. 1. ad 4.

sonally united to the Word of God[35] but rather the particular sacraments[36]; nevertheless, these special sacraments are personal acts of the risen Christ in ecclesial form. Therefore they are, in ecclesial visibility ("sign"), Christ's eternally actual act of redemption ("cause of grace") as personally affecting a particular man. They confer grace precisely as a sign of the redemptive act. The sacraments thus confer grace because they are the redemptive act in sacramental visibility. Therefore the effective sign of grace indicates the fact that grace comes visibly and is not merely a "purely inward" matter.

If then we examine the sacraments as it were from below, we may say that they are the specific ritual activity of a particular religious community, the Church, in which Christ glorified is perfecting a deeper mystery through the sending of the Spirit. Seen in this manner the ecclesial symbolic act ("sign") is imbued with the divine saving power of Christ's redemptive act. But if we look at the sacraments from above—that is in the light of the heavenly redemptive act which Christ realizes sacramentally in an act of the Church, and thus as a personal symbolic act of Christ through the institutional medium of the Church—we see the sacraments immediately as the ecclesial visibility of Christ's redemptive will applying to the recipient of the sacrament. The sacraments are this redemptive will itself in visible and tangible ecclesial form. They are thus the actual gift of grace itself coming and appealing to us in historical visibility. The sign itself makes the actual gift of grace here present. It is not of course as if the sign, as sign, could have an actual effect, but rather the other way about; the gift of grace comes in its own visibility; it makes itself here present visibly (thus "in a sign") and therefore "works" in visible presence. Certainly the gift of grace makes itself present in an embodiment borrowed from this world or, more precisely, in a human act of the ecclesial minister.

In actual fact we are confronted with two realities; one an act of Christ, the other a personal act of the Church's minister. But upon

[35] *Sacramentum coniunctum.*   [36] *Sacramenta separata.*

the plane of sacramentality or sign-activity this human act is personally the act of Christ the High Priest. Of this unity in duality we cannot do better than to say with St. Thomas that it is an instrumental efficient saving causality. And this is quite free from any taint of "physicism"; it is the efficacy of the grace of Christ himself, in and through an ecclesial act which is the sacramentalization of Christ's own redemptive act. Thus in baptism, for example, the washing is the divine and cleansing grace itself in earthly visibility. If we appreciate "sign" in its true human significance, as soon as we have said "sign" we have already said "efficient causality." For here "sign" means the visible presence of a grace-giving activity. In formal terms, the sign-value and the causal value remain distinct. (To have emphasized this is a lasting achievement of the Thomist school; it is not possible to confuse the efficiency with what Billot calls the efficacy of a sign as such.) Nevertheless one cannot consider the sign as constituted first of all in its full human value as a sign, in order then to load it with a coincidental power as well. That would be physicism. We must hold that the bodily washing in baptism, as the symbolic realization of Christ's own act, is more than bodily washing is on the merely human plane; it is indeed the gift of grace in tangible visibility—the outward sign of something inward.

Consequently we must say that because it realizes the symbolic activity of Christ in his Church, the sacrament causes salvation as a sign in the full human sense of the word (and thus not as a mere indication of something "beyond"). "Significando causant," St. Thomas has already said,[37] yet in our opinion the term "causality of the symbol"[38] is by itself inadequate in the case of the sacraments. Indeed, even if this term may be appropriate for the explanation of the immediate symbolic acts of Christ himself (e.g., of Christ on earth), it is not suitable as an explanation of the symbolic acts of Christ through an ecclesial act. Since the body of Christ is

[37] *De Veritate,* q. 26, a. 4, ad 13; *ST,* III, q. 62, a. 1, ad 1.
[38] Cf. L. Monden, "Symbooloorzakelijkheid als eigen causaliteit van het sacrament," in *BJ,* 13 (1952), pp. 277–85.

the visible realization of his human interiority and thus belongs hypostatically to the person of God the Son, the term "instrumentality" presents difficulties when used of his incarnate human acts.[39]

For human nature is certainly not an instrument of the person, but rather the mode of his existence. Thus the (bodily-spiritual) humanity of Christ is a mode of existence of God the Son himself. But the case is not the same with *ecclesial* symbolic acts of Christ. For in its human reality the Church's symbolic act is quite clearly separate from Christ. Even so, it becomes identified sacramentally with the body of Christ which is active in heaven. In this case, therefore, instrumentality retains its precise meaning (*sacramentum separatum*). The organic unity of "sign" and "instrumental efficient cause of salvation" can therefore best be expressed by the term "instrumental causality of the symbol."

The following will help to clarify this. One man's inward act of will with regard to another man only becomes a completely human reality with meaning for the other man when this inner intention has been manifested in an external act. Only in the expressive word or gesture does a human intention directed to some other person receive its perfect meaning. Now as man Christ is the mediator between God's love and ourselves. Consequently his mediation takes place through human acts, through loving saving acts of will which find their full expression in an expressive and loving gesture. The specific expressive "gesture" of Christ's saving love is his exalted and glorified body, the established sign of the victorious redemption. It is in the Church's sacraments that Christ wants to make this expression of love visible within the sphere of our earthly life and earthly world, which through our human activity is made into an extension of our humanity. In this way material things of the world around us are taken and humanized through our own proper corporeality: that is to say, in a union with our own bodies they become an expression of our spiritual thoughts.

We find something of the same kind in Christ, who through his glorified body takes up material things of our human world into a

---

[39] St. Thomas too is aware of this distinction, for though he speaks of instrumentality, he adds the nuance, "instrumentum coniunctum."

dynamic unity with his risen and active body. I hope I may be forgiven for drawing a likeness between the sacred sacramental event and present-day jazz, but perhaps the coherence of the sacramental whole can best be suggested by means of the image of a drummer. Just as when a drummer is playing he is extending himself through all his bodiliness into the instruments grouped about him, so that these instruments dynamically participate in the expressiveness of his rhythmic movement, making but one total movement which, arising from within the drummer, flows through the rhythm of his body, of his beating hands and stamping feet, and produces a varied harmony of percussion—so too the heavenly saving will of Christ, through his glorified body, makes one dynamic unity with the ritual gesture and the sacramental words of the minister who intends to do what the Church does.

It is only when a person's love is manifested in some telling and appealing gesture, through which it becomes possible for me to enter into this love, that I become personally confronted with this love for me. The flowers which I have an agency deliver to friends overseas on their wedding day are to them the concrete presence of my love and friendship; the concrete interpretation of my love; love in a form that is visible. This, but in infinitely greater measure, is the case in the sacraments too. For the proof Christ gives us of his love is not turned into a lifeless thing. It is not merely an indication of an absent love which nevertheless in the indication somehow becomes present. The sacramental proof and token of love makes a living unity with the human saving will of Christ in heaven. Because this is a personal act of God the Son—even though done in human form—it transcends time and space, and therefore in the literal sense of the word, like the soul in the body, becomes incarnate in the outward rite.

In this light we see more clearly the unity of the sacramental signification of grace and the sacramental bestowal of grace. In human encounter love's visible expression is an appeal and an offer, not the production of a physical effect. Love is freely given and must be freely accepted. Therefore love's expressive gesture is appealing, inviting, seeking; it is the making of an offer. This gesture of love has a certain effect. It is not an indifferent sign of love; it is a compelling sign. The firm handshake just naturally draws the firm grip in reply. Within the confines of the limited influence of one man upon another the expressive gesture of love is a *signum efficax,* a sign that effects what is signified.

Now Christ is truly man. During his life on earth the manifestations of his saving love took place on the plane of expressive human acts and gestures. Christ remains man in heaven. His saving will encounters us in an expressive personal gesture of his own, though now through the mediation of his mystical body on earth. In this the human sense of the efficacy of love's expressive gesture does not lose its force, but it does take on an unexpected profundity on account of the fact that the one who makes the loving gesture is God himself, the Son, even though in human form. While a gesture of human love directed towards us shares in the relative limitation and impotence of personal influence and remains powerless before the essential core of our personal liberty, the gesture of Christ's human love, precisely because this human act is a personal act of God the Son, enters into the centre of our personal freedom if we but hold ourselves open to it. Christ's gesture of human love is able truly to effect an answering love. The quality of appeal which does not wish to constrain our freedom remains intact. But it is, in human form, a divine appeal, and in a man of good will this infallibly attains its goal. Thus the encounter is entirely the work of grace, and yet it does include the personal response of a man—and this in itself is grace.

This is encounter which would not even be possible did not the God who comes to meet us raise us up from within to an ontologically higher plane. For since Christ's loving gesture brings about a responsive love in us, it also brings about the ontological basis upon which we, while remaining men, become capable of the theological act of encounter with God in trusting and loving surrender. If we but think what one human glance, one human smile, can do in our lives, how by such a smile we seem in a moment to be turned into a new man who in the strength of the love which comes to him in that small token can begin life anew, apparently with powers that were not there before—should we not be able to conceive how a smile of the man Jesus, God's smile, how the God-man's glance at us, can change our whole life? And this is what the sacraments are: the God-man's expression of love—with all its consequences.

3. Sevenfold Ecclesial Realization of the One Mystery of Redemption

Since it is in the power of his personal act of redemption that Christ makes himself here present in an ecclesial symbolic action, the various specific goals of signification within the sevenfold sacramental symbolism will cause the eternally actual redemptive act of Christ to be shown forth in different ways. This is proper to the structure of human symbolic activity. A sacrament is not redemption pure and simple, but rather redemption as directed to a particular human and ecclesial need for it, differentiated according to the seven sacraments (always allowing for the universal character of the eucharistic sacramental sacrifice). The outward sign therefore gives the manner in which Christ becomes actively present in each of the seven sacraments in virtue of his eternally actual redemptive act. For indeed the outward element of the sacrament is the visible manifestation of the act of redemption, and therefore indicates the particular aspect under which the redemptive act is here present. The creator of a symbol determines freely the meaning his act expresses. In this case it is Christ himself who determines the meaning of the symbol, and in consequence it is only in faith that the Church can approach and appreciate the sevenfold manner in which Christ's act of redemption is sacramentally realized.

This is a first and limiting function of the sacramental presence simply of Christ's heavenly act of redemption, in contrast to the Eucharist, where redemption as such, including therefore the aspect of sacrifice, is really present.

4. The Sacramental Presence of Christ for the Recipient

While making an exception for the special case of the Eucharist as a sacrifice, we must add yet another limiting function to the one mentioned above, in virtue of the specific structure of symbolic activity. A sacrament is essentially Christ's redemptive act being perfected with regard to a particular subject in such a way that the recipient subject is an integral and essential element within the definition of the sacrament. Quite rightly, this aspect was urged by G. Sohngen and L. Monden, in reaction to the exaggerated objectivization of Casel's view. The question, however, is this: How is one to clarify and interpret this reality? We offer the following explanation.

Upon the Cross the God-man intended his act of redemption for all men without exception. The sacrifice of the Cross, in its eternal actuality in mystery, is still intended for all men, for each one personally. Now it is this personal intention of Christ's act of redemption for a particular man that is brought out in the sacraments. It is clear, from the specific nature of the realization of eternally actual redemption in an ecclesial symbolic act, which essentially is performed for a particular man, that the presence of the redemptive act is essentially intended for the recipient of the sacrament. This being intended for a particular individual belongs to the essence of the sacraments, which after all presuppose the objective redemption, and the purpose of which is to introduce individuals personally into this redemption. The eternally actual redemptive act, already "focused" by the particular mode of signification of each of the seven sacraments, becomes actively present in being orientated towards or channeled to the recipient himself.

As the personal redemptive act of Christ in his Church, a sacrament is therefore the personal approach of Christ to a particular man. In the fullest sense of the word, a sacrament is the pledge of Christ's availability to a particular individual; the tangible pledge of his willing readiness to enter upon an encounter. The sacramentality of the economy of grace, in which grace comes from the Church to encounter us in visibility, gives rise to the quality of human peace and satisfaction peculiar to the sacramental bestowal of grace in contrast to the so-called extra-sacramental bestowal of grace. For indeed the sacrament itself is the open, frank and unambiguous pledge of the fact that Christ really wants to give grace to this man who is receiving the sacrament, and in fact does thereby give it to him unless he shuts himself up inwardly against it.

The aspect of being realized for a particular subject enters therefore into the essence of a valid sacrament, and therefore this aspect remains even if the sacrament should nevertheless be fruitless. For the specific contact with the visibility of the saving Church is still achieved. And given the inner receptivity of faith, this contact itself effects the bestowal of grace. Consequently a sacrament is the sign or the visibility of Jesus' act of redemption considered not in itself but precisely as affecting this particular man.[40]

The sacraments are signs of Christ's redemptive act in its actual grasp of a particular individual. For this reason, even when on account of the recipient's interior dispositions a sacrament remains (probably only for the time being) fruitless, every valid sacrament achieves a certain fruitful effect. It cannot be an empty sign, for even in such a case it is still a sacramental prayer of Christ and his Church for the person receiving it. And precisely on these grounds a sacrament can, as it is said, "revive." If, however, the personal

---

[40] St. Thomas has already formulated it in this way: "In hoc quod [sacramentum] significat rem sanctificantem [namely, the redeeming passion of Christ], oportet quod significat effectum, qui intelligitur in ipsa causa sanctificante prout est sanctificans." (*ST*, III, q. 60, a. 3, ad 2.) In *SH* (p. 145) the author remarks: ". . . the fact that St. Thomas, in indicating the threefold *significatum* (cf. III, q. 60, a. 3), does not stress the historically past events of the mystery of Christ, nor the eschatological bias in the sacraments, but rather the actual bestowal of grace symbolized in them is . . . characteristic of his view of the sacraments as formally a ritual symbolic action. The sacraments presuppose faith in the historically past acts of the mystery of Christ, and in this sense they are fundamentally signs of the objective redemption. But the sacramental significance refers to this mystery *prout est sanctificans,* i.e., the formal and immediate reference is to the bestowal of sacramental grace as a bestowal, here and now, upon the recipient of the sacrament.

power of supplication of the recipient is joined with the power of the ritual supplication of Christ and his Church, so that the outward sign which the recipient makes is not a fiction with regard to his inward dispositions, then the outward sign by that very fact becomes effective bestowal of grace, and in consequence its full significance is also realized. For then the sacrament is indeed the visible realization of that which takes place through Christ's redemptive act grasping this man in the sacrament. Then it is quite straightforwardly a true sign; a sign that in no way at all involves a lie and therefore *ex opere operato* is factually effective.

In this aspect as well Casel was mistaken in positing a kind of objectivized *Mysteriengegenwart*. The presence-in-mystery of Christ's eternally actual redemption and thus of all the mysteries of his life in their perpetuity is, on the contrary, essentially an active presence of the redemptive act as taking hold of a particular individual. So this presence is completely realized only when it is reciprocal and develops in consequence into an encounter in the fruitful sacrament. The "merely valid" sacrament is nevertheless still Christ's personal redemptive act in the midst of his ecclesial community and, indeed, as directed to a particular person. This simply shows that a sacrament in the full sense of the word is realized only when it is fruitful, but that even so the unfruitful though valid sacrament is truly a ritual prayer of Christ and his Church for the recipient, and is therefore the presence on earth of the heavenly reality of salvation. The recipient has but to reach out and hold on to this presence in faith.

APPENDIX

ST. THOMAS' CHRISTOLOGICAL INTERPRETATION OF SACRAMENTAL EX OPERE OPERATO CAUSALITY

As far as we have been able to discover, St. Thomas uses the term *ex opere operato* twenty times in a sacramental context in the *Scriptum super Sententiis,* but in the *Summa* not at all. This is an indication that St. Thomas, in whose day *ex opere operato* was already a traditional technical term, found that it was not really needed in order to present a genuine view of Catholic sacramental doctrine, for the truth which this terminology was intended to bring out was presented satisfactorily, and even in finer detail, in his Christological appreciation of the sacraments. The passages in which St. Thomas has used this term can be classified under four headings according to the precise sense in which it is employed.

(A) First we have those passages in which it has the old meaning given it by the earlier masters. The sacrament itself is the *opus operatum;* the use of the sacrament is the *opus operans.*[41] In this, the old sense, the term is used especially in connection with different aspects of Christ's death on the Cross; indefensible murder and a meritorious death of reconciliation.[42]

(B) In other passages St. Thomas contrasts *ex opere operato* with "faith alone" on the part of the recipient. The "sacraments of nature" are not efficacious *ex opere operato,* but by faith alone; the Christian sacraments, on the other hand, have their effect *ex opere operato.*[43] Elsewhere he makes a similar but already more profound distinction between the part played by personal faith (and hope) with regard to the sacrament, and with regard to the bestowal of grace—the *res sacramenti.* The personal faith of the recipient has considerable effect upon the measure of what the sacrament brings about, but it has no effect on the sacrament itself; in other words, the validity of a sacrament does not depend upon the faith of the recipient, "because the sacraments of the New Law are efficacious by the very fact that the rite is performed."[44] The particularly Thomist use of the term is very often found to convey this meaning; the sacrament is an "outward sign"—the objective embodiment in a sign of God's will to bestow grace, or as an objective source of

[41] *IV Sent.,* d. 1, q. 1, a. 5, sol. 1 (p. 41) and sol. 2 (p. 42): St. Thomas says: "dicitur a quibusdam. . . ." Note: the pagination refers to the critical edition of E. Moos, Paris (1947), vol. 4, for texts from *IV Sent.,* d. 1–d. 22. Other loci in *IV Sent.* are from the *Opera Omnia,* Parma (1858), vol. 7.

[42] *III Sent.,* d. 20, a. 5, sol. 2, ad 3. (Moos, vol. 3, p. 627.)

[43] *IV Sent.,* d. 2, q. 1, a. 4, sol. 4, ad 2 (p. 92).

[44] *IV Sent.,* d. 2, q. 2, a. 4 (p. 101).

power—is in fact realized quite independently of personal faith. "In baptism, as far as the work done [*opus operatum*] is concerned, the merit of the person baptized has no effect."[45] In other words, sacramentality, or the *veritas signi,* is quite independent of the subjective religious purposefulness of the one for and upon whom the sacrament is being performed. In this context St. Thomas usually contrasts the *opus operatum* with the *opus operans* as well, so that we already see that this terminology does not concern or convey a relationship between the gift of grace (the *res sacramenti*) and the personal act of the minister (the *opus operantis*), and this is of capital importance for a correct appreciation of sacramental efficacy *ex opere operato.*[46]

(C) In passages of the third group, *ex opere operato* indicates that the efficacy of sacramental grace does not depend on the moral and religious dispositions of the minister.[47] The contrasting of the *opus operantis* and the *opus operatum* also sometimes refers to this independence of the sacrament with regard to the minister's dispositions.[48]

(D) A final category of texts shows us the fundamental idea underlying the term *ex opere operato:* the idea upon which the two previous senses (B and C) are based. In these passages it is precisely the Christological character of the sacrament as the "work of God" and the "work of Christ" that is emphasized. "Baptism justifies *ex opere operato:* this is not man's work, but God's."[49] Elsewhere the same thing is said in a different way: "Baptism does

[45] *IV Sent.,* d. 4, q. 2, a. 2, qla. 2, ob. 1 (p. 171); cf. also d. 45, q. 2, a. 3, sol. 1, ad 3 (Parma ed., vol. 7, p. 1126), and compare d. 45, q. 2, a. 2, sol. 2, and 4 (p. 1124).

[46] *IV Sent.,* d. 1, q. 2, a. 4, sol. 2 (p. 58); d. 4, q. 3, a. 3, qla. 3, ob. 1 (p. 191) and ad 1 (p. 194); d. 5, q. 2, a. 2, qla. 3, ob. 1 (p. 216) in connection with sol. 1 (pp. 218–19).

[47] *IV Sent.,* d. 13, q. 1, a. 1, sol. 5 (p. 550); d. 5, q. 2, qla. 3, ob. 2 (p. 216); d. 13, q. 1, a. 3, qla. 3, ob. 3 (p. 560).

[48] *IV Sent.,* d. 5, q. 1, a. 2 (p. 204); d. 6, q. 1, a. 2, sol. 2, ad 2 (p. 238). In this latter text *ex opere operato* does not appear, but the *bonitas ex opere operante* is distinguished from the *bonitas* of the sacrament of baptism itself.

[49] *IV Sent.,* d. 15, q. 1, a. 3, sol. 3, ad 2 (p. 656).

not have its effect because of the merits of the person being baptized, but because of the merits of Christ"[50]; ". . . baptism with water [is efficacious] because of the passion of Christ."[51] Thus in these last two texts the notion *ex opere operato* (the term itself is not used, but the meaning is clearly there) refers to efficacy in virtue of the passion of Christ. We have a further example in this objection: "Baptism confers grace *ex opere operato*. Likewise it is clear that holy men by the work they actually do [*ex opere operante*] merit the beginning of grace for someone else. Therefore if the *opus operans* of the minister is joined with the efficacy of baptism a greater grace will be given." To which St. Thomas replies that something can have an essential effect and an accidental effect. Now "the essential [*per se*] effect of baptism remains the same whoever does the baptizing, a good man or an evil man—all being equal as far as the person to be baptized is concerned. In virtue of the merits of the baptizer something can be conferred along with the effect of the baptism itself. . . . But this is not the essential effect of baptism because baptism is only an instrumental cause; an instrument which does not have its effect by the power of the minister, who is an instrument himself, but rather by the power of Christ and God."[52] *Ex opere operato* therefore means exactly the same as "by the power of Christ and God." It is the sovereign efficacy of Christ which makes the *opus operatum* itself independent of either the merits of the minister who baptizes or the merits of the one to be baptized.[53]

This Christological foundation of the *ex opere operato* efficacy is brought out still more clearly when St. Thomas connects this efficacy with the sacramental character. "The sacraments of the old Law conferred nothing *ex opere operato* and therefore those acts

---

[50] *IV Sent.*, d. 6, q. 1, a. 3, sol. 2 (p. 242).

[51] *IV Sent.*, d. 4, q. 3, qla. 4, ob. 1 (p. 191).

[52] *IV Sent.*, d. 5, q. 2, a. 2, qla. 3, ob. 1 (p. 216) and sol. (pp. 218–19).

[53] Cf. *IV Sent.*, d. 6, q. 1, a. 3, sol. 2 (p. 242); d. 4, q. 2, a. 2, qla. 2, ob. 1 (p. 171) and sol. 2, ad 1 (p. 174): ". . . in baptism it is not the merits of the one to be baptized that have an effect as far as the *opus operatum* is concerned but the merits of Christ."

required no spiritual power, neither, therefore, was a character conferred by them or for [the purpose of performing] them."[54] Since the power of the redemptive mystery of Christ comes to us in the sacraments in a ministerial, instrumental manner, and since there is thus a "spiritual power" in the sacraments, they are efficacious *ex opere operato*. In other words, since the sacraments are ministerially an *opus Christi* they have an objective salutary power which in its constitution is entirely independent of the religious dispositions of either minister or recipient. *Ex opere operato* is therefore a mode of reference to the mystery of the sacraments, which are the celebration in mystery of the historical mysteries of Christ. In both the *Sentences* and the *Summa* St. Thomas poses an objection which in the former he answers by referring to the *ex opere operato* efficacy of baptism, while in the latter the answer given is the affirmation that baptism is a "work of God, not of man."[55] The same thing is suggested by the distinction made between liturgical sacerdotal prayers and the essentially sacramental prayer; the priest is "the principal (although secondary) agent" with regard to the former, while in the latter (i.e., the works done, the *opera operata*) he is purely an instrumental cause in relation to Christ's saving activity.[56]

In connection with the idea that the sacraments have their power from the redemptive mystery of Christ and, in this sense, are efficacious *ex opere operato,* we can cite another passage in which a "quasi *ex opere operato* efficacy" is ascribed to circumcision, in virtue of Christ being the object of the faith of the parents of the child, and not in virtue of the faith as such, subjectively considered.

[54] *IV Sent.*, d. 4, q. 1, a. 4, sol. 1, ad 2 (p. 163). The same doctrine is in the *Summa* too, but without the term *ex opere operato*. (*ST*, III, q. 63, a. 1.) Therefore the term is used only of the efficacy of sacramental symbols that are not signs only, but signs and causes. Cf. *IV Sent.*, d. 8, q. 1, a. 2, qla. 2, ob. 5 (p. 312), sol. 2 (p. 314) and ad. 5 (p. 315).

[55] Cf. *IV Sent.*, d. 15, q. 1, a. 3, sol. 3, ad 2 (p. 656); *ST*, III, q. 69, a. 10, ad 1. The omission of the term *ex opere operato* from the reply in the *Summa* is in all probability deliberate, since this term is absent from the *Summa* altogether in a sacramental context, in contrast to the relative frequency of its occurrence in the *Sentences*.

[56] *IV Sent.*, d. 5, q. 2, sol. 1, ad 2 (p. 218).

In this, circumcision "has a certain similarity to our sacraments, inasmuch as it brought justification on account of the object [of Old-Testament faith, i.e., implicitly, Christ], *quasi ex opere operato* and not on account of the one performing the work [*ex opere operante*]."[57]

Finally St. Thomas gives a definition of a sacrament in which the essentially definitive element is the sacramental efficacy in the bestowal of grace *ex opere operato*—in the fundamental meaning of this term (D above) with its two immediate consequences (B and C): "Omnis actio per ministros ecclesiae dispensata, in qua ipso opere operato gratia confertur, est sacramentum."[58]

From all this we have a clear idea of the many shades of meaning St. Thomas gives to the term *ex opere operato*[59]—a term which was later to be taken over and used in official definitions by the Church. In no place at all does it imply a contrast between the bestowal of grace (the *res sacramenti*) and the subjective religious intention of the person; the contrast is found only between the constitution of the sacrament or the outward sacramental sign and the subjective states of the minister or the recipient. It is not the *opus operantis* of the minister, or of the recipient, that constitutes the sacramental sign; the *opus operantis* is quite external to sacramentalism in this sense (i.e., as the actual administration and reception of a sacrament). However, the *opus operantis* of the recipi-

---

[57] *IV Sent.*, d. 1, q. 2, a. 6, sol. 1, ad 2 (p. 70). The meaning of "quasi" in this passage (and its usual meaning in St. Thomas) is pure comparison, the equivalent of "like" or "in the manner of"; it does not have the ironical flavour often attaching to it in English usage or in classical Latin. Thus, circumcision in the Old Law really justified *ex opere operato,* since its efficacy derived from Christ himself. It differs from the sacraments in this: Circumcision was not instrumentally imbued with the power of Christ. This latter wording taken from the *Summa* represents an alteration in St. Thomas's view; in his earlier works he denied a bestowal of grace in circumcision.

[58] *IV Sent.*, d. 8, q. 1, a. 1 gla. 1, sed contra 2, (p. 304).

[59] As far as I know, we have seen all the instances in which the term is used in the *Sentences*. Apart from the *Sentences* I have found it used only once in a sacramental context by St. Thomas: in *Commentum in Johannem*, c. 6, lect. 6 *in fine*. The search, however, could not be exhaustive.

ent does have a part to play in sacramentalism considered as the actual reception of grace bestowed sacramentally. With regard to the sacramental sign, all that is necessary on the part of the minister is to do what the Church does; all that is necessary on the part of the recipient is to receive this. Hence *ex opere operato* efficacy means that the sacrament, as an act which is done in virtue of a character, is objectively and ministerially an act of Christ, an objective celebration in mystery of the historical, redemptive mystery of Christ, in such a way that it brings about the unmerited application of the redemption, a work of pure mercy, to *this* person. In this sense *ex opere operato* is a reference to the universal causality of Christ's grace, to the unicity of Christ's mediation, to the pure gratuity of redemption; it says, in other words, *gratis estis salvati* by sacramental means; sacraments effect what they signify.

In consequence it is not possible to agree with the purely juridical interpretation of a correct administration of the sacraments which many moralists attach to the term *ex opere operato,* and in which they are altogether silent about its profound Christological sense. Prummer, for example, writes: "The term 'ex opere operato' is explained in two ways: (a) as the valid administration of the sacrament itself, provided there is no obstacle . . . (b) as the work of redemption done by Christ. This latter explanation, proposed by few theologians [he cites Möhler and Hilgera], is not so correct [*minus est recta*]."[60]

St. Thomas, on the contrary, unites both meanings in one fundamental notion, in which the central and essential factor is the meritorious and efficient activity of the historical mystery of Christ.

[60] D. Prummer, *Manuale Theologiae Moralis,* 12th ed., Freiburg and Barcelona (1955), vol. 3, p. 29. As his reason, the writer gives: "Etenim Christus Redemptor per suam passionem est quidem causa meritoria gratiae sacramentalis . . . [blithe omission of the *causa instrumentaliter efficiens* of which St. Thomas speaks], sed in sacramentis novae legis gratia causatur effective (licet instrumentaliter) per ipsum signum sensible, i.e. per debitam applicationem formae ad materiam." This is the headless corpse of sacramentalism if St. Thomas's explanation is the right one.

A sacrament, the *opus operatum,* is valid when the ministerial act is an act of Christ (*opus Christi*); it is valid therefore when it is authentic sacramental representation of the acts of the mystery of Christ in and through his ecclesial community. The constitution of the sacramental symbolic act is not dependent on the dispositions of the minister or recipient, as long as each has the required intention. Already in principle any tendency towards a magical or mechanical concept of *ex opere operato* efficacy is excluded. Loyal human care for correctness concerning the "matter" and the "form" is quite simply care authentically to extend Christ's work of redemption in and through the sacrament; contact with the saving mystery of Christ comes about only when the sacrament is really valid, only when the sacramental act is really a symbolic act of Christ himself through his Church. If "bringing together matter and form correctly" gives grace efficiently, this happens in virtue of the fact that, through this correctly performed action, the ecclesial symbolic act really becomes an act of Christ through the minister and really is, therefore, the re-presentation of his effective work of redemption.

This beyond doubt is St. Thomas's view of sacramental efficacy *ex opere operato.* Since the time of the Council of Trent some theologians, as far as their systematic treatises are concerned, have separated their sacramental doctrine far too much from the mystery of Christ; the term *ex opere operato* thus degenerated into an emphasis of one element only of the scholastic, and especially Thomist, doctrine, and gave the impression of a purely materialist juridical approach to the sacraments. However, this is no more than an impression; it was not the deliberate intention of these writers, and certainly was never the intention of the Church, to approach the sacraments in this way.

3

IMPLICATIONS OF THE ECCLESIAL
CHARACTER OF SACRAMENTAL ACTION

The sacraments are the personal saving act of the risen Christ through his visible Church. For this symbolic action to be truly ecclesial, and thus for it to be the authentic sacramentalization of the redemptive act of the risen Christ, there are, broadly speaking, four basic conditions that must be fulfilled. (For some particular sacraments other conditions over and above these four are necessary.) First, for the symbolic action itself, there must be its two-fold liturgical structure.[1] Second, for the Church's minister there must be the "intention to do what the Church does."[2] Third, for the recipient there must be the intention to receive the sacrament.[3] In the fourth place, and fundamentally, there must be the institution of the Church's sacraments by Christ. Since this matter has been investigated closely and at length in our earlier work, *De Sacramentele Heilseconomie,* we may confine ourselves in this chapter to a précis of that discussion, developing certain points in the process.

---

[1] A full treatment of this and the following points has been undertaken in *SH*, pp. 239–454.

[2] *SH*, pp. 457–79.

[3] *SH*, pp. 481–4.

1. THE TWOFOLD LITURGICAL STRUCTURE OF THE SACRAMENTS: "SACRAMENT AND WORD"

1. Historical Survey of Teaching on Liturgical Action and Liturgical Word

Since the Middle Ages sacramental theology has distinguished between the matter (*materia*) and the form (*forma*) of the sacrament as the two constitutive elements of the outward sacramental sign. This understanding depends on a view of the actual structure of the Church's sacramental practice. In Scripture itself the liturgical action (for example, washing with water, the laying on of hands, the breaking and sharing of the eucharistic bread) was always coupled with a prayer or a "word." Following this lead, the Fathers thought of the sacraments as the bringing together of an earthly and a heavenly element, which was manifested externally in the liturgical action and a prayer of petition or *epiclesis*. The sacraments (they thought above all of baptism, confirmation and the Eucharist) were considered to consist of "matter and spirit"; of an element or a thing (water, oil, bread, the laying on of hands) and the *pneuma* of the *Logos* which, in the power of the *epiclesis*, came down upon the material element. "Accedit verbum ad elementum et fit sacramentum," as St. Augustine so concisely formulated it—"A word comes to an element and a sacrament is there."[4] This word is a confession of faith, a *verbum fidei*. It is, that is to say, Christ's own proclamation of the word, made known by means of the Gospel, accepted through the faith of the Church, and confessed with regard to the sacramental action in a *verbum fidei,* a word of faith. Unquestionably the Fathers attributed a value to the word of faith above that of the element in the sacraments.

Later on, in the age of the great scholastics, this *verbum* and *elementum* of patristic doctrine developed into the matter and the form of the sacraments. This development represents in a certain sense a different orientation, but it was not until much later than

---

[4] *In Evangelium Johannis,* tract 80, 3 (*PL,* 35, col. 1840).

the time of the great scholastics that it lost its underlying harmony
with patristic thought. The Fathers of the Church were concerned
immediately with a mystical bringing together; heaven and earth
work together in the sacraments. Among the scholastics on the
other hand (at least after the period of Hugh of St. Victor and
Peter Lombard) attention was more directly turned to the constitutive elements of the outward sacramental sign.[5] The word and
the element (thing or action) now come to be seen as constitutive
parts without which the outward sacramental sign cannot be present. These two parts together form what is called the substance
of the sacrament. Even before the influence of Aristotelian hylemorphism[6] had been brought to bear these two parts had already,
as it happened, been called *materia* and *forma*.[7] Hence among the
Aristotelians of the first half of the thirteenth century, when the
current non-Aristotelian terms of sacramental *materia* and *forma*
came into contact with the similar terminology of hylemorphism,
quite naturally these sacramental terms acquired Aristotelian over-
tones. The problem began to be considered in this way: Just as in
the material world the essential form and the *materia* make the
substance of a material thing, so too the substance of a sacramental
sign consists of an indeterminate material principle (the liturgical

---

[5] "Quoniam de verbis audibilibus et speciebus visibilibus ipsum sacramentum, i.e., rei sacrae signum, perficitur," wrote Gerhoh of Reichersberg
(*Liber de Simoniacis, in Libelli de lite Imperatorum et pontificum saec. XI
et XII, III*, ed Soc. Aperiendis Fontibus, Hanover, 1897, p. 255 [*Monumenta
Germaniae Historica*].) Cf. *SH*, p. 367.

[6] Hylemorphism is the Aristotelian doctrine according to which every
corporeal being consists essentially of *materia*, a principle of indetermination,
and *forma*, a principle of completion and determination; the essential form
and the matter together make up the substance of every corporeal being.

[7] *Materia* here has simply the meaning of "element": water, bread, oil,
etc. *Forma* has the common meaning of "an outward shape." Both the
liturgical action and the liturgical word could thus be called *forma,* and this
gave rise to the technical terms *forma verborum*, the outward shape
(formulation) of the sacramental word (later, the *forma* of the sacrament)
and *forma facti* (the *materia*, strictly speaking, of later terminology). Cf.
SH, 1, pp. 368–9, and also the article by D. van den Eynde. "The Theory of
the Composition of the Sacraments in Early Scholasticism," in *FS*, 12
(1952), pp. 1–26.

action or the element) and a principle of determination (the liturgical formula of words), through which the indetermination of the action is taken away and it is made precise. The liturgical word thus fulfils the function of *forma*. Ever since that time scholasticism has applied the hylemorphic theory as the principle of theological intelligibility allowing the essential core of the sacramental sign to be determined precisely for each sacrament. In the course of time the theory even came to be used as a principle from which conclusions could be drawn, and the original, merely comparative, character of its terminology was forgotten.[8]

From this short sketch of what happened it is clear that the so-called sacramental hylemorphism was only an incidental aid, characteristic of a particular time, to the presentation of the more profound traditional idea that a sacramental action is coupled with a confession of faith or a prayer of petition which in a certain sense possesses a value superior to that of the action. Since the fifteenth century this terminology has been adopted in the Church's official documents.[9] However, it is not the Church's intention to bind her-

[8] St. Thomas writes, "In sacramentis verba se habent per modum formae, res autem per modum materiae" (*ST*, III, q. 60, a. 7), and ". . . et ideo ex verbis et rebus fit quodammodo unum in sacramentis sicut ex forma et materia." (*ST*, III, q. 60, a. 6, ad 2.)

[9] Cf. *SH*, 1, pp. 338–91. In that place the author refers to the following: the Bull *Inter Cunctas*, Martin V (*MC*, vol. 27, col. 1212; *DB*, 672); the Council of Florence, *Decretum pro Armenis* (*DB*, 695); the Council of Trent, Session XIV (*DB*, 895); Benedict XIV, *De Baptismo Iudaeorum* (*Bullarium Sanctissimi Domini Benedicti XIV*, ed Mechelen [1926], vol. 5, t. 2, p. 46); Leo XIII, *Apostolicae Curae* (*DB*, 1963, 1964, 1966); Pius XII, *Constitutio Apostolica* of 30 November 1947, *Sacramentum Ordinis* (*AAS*, 40 [1948], p. 6). In none of these documents does a definition of faith concern the *materia-forma* terminology directly. The most important among these, because the only document having a direct dogmatic bearing, is the *Decretum pro Armenis*. "Haec omnia sacramenta tribus perficiuntur: videlicet, rebus tamquam materia, verbis tamquam forma, et persona ministri. . . ." In no sense was it the Council's intention to define that matter and form constitute the substance of the sacrament. Moreover, when dealing with matrimony the Council did not use the *materia-forma* terminology. If this decree does define the structure of a sacrament, it refers formally to the twofold nature of the external sign, viz., the *res et verba* brought together by the intention of the minister. *Tamquam forma* and *tamquam*

self to the use of this terminology, which she herself indicates is merely an adaptation of a prevalent theological way of speaking[10] that has been found suitable in practice.

2. Sign-Activity in Action and Word

Now in what sense are the liturgical action and the liturgical word intrinsic components of the outward sacramental sign? In order thoroughly to understand this matter it would be necessary to trace the historical development of ritual in each of the seven sacraments. In our day the broad lines of this development can be indicated with some degree of certainty. From an investigation based on an historical study of this kind the following comes to light. First of all, the liturgical action is always coupled with a sacramental prayer. (In former times this prayer was in deprecatory form; later, at least in the West and owing partly to the influence of sacramental hylemorphism, partly to a fuller appreciation of the instrumental role of the minister in the sacrament itself, it became more usual to use an indicative formula.) Next, the shape of both the liturgical action and the liturgical word underwent far-reaching changes in the course of the Church's history. If, then, in the Council of Trent the Church defines that the essence of a sacrament cannot be changed,[11] and if on the other hand the councils of

---

materia are simply put in by way of illustration and are not formally the object of the definition. The terminology in all these documents merely follows the *usus receptus;* as Leo XIII writes, ". . . quae materia et forma appellari consuevit." (Tr.)

[10] Cf. Leo XIII, cited above.

[11] *DB,* 931. See *SH,* pp. 421–3, which, briefly, states the following: the Council of Trent teaches (a) that all (seven) sacraments were instituted by Christ (Session VII, *DB,* 844) and (b) that the Church has the power to make alterations in the sacraments provided that the *substantia sacramenti* is maintained unaltered. (Session 21.) Therefore it must have been this *substantia sacramenti* that Christ instituted "once and for all." Now the Council (this is clear from the *acta*) did not set out to resolve differences of opinion within the Church. The exact meaning of the terminology used—*materia; forma; substantia sacramenti*—remains an open question. *Substantia sacramenti* clearly cannot be taken in a strictly hylemorphic sense, for

Florence[12] and Trent,[13] and also the Brief *Apostolicae Curae* of
Leo XIII[14] all say that "the essence of a sacrament consists in matter and form," it is evident that this essence cannot consist, formally, in the outward shape of the liturgical action and the liturgical
word considered in themselves, but rather that it must lie in them as
aspects of the ecclesial symbolic activity. The essence of a sacrament lies therefore neither in its spiritual significance on the one
hand nor in its outward shape on the other, but rather in the manifested signification. In other words the essence of a sacrament consists in the spiritual signification as this is made manifest in the
liturgical shape of the rite. This may also be stated the other way
about: The essence of a sacrament lies in the outward shape of the
rite as this participates in the sacramental spiritual meaning. Because a sacrament is a symbolic act of Christ in his Church, it is
only through faith in Christ that the Church is able to make this
spiritual signification manifest in her sacraments, and so the faith
of the Church is necessary for the constitution of an outward sacramental sign. Moreover, this outward making-manifest of the spiritual signification takes place in an action and in a word, each of
which is properly suited to give meaningful expression to the sacramental meaning. Thus while making reservation for the fact that
Christ himself may explicitly, or possibly implicitly, have determined the shape for one or another sacrament (e.g., water for
baptism; bread and wine for the Eucharist), we may say that this
shape of the ritual may undergo all sorts of variations and amendments. It is only in their signifying, as the visibility of the Church's
spiritual activity in faith, that the liturgical actions and words belong
to the essence of a sacrament.

---

otherwise the Council would be contradicting the authentic historical fact of
the alteration of the *materia* and *forma* in the hylemorphic sense of these
terms. The problems of the precise mode of the institution of the sacraments
by Christ, and of the manner in which the unalterable *substantia sacramenti*
is in fact embodied, are therefore still matter for theological solution.

[12] *DB*, 695.   [13] *DB*, 895.
[14] Cf. note 9 above.

3. The Relationship of the Word to the
Sacramental Manifestation of Salvation

Now why must the outwardly manifested shape of the Church's sacramental activity-in-faith comprise a double element, an action accompanied by a word? This is partly a matter of the nature of human beings, but the twofold structure also has a formal theological significance.

Even on the human plane, action, speech and silence are essential elements in symbolic activity, forming a single pattern. The play of gestures alone can be so expressive that it does not require the help of words to indicate its meaning, as in pantomime. Again, it may happen that the explanatory word precedes, or follows, or is simultaneous with, the symbolic action, without the unity of the symbolism being broken, so that the spiritual intention is brought by stages to a full expression. Furthermore, it is possible that where the symbolism is insufficiently determined it can be given a more precise determination by a second, and even a third, symbolizing action, or re-emphasized by the employment of new symbols. Thus we may have a complex unity of symbols, varyingly accompanied by a deep and telling silence or by words of explanation, developed into a single play of mystic symbolism, in all of which there is but one manifestation. In this complexity of symbolism all ordered to a single meaning, there is nothing to prevent there being a central symbolic factor, which by its shaping power, because it is the essential formula, enables the fundamental intention dominating the whole to be realized. In this way all the other partial symbolic factors are directed to this central point and draw from it their meaning within the whole.

This same structure of human social symbolic activity may be recognized in all the sacramental liturgy. The sacramental meaning, which can be approached only through the faith of the Church, is the factor which dominates the whole; it is this which makes symbolic activity ecclesial. The word, of its nature an expressive and clear bearer of meaning, can often possess a psychological value superior to that of the action, and can thus fulfil the formal role of the factor clarifying the meaning.

Yet all this has a more profound theological dimension. Sacramental symbolic activity, although performed through the Church by the mediation of the minister, is fundamentally a personal act of the *Kyrios,* who is the actual High Priest throughout the action. Therefore that which ecclesial symbolic activity expresses first of all is the *fides Ecclesiae,* the faith of the Church in the (eternally actual) redemptive act of the Saviour. The prayerful orientation of the Church's sacraments towards the mystery of Christ is fundamental. And conversely in all this the Church is also fulfilling her role as the sacramental Christ in his capacity as Head; in its sacraments the Church, as the servant of Christ, really gives us the grace of redemption. Deeply convinced that God alone is the giver of grace, the ancient Church, and still in our day the Eastern Church, holds to the deprecatory form—"May God absolve you. . . ." The Church of the West, deeply convinced of the Church's role as the sacramental Christ, says "I absolve you . . . I baptize you. . . ." Both elements, however, are essential, and both receive their liturgical embodiment in the entirety of the sacramental ceremony. Even in the West the deprecatory form has been preserved for the central and essential element in the rite of some sacraments (for example, in the last anointing and in ordination to the priesthood according to the modern ritual).

It is in this view of the sacramental realization of Christ's personal act of redemption in the Church that we must appreciate the dominant importance of the word of faith, the *verbum fidei,* though this is given a special meaning according to the special character of each sacrament. By the sacramental word the symbolic activity, which is to a certain extent a religious activity common to all human society, is integrated into the Church as the sacrament of Christ. The ecclesial sacramental confession of faith makes the symbolic action into a sacramental realization of Christ's personal act of redemption; makes it, that is to say, into a sacrament. To formulate the matter in precise terms, we may say it is in the Church's sacramental (deprecatory or indicative) confession of faith that the risen Christ can make an earthly element or a human action into a sacramentally visible manifestation of his heavenly act of salvation. In this sense the Church's sacramental confession of faith is the formative or determining principle with regard to the earthly symbolic activity. In other words, through the sacramental confession of faith human symbolic action becomes the visible prolongation and presence on earth of the invisible saving act of the risen Christ. This seems to me to be the strictly theological sense of the datum preserved by tradition, according to which the sacraments' exterior structure must always be a twofold one. It is this that gives meaning to the twofold structure, and that also, therefore, determines its extent or even its possible limitation.

Thus in each of the seven sacraments we recognize in miniature the same thing that constitutes the Church as Church: the sacrament, or the revelation-in-reality, and the word, or revelation-by-word. Christ is our High Priest in his sacramental manifestation of salvation and through his preaching of the word. The spoken revelation is intrinsically required by the revelation in reality, precisely because this latter is a manifestation of something supernatural in that which is natural. In the word this saving reality is manifested as revealed and given to us. In this way the word belongs to the intrinsic constitution of the presence of a supernatural reality among us.[15] Only in this light is it possible correctly to understand how the sacramental word possesses a value superior to that of the sacramental action. A comparison between Christ's action and that of the Church may help to clarify this. It was the saving reality actually present on earth—Christ himself—who manifested himself for men in his word, and by it established contact with them and presence among them. In the sacraments of the Church, on the other hand, it is the Church's sacramental word of faith that actually

---

[15] See Karl Rahner, *Priesterliche Existenz*, Einsiedeln (1956), p. 291 (*Schriften zur Theologie*, 3), where, however, this point has been developed in its application to priestly preaching.

brings about the saving manifestation of Christ's redemptive act in the sacrament. Through an *epiclesis,* that is through a word or prayer by which God is "called down,"[16] Christ's act of redemption comes into the Church's symbolic act.

Saving reality is thus given a twofold outward expression in the sacraments, although the precise values of the two factors in this expression are not identical. The expression is achieved through the liturgical action which by the power of the sacramental word of faith becomes the celebration in mystery of the heavenly saving act of the Lord.

If in this context we wish to speak of the matter of sacrament, we shall have to understand this rather as consisting in the basic natural symbolism of the actions performed; in the human substratum of ecclesial symbolic activity. Through the ecclesial word of faith a natural symbolic action, often one that already had its place in human ritual in virtue of its own meaning and power to signify, is given a similar but transcendent (and in this sense entirely different) ecclesial signification; in this way a Christian sacrament is constituted as a sacrament of ecclesial faith and, although it bears a relationship to the sacramental symbolic activity of mankind in general, becomes something entirely unique.

2. THE ECCLESIAL ADMINISTRATION OF THE SACRAMENTS

1. *The Necessity of the Intention of the Church's Minister*

As an ecclesial symbolic act which is a saving act of Christ, a sacrament is of its nature not a "thing" but a human action performed by a man in the name of the Church, and thus ultimately

---

16 *Epiclesis* derived from the Greek *epi-kaleo,* i.e., "call upon," "call over here" (in the sense of calling someone to do something). The author suggests, by way of illustration of the meaning, the old Dutch saying *God uit de hemel smeken,* which may loosely be rendered, "Pray so hard that you call God out of heaven."

in the name of Christ himself. We have said that the connection between the Church's earthly symbolic act and the personal act of the risen Christ is established in the sacrament itself by the faith of the Church.[17] In practice this takes place through the minister who administers the sacrament. He as minister performs a ministerial action, an official action, inasmuch as he is delegated and sent by the Church to this end. The administration of a sacrament, as a human act, must certainly be voluntary. As a ministerial act, the conferring of a sacrament requires that the minister fulfil precisely the intention of the Church. In some way he must therefore voluntarily carry out the intention of Christ and the Church in the actual administration of the sacrament, or else the rite performed will not be the Church's authentic rite, and thus will not be a sacrament, even though the whole ceremonial is mimicked. The intention of the minister is therefore necessary for the validity of the sacraments.[18] The question, however, remains: To what in fact must this intention, the constitutive intention of an ecclesial and ministerial action, refer? Usually this question is studied from a merely casuistic standpoint: What, it is asked, is the minimum required for the sacrament administered to be at least valid? Of course this is of the greatest practical importance. But we must rather ask what, from the theological point of view, are the necessary conditions for an entirely worthy administration of the sacraments, and then from this we can descend to the borderline cases.

2. Office and Charism; the Ideal Conditions Intrinsically Required by the Essence of the Church

Since the Church is essentially grace realized in institutional and apostolic form, the conferring of an ecclesial office is always associated with a bestowal of grace. For the Church is a sign of

[17] St. Thomas, *IV Sent.*, d. 1, q. 1, a. 4, sol. 3.
[18] "Intentio est necessaria qua copulatur actus ille fidei Ecclesiae, tamquam actus particularis et actualis in ministrante." (St. Bonaventure, *IV Sent.*, d. 6, q. 2, a. 2, q. 1.)

grace charged with the reality it signifies. The Church is holy and
makes holy, so ecclesial office of itself implies sanctifying grace. We
know that ordination to the priesthood, by the fact that it confers
the character of the office, at the same times bestows a sacramental
grace. This is inseparably bound up with the essence of the mystery
of the Church. In God's plan, by the nature of the Church, personal
holiness with its apostolic will to sanctify necessarily belongs to
an official ecclesial act. A rupture between personal religious intention and the authentic official act of the Church can come about
only as the result of interior dispositions and personal opposition.
In this sense Christ's ministration of the sacraments is independent
of a minister's personal possession of grace and his personal sense
of the apostolate. But along with this we must not forget that,
although it does not invalidate a sacrament, such a rupture is an
anomaly when considered in relation to the essence of the Church.
The normal situation required strictly by the fullness of the
Church's being is that of a sacramental ministration in which the
minister performs the acts of his office in such a way that they are
at the same time an expression of his own personal dedication to
the apostolate, and of his will really to sanctify the persons to whom
he administers the sacraments. Because the Donatists of old, and
Luther at a later date, held the power of the sacraments to be
dependent upon the personal intention of the minister, it is not now
necessary for us to go to the other extreme, thinking that on
ecclesial and sacramental grounds all is well if the sacraments
administered are merely valid. Certainly there is no positive loss to
the recipient in such cases. Nevertheless the intrinsic nature of a
sacrament calls for something more.

We have already said that a sacrament possesses not only grace-
giving character but also the character of ritual worship. It is a
sacramental act of worship or a sacramental prayer of both Christ
and his Church on behalf of the one who is receiving the sacrament.
Thus as long as the minister does not also make this prayer of ritual
worship his own personal prayer for the recipient, his official action
is, at least as far as the minister is concerned, not all that it should

be in the light of what the Church essentially is. Precisely because the minister is carrying out an administration, this ecclesial performance of his office requires, of its nature, that he identify himself personally in a religious and apostolic sense with the sacramental prayer of Christ and his Church. In keeping with the essential character of the Church, the normal administration of the sacraments should therefore be a personal act of faith made manifest in the ministration itself; an act of apostolic hope and of sanctifying fraternal love, as an intercession for the person who is receiving the sacrament. The minister must act, not as minister merely of the visible Church, but as minister of the Church which is mystery.

This comes to the fore very clearly even in the case of giving Holy Communion, where the minister prays, "May the body of our Lord . . . preserve you unto life everlasting." It is surely not possible to maintain that this ministration is all that it ought to be when this prayer is not also a genuine personal prayer. Christians are instinctively aware of this, and on their part they are certainly not misjudging the true nature of sacramentality and its *ex opere operato* effectiveness when they prefer to give a Mass stipend to a priest who in their opinion is a holy man rather than to one who lacks all but the "intention to do what the Church does." In this ecclesial perspective we can understand, too, the exceptional power of the absolutions of a Curé of Ars, who in *oratione et jejunio* (in prayer and fasting) first battled in his own body for their fruitfulness.

St. Thomas himself held that the faith and the devotion of the whole Church is operative in the sacraments.[19] For the sacramental

---

[19] The author refers to *SH*, pp. 647–57, a chapter on St. Thomas's synthesis of efficacy *ex opere operato* and efficacy *ex fide*. St. Thomas is very explicit on the part played by the faith of the Church in the sacraments. Whereas the sacraments of the Old Law were efficacious *ex sola fide*, in the Christian sacraments "fidei efficacia non est diminuta, cum omnia sacramenta ex fide efficaciam habent." (*IV Sent.*, d. 1, q. 2, a. 6, sol. 2, ad 3; Moos, p. 171.) Cf. note 17 above: that text continues: ". . . et ideo efficacio instrumentorum vel virtus est ex tribus, scilicet ex institutione divina . . . ex passione Christi . . . ex fide ecclesiae." In the *sacramentum simpliciter verum,*

rite is indeed an act of Christ together with his mystical body; an act of Christ in and through the Church. The faith and devotion of all who are united with Christ in grace, as a participation in the fullness of Christ, contributes to the fullness of the sacrament. Therefore clearly it is required of the minister himself in the first place that he should participate in this *devotio Ecclesiae*.

From this we see that the normal ecclesial requirement is as much as possible of the minister's intention intrinsically called for by the nature of the sacramental administration, and that this is achieved only when the minister, beyond merely performing the external rite, enters with the fullness of his apostolic purpose into the mystery which is realized through his act. We see that the minister must therefore identify himself in an apostolic spirit with the whole of this process of sanctification, and in the ritual mystery of worship express his own prayerful desire for the sanctification of the recipient.

3. Break between Office and Charism; the Necessary Minimum for the Minister's Act to be a Participation in the Visibility of the Church

The ideal fulfilment of the minister's commission therefore lies in his doing what the Church does in the fullest sense of the phrase; he must, in other words, identify himself personally with the sacramental sanctifying will of the Church. The minimum requirement

---

the minister's action plays an essential part as being the representation in the minister of the *fides Ecclesiae*. Even more explicit is St. Thomas's teaching on the necessity of the faith and devotion of the recipient in the true sacrament (i.e., not only valid but fruitful): "Operatur ad efficaciam baptismi fides Ecclesiae et eius cui baptizatur" (*ST*, III, q. 39, a. 5): "Necessarium est quod recipiens sacramentum quodammodo contingat ipsum, et per intellectum, quem quidem contactum facit fides, et per affectum, quem contactum facit devotio." (*IV Sent.*, d. 4, q. 3, a. 2, sol. 2; Moos, p. 188.) (Tr.)

is thus his willing participation in the visibility of the Church, even though he does not enter into the reality expressed by this sign and participates only by his performing of the sacramental action. What exactly does this mean? We said above that as a human act the administration of a sacrament must be a voluntary one; voluntary in such a way that by the intention of the minister the action performed really is an ecclesial symbolic action. Now what is the minimal content of this intention for which the act is still truly ecclesial, even though on the borderline? The Council of Trent resolved the question in this way: "If anyone should say that the ministers, when they administer sacraments or celebrate [the Eucharist], need not have the intention at least to do what the Church does, let him be anathema."[20] The intention to do what the Church does is the strictly necessary minimum.

In the sacraments grace comes to us in ecclesial visibility. A sacrament is valid only when it is ecclesial. So if the intention of the minister is necessary for validity, it means that this intention must in some way concern at least the visible ecclesial character of the sacrament. The minister must inwardly intend to perform the Church's outward rite. All theologians agree that for validity it is not necessary that the minister should believe personally in the mystery and the meaning of the Church's sacraments. If he does not believe, of course, the minister cannot have the intention to administer a sacrament precisely as sacrament (this would be a psychological impossibility). A non-believer, however, can want to perform an act (and in fact perform it voluntarily) which has meaning only in the perspective of the economy of salvation, even though he cannot appreciate it in that light himself. In this case, in the performance of the visible ecclesial act he fulfils the intention of Christ and of the Church as an outsider would. He must have, therefore, at least some vague knowledge of the fact that the act asked of him is ecclesial. In this he might be acting out of respect for the religious opinions of a fellow man who has asked him to do this, or he might merely ridicule the practice; still, as soon as he consents to the request and performs the act voluntarily, he performs an ecclesial symbolic action.

Thus the honest inward will to perform the Church's outward rite is sufficient. So when a person has the inward intention truly to perform a visible act of the Church (the intention to do what is accepted by the faithful as an act of the Church, of which the minister must have at least an elementary awareness) what is done is truly an act of the Church, and consequently is valid. From the psychological point of view this intention may, naturally, be reflexively conscious; you can think of the fact that you are intending to act (a reflection that not infrequently leads to scrupulosity in forming an intention). But the intention may simply be implicit in carrying out the act; going ahead and doing the act, you intend it (which psychologically is the healthier way).

By the necessity of the minister's intention it is clearly shown, once again, that the sacraments are ecclesial acts. The minister performs the ritual act in the name of the Church and thus in the name of Christ; therefore he must will to do precisely what the Church asks. When the visible act is ecclesial it also manifests the sacramental meaning: viz., a ritual prayer of Christ and the Church which by that very fact bestows grace. This is equally true of matrimony, in which the contracting parties themselves are the chief ministers of the sacrament.

Note

In the history of theology there has been a great deal of controversy about the intention of the minister. Not infrequently, however, this problem has been confused with a second question, of how an observer is to decide from the correct outward performance (as the Church requires) that the minister did truly intend to perform the ecclesial rite. For he is able to pretend, to act "as if." And if this is all he does, it is evident that the sacrament is not valid. In practice it is prudent to suppose that when the Church's outward rite is performed at the request of a believer it is genuinely performed. If a case does occur in which, for example, a doctor who is an unbeliever, on being asked to baptize, merely pretends, or in which a priest in difficulties makes a pretence of his administration, then there is of course no sacrament, but "God will provide." And so, again, after a sincere and perhaps urgently necessary confession, there is no reason at all to worry anxiously whether the priest on his part had the genuine intention to absolve.

It was nevertheless problems such as these that gave rise to the dispute about the so-called "internalist" and "externalist" theories. "Externalism" is the theory of theologians who hold that when the outward performance of the ecclesial act is correct, even when it is not willed inwardly and is thus pretence, the sacrament is valid. This theory of Fr. Farvacques was condemned by Rome.[21] The inward intention is therefore necessary too. This is called "internalism." Historically, the controversy concerned only whether Lancelot Politi (Ambrogio Catarino) defended the externalist theory or not. The core of his teaching is that there must be the inward intention to perform the outward rite of the Church. And that is right enough. Unfortunately, however, in Catarino's works there are passages that contradict his basic position.[22] In fact the

---

[21] *DB*, 1318.

[22] Catarino says, on the one hand. "Who in [full] possession of his faculties would do something that he did not actually intend to do?" (*De Intentione Ministri Sacramentorum*, Rome [1552], col. 208.) But on the other hand he says that when the minister does what the Church does, "intus aliud servare in animo, ita ut itendat derisorie batptizare" (*De Intentione*, col. 207), the baptism is nevertheless valid. My interpretation of this text was as follows: When the minister really does voluntarily what the Church asks, but because of his inward disbelief can only deride the practice of baptism, then the baptism is valid. (*SH*, p. 470.) However, L. Renwart, "Intention du ministre et validité des sacraments," in *NRT*, 77 (1955), p. 806, has since given an entirely different interpretation: When the minister outwardly performs the Church's ceremonial, while nevertheless in reality only "wanting to play at baptism," then, according to Catarino, the baptism is still valid. If this is the correct interpretation, then Catarino's theory agrees entirely with the condemned theory of Farvacques. It seems to me

whole problem of internalism and externalism has become the historical one of discovering the actual opinion of this or that author.

3. THE INTENTION OF THE RECIPIENT

1. Free Acceptance of the Visibility of the Church

The necessity of the intention of the recipient, unlike that of the minister, up to the present has not been the subject of a dogmatic definition. It is, however, a matter of faith to which the whole of tradition witnesses, asserted in the *Rituale Romanum*[23] and sanctioned by Canon Law.[24] However, these two documents do not state that this intention is necessary for the validity of a sacrament. The general principle governing this doctrine on intention is the constant attitude of the Church on the matter of "conversion"; no one can be brought into the Church by force and against his will. The life of religion is of its very nature a free acceptance of the God who condescends to meet us.

Since a sacrament is essentially realized for a particular individual, so that it is precisely for him, the recipient, that Christ's act of redemption becomes present, it is not possible that a sacrament should have any significance for an adult if he is not at least willing to listen. If he is not willing, then the sacrament is not performed for him; at the most, all that happens is that he undergoes the rite. This "listening" as the minimum requirement[25] for the

---

that Catarino allowed the problem concerning the certainty a third party is able to have about the minister's intention to intrude in his discussion of the totally separate question of the necessity of the intention as such, thus giving rise to confusion. It is only when these two problems are clearly and carefully distinguished that the points at issue can be clarified.

[23] Tit. 2, c. 3, nos. 1 and 9.   [24] Canons 752 and 754.

[25] Full readiness to hear and accept (the optimum requirement) which develops into a genuine encounter with Christ is considered in a later chapter.

validity of a sacrament means that the recipient truly desires the ecclesial rite to be performed upon him; then at least he accepts the direction of this rite to his own person. It is not necessary for validity that he should desire the actual bestowal of grace, and thus in faith and love hear and enter into the sacramental offer of it. As the minimum it is sufficient that he willingly has the rite performed on himself knowing, at least vaguely, that it is an ecclesial religious rite. (Throughout this discussion we make a reservation for the special nature of the sacrifice of the Mass.) Personal faith in the sacraments is therefore not necessary for their validity—although here we approach the borderline. For psychological separation of faith from intention is indeed possible for motives of utility (for example, should a dignitary in a village have himself baptized from motives of political gain).

From the necessity of the intention of the recipient (at least should he be an adult), it is clear that on his part too the sacrament must be a human act and that it requires at least a minimum of personal involvement if it is truly to be a sacrament. Without this intention the sacrament does not have its special relationship, accepted by an act of will, to this particular person. In no other way than by voluntary acceptance of and involvement in the rite can this become a ritual and effective manifestation of saving power for the benefit of the recipient in person. The necessity of the intention is founded on the personality of man in relation to the ecclesial reality in which grace comes to meet him.

2. The Problem of Sacraments for Infants; the Assurance of God's Redeeming Love towards Those Who Can Have No Knowledge of It

From the above it follows immediately that as the recipient of a sacrament of which he is capable (infant baptism, for example), an individual who is psychologically still undeveloped need not himself form any intention with regard to its reception. This does not involve some sort of dispensation from a condition that would otherwise be necessary *per se*; it is rather the nature of symbolic action as performed on and for an individual who is psychologically an infant, just as the nature of symbolic action performed for a conscious person makes his personal intention necessary. The objection that persons who are baptized in infancy, when they reach the age of reason, are obliged (and perhaps against their will) to live according to their baptism presents no real difficulty. None of us were asked whether we wanted to be born. And yet we are obliged to take upon ourselves, in free responsibility, our actual existence and all its consequences. Or is a baby less the child of its father and mother because it does not know that it is their child? Does it receive less love and care because it does not know what its parents are doing for it? Against this it cannot be objected that birth is unavoidable while baptism, on the contrary, is not. The personal love of God, of Christ who gave his blood for love of this child, is a primordial fact impossible for us to ignore. And in baptism Christ wishes to pledge and bestow this, his love which will not take "no" for an answer.

The unavoidable fact of God's love always requires a response from created beings. It is true that a dormant personality is not yet capable of an encounter. But because a baby is still not capable of meeting its mother, she surely does not withhold from it all her care. She speaks to her child, smiles at it and fondles it, as if the child were already aware of it all. Dr. F. J. J. Bujtendijk has given a masterly description of this in his essay on the child's first smile. All the little things done for the baby, every loving gesture of motherly watching by the cradle, represent an eager expectation of response, an enticement to the dormant personality. It is in the world of people, not of things, that a baby grows to conscious awareness. The personality, still dormant, gradually blossoms forth under the cherishing care of motherly love. Here too bodiliness, as the manifestation of loving care, is the medium through which the child will eventually respond to so much, and such expressive love.

This is the psychological foundation of infant baptism in which the Church, in her sacramental personification of Christ, turns the bodily care of washing clean into the manifestation of Christ's saving love; it is a maternal gesture that of its nature expects a response which will be given later on. It will be able to be given precisely in virtue of that bodily care of "bathing the baby" as the sacrament of Christ's saving love for this child. And at the moment in which it is made, the sacramental gesture has a more profound effect than the motherly care bestowed on the psychologically still unconscious child; for the sacrament produces within the child the ontological foundation which makes the future response possible; the foundation of the encounter with God is laid. In other words, sanctifying grace is now present as the positive possibility of an encounter with God when the child's psyche awakes, and has an effect in this very waking, at least as far as religion is concerned.

The fact that infant baptism (and certain other sacraments of which people are capable before the age of reason) is a right and intelligent thing to practise points to the tremendous significance of "preventive grace," which initiates and logically precedes every human action in adults as well. A religious act is always the human willing of something that God "previously" does in us in free sovereignty. A person because of his essential personality must freely will and accept the divine initiative immediately. An infant can do this in its own time; once grown up, it must make the grace it has received personally its own.[26] This shows that the negation of infant baptism in some Protestant Churches goes against the deepest meaning of the redemption.

We must also keep in mind the ecclesial communal character of the sacraments and our human, especially our ecclesial, co-responsibility for the destiny in life of our fellow men. For a man never goes to his God in isolation. For this reason St. Thomas says, "children can be considered to have an intention in virtue not of their own

[26] More precisely, the spiritual development of a baptized child, especially in a Christian milieu, is at the same time the gradual personal acceptance of its baptismal grace.

personal act . . . but of the act of those who bring them to be baptized."[27] Christian destiny is a divine command, and at the same time a divine promise which really takes hold of the child through its Christian parents and ultimately, therefore, through the visible historical fact of the Church.[28] There is a social co-responsibility for the realization of the aim in life of our fellow men. The Church has this apostolic aim with regard to all men; it is realized both in the Christian parents who bring their children to baptism and in the one who administers it. Hence it cannot be objected that the intention of the parents and, as the character of the communal liturgy requires, the intention of the faithful there present concerning the infant to be baptized are alien to the inner significance of the sacramental event as visible expression of the sanctifying will of God in Christ. This co-responsibility and thus this communal intending of the sacramental act must, for that matter, play their rightful part in the sacraments received by adults as well; they are not a feature of infant baptism alone.

4. THE CONDITION UPON WHICH THE VALUE OF THE SACRAMENTS AS PRAYER AND SANCTIFICATION DEPENDS: INSTITUTION BY CHRIST

As we have seen, by the sacraments Christ's personal act of redemption, which is eternally actual, becomes sacramentalized in the Church. In their employment the sacraments are therefore acts of Christ. But this immediately implies that the Church cannot have established the sacraments on her own initiative. Christ himself, before leaving this world to go to the Father, must have entrusted to the Church (explicitly or implicitly, but really) the commission to bring his heavenly saving act to effective manifestation. In other

---

[27] "Possunt dici [infantes] intendentes, non per actum propriae intentionis . . . sed per actum eorum a quibus offeruntur." (*ST*, III, q. 68, a. 9, ad 1.)
[28] Cf. H. Schlier, *Die Zeit der Kirche*, Freiburg (1956), ch. 9. "Zur Kirchlichen Lehre von der Taufe," p. 125.

words the nature of the sacraments demands that he must in some way have instituted them himself. The Council of Trent therefore defined as a dogma that "the sacraments of the New Covenant are all instituted by Christ.[29] In its actual context this definition of faith was directed against the Reformation, which accepted only some of the sacraments. The Church said there are seven, no more, no less,[30] and these seven are instituted by Christ. Consequently it was also defined that the Church, on account of this, does not itself possess the power to alter the substance, the essential core, of the sacraments.[31] This essential core is, as Pius XII defined it, "that which, according to the witness of the sources of divine revelation, Christ the Lord himself laid down to be preserved in the [sacramental] sign."[32] What precisely did Christ institute?

Since the teaching authority of the Church has not decided this question, several attempts have been made to find a solution. In the Middle Ages there were already differences of opinion on the matter.[33] The various tendencies which have appeared in the course

---

[29] *DB*, 844.   [30] *DB*, 844.

[31] *DB*, 931.

[32] "Ea quae testibus divinae revelationis fontibus ipse Christus Dominus in signo servanda statuit." (Constitutio Apostolica "Sacramentum Ordinis," in *AAS*, 40 [1948], p. 5.)

[33] The author has investigated this in *SH*, pp. 416–19. Briefly we note the following. As examples of the different opinions: Alexander of Hales, speaking of confirmation, held that the matter of this sacrament was instituted by the Church at the (historically unidentified) Council of Meaux (his *ST*, IV, q. 9, nos. 1 and 2); thus a case of institution by the Church. St. Bonaventure held that the Apostles instituted the matter of confirmation (*IV Sent.*, d. 7, a. 1, q. 1 and 2); thus mediate institution—institution by Christ through his immediate witnesses. St. Thomas held the "institutio immediata materiae et formae" by Christ. (*ST*, I–II q. 108, a. 2; *ST*, III, q. 60, a. 5c and ad 1.) It is important to notice that the modern problem concerning the institution and the unalterable substance of the sacraments is not exactly the same problem that occupied the theologians of the twelfth and thirteenth centuries. These questions were seen as part merely of the wider controversy around the "delegatio potestatis excellentiae" (cf. A. Landgraf, "Der fruhscholastische streit um die 'potestas quam Christus potuit dare et non dedit,'" in *GM*, 15 [1943], pp. 524–72). It was generally held that the external rite of all the sacraments had been substantially (i.e., as to matter and form) the same since the time of their institution; the historical data

of the Church's history, especially in scholastic theology, can be reduced to four. First, Christ is said to have established the outward sign and therefore the sacramental action and the sacramental word, each individually in its actual form.[34] A theory of this kind could arise only at a time in which theologians were totally unaware of the historical alterations which the sacramental rite has undergone. Second, Christ is said specifically to have determined both of the elements of the sacramental rite in their outward embodiment.[35] The conditions which the Church subsequently superimposed are said to concern the licitness, never the validity, of a sacrament. Third, Christ is said to have determined the basic or specific outline of the liturgical actions and words according to their outward embodiment, but nevertheless in such a way that the Apostolic Church could give this outline a closer precision to which now the post-Apostolic Church remains bound.[36] Some formulate this theory differently: Christ determined the outward sign specifically, but the Church is able to impose conditions which affect validity. Finally, constrained by historical facts, theologians in modern times have come to affirm that Christ instituted the sevenfold sacramental grace alone, and determined that this grace represented in seven outward signs should be bestowed in the Church.[37] The actual determination of the seven outward signs Christ will have left to the Church, on the condition that the sign the Church adopts should of its nature be intrinsically suitable as a representation of the relevant sacramental grace. This theory is put forward with a reservation:

---

necessary for a true appreciation of the problem were simply not available. Therefore any suggestion of even a mediate institution of one or other of the essential elements in a sacramental rite would have meant *ipso facto* that Christ had delegated his *potestas excellentiae,* that other men had shared with Christ his position as Head, Lord and Mediator, since it pertains to the giver of grace alone to determine the signs in which grace is given. (Tr.)

[34] The *determinatio in individuo* theory.

[35] The theory of the *determinatio in specie immobili et infima.*

[36] *Determinatio in specie mobili* (with the exception of baptism and the Eucharist).

[37] The theory of the *determinatio in forma generica tantum,* excepting baptism and the Eucharist.

In some sacraments (for example baptism and the Eucharist) the specific determination of the outward sign itself may derive from institution by Christ.

1. The Fundamental Institution of the Seven Sacraments as Implicit in the Establishment of the Sacramental Church

In order to have a clear appreciation of this question, we must keep it in the context of the ecclesial significance of the sacraments. A sacrament, as we have said, is a special vital contact with Christ in a visible act of the Church. In each of the seven sacraments there is thus a particular kind of encounter with Christ; there is, we may say, one of the seven possible aspects of sacramental grace made manifest in a visible act of the Church—precisely because that act is the symbolic realization of the risen Christ's act of salvation. For in the sacraments the eternally actual redemptive act takes a hold on us by way of the special significance of the outward sign. And this makes two things clear.

First, the Church as the visible earthly representation of the grace of redemption is the great saving sign of the grace of Christ. This means that the Church's fullness of grace in its "establishment in power," which took place on the Cross, culminating in the resurrection and the exaltation of Christ to be *Kyrios,* is connected with the great outward sign that the visible Church itself is. The Church as primordial sacrament and as community of worship already is the fundamental institution of the seven sacraments by Christ. The Church is the earthly "body of the Lord"; is therefore the representation of the primordial sacrament which is the glorified body of Christ. Hence even if Christ before his death indicated the structure of his Church and in this sense "founded" it, the actual founding or, more precisely, the "establishment in power" of the Church, took place only upon Christ's resurrection from the dead and exaltation by the Father's side. From that moment, and not before, the Church is the sign of grace imbued with the reality it signifies; the earthly sign of redemption.

But at the same time this fundamental institution of the Church as the primordial sacrament in which the seven ritual sacraments are implicitly instituted is not entirely sufficient. It does not suffice because in the seven sacraments the actual saving act of the *Kyrios* takes a hold on us in a direction indicated by the outward sign. So Christ himself must have had some immediate part in directing the meaning, since this implies directing his own redemptive grace to a specific need of Christian life. This further implies that Christ, who wills to bestow a share in his grace through the Church, or rather through a visible act of the Church, must himself have established the sevenfold direction of grace, of which a visible act of the Church is the medium. Otherwise it must have been the Church that established the sevenfold direction of grace, presumably in virtue of its own establishment as the primordial sacrament. But it is difficult to reconcile this with either the Tridentine dogma or the nature of a sacrament as the ecclesial symbolic act of Christ himself.

2. *The Problem of the Separate Institution of the Seven Sacraments*

(a) *How Christ Himself Indicated the Sevenfold Direction of Sacramental Meaning*

It follows from what we have just been saying that the principle upon which we must work is that Christ himself laid down the sevenfold direction of the sacramental visible acts of the Church. This implies that the meaning of each sacrament was determined by Christ. The way in which Christ manifested his will in this regard may have differed from one sacrament to another, and as a matter of fact cannot be discovered with certainty for all of the sacraments. His will did not need to be expressed with explicit clarity, for there is such a thing as an implicit, unparticularized, but nevertheless real manifestation of will.[38] Nevertheless we do find in Scripture data which manifest sufficiently, for some sacraments more clearly than for others, Christ's will with regard to a visible ecclesial saving act in different directions. This is so especially when we consider the question in the light of the consciousness of the Faith which evolved subsequently and in the light of the Church's sacramental practice.

The scriptural data are there, at least for baptism, confession or the sacrament of penance, the Eucharist, the apostolic office (priesthood) and, to a certain extent, confirmation. As far as matrimony and the sacrament of the grievously ill and dying are concerned, it is more difficult to indicate data referring immediately to Christ's will in these matters. Hence we must presuppose an implicit will of Christ, and we are clearly led to do so by reason of the Apostles' immediate practice of anointing the sick,[39] for example, especially since the messianic healing of the sick was quite evidently intended, according to the will of Christ, to devolve upon the primitive Church. Furthermore St. Paul gives, in a most special way, a Christian and ecclesial appreciation of marriage, and sees the conjugal relationship of man and wife as an image of the relationship between Christ and the Church,[40] which brings out the fact that the connection between the Church (the sacramental sign of salvation) and matrimony had already been established. From this it is no great step to a special visible act of the Church concerning matrimony, and thus to the sacrament.

This makes it clear that even in the more explicit institution of other sacraments by Christ the fundamental institution of the Church, as the sacramental saving sign, remains the essential factor. For as we have seen, this fundamental institution of the mystery of the Church is an implicit institution of the seven sacraments.

---

[38] Cf. D. van den Eynde. "De modo institutionis sacramentorum," in *AAM*, 27 (1952), pp. 3–10. This writer, however, makes the question turn upon the outward rite, which, as far as I can see, is not at all necessary.

[39] Jas. 5.14–15.   [40] Ephes. 5.25–33.

And perhaps this implicit institution is the only manifestation of Christ's will regarding one or another of the sacraments—matrimony, for example.[41] Furthermore, we must not lose sight of the fact that even those sacraments of which Christ spoke more explicitly during his earthly life were established "in power" only by his death and resurrection. Before then they were for that matter not needed, since the Apostles lived in immediate contact with the primordial sacrament, Christ himself. Especially when we see how the seven sacraments enter into the constitution of the Church, and thereby indicate the ecclesial reason why there are seven of them,[42] it becomes clear that Christ's fundamental institution of the Church as primordial sacrament is, immediately but implicitly, also the institution of the seven. So we see that reasoning from the function as constituting and propagating the Church we may conclude immediately that there was at least an implicit and unparticularized manifestation of Christ's will concerning the seven sacraments.

(b) The Role of Christ, of the Apostolic Church, and of the Post-Apostolic Church in Determining the Outward Shape of the Sacraments

Thus Christ himself, in some cases explicitly, in others probably merely implicitly and without particularization, determined the sevenfold direction of the signification which is brought out in the ecclesial saving acts that are the sacraments. Whether he deter-

41 This becomes all the more intelligible now we know that a valid matrimonial contract entered into by baptized persons is of its nature a sacrament. Originally, therefore, the Church did not lay down any special conditions (apart from those required by civil law) for the validity of a marriage.

42 Karl Rahner has attempted this in broad outline in the article, "Kirche und Sakramente. Zur theologischen Grundlegung einer Kirchen und Sakramentenfrömmigkeit" in *GL*, 28 (1955), pp. 434–53.

mined the nature of these visible acts or left this to the Church, so long as the act determined upon manifested its purpose in the direction he laid down, is another question. And there is no *a priori* solution to this question in favour of either alternative. To arrive at any solution a preliminary and positive theological study of the Church's ritual for each of the seven sacraments is necessary.[43] The positive data provided by an investigation of this kind show clearly that there has been enormous variation in the shape of the liturgical word and the liturgical action (the so-called form and matter) but that, even so, the general direction of the sense manifested in each sacrament has remained constant. What was instituted by Christ— and so, according to the Council of Trent, what the Church neither may, nor indeed can, alter—cannot, in all these variations, be the shape of the matter and form of the sacraments.

Consider the question of confirmation, for example. Christ did not say to his Apostles, even by mere implication, "Today I am instituting confirmation, which you are to administer in this fashion . . ." What actually did take place? During his earthly life Christ had promised the Holy Spirit to the Apostles. He had, moreover, laid down the outlines of the structure of his visible Church. After Easter the Apostles, in the Cenacle, experienced the sensational effusion of the Holy Spirit, along with what seemed to be

---

[43] We have undertaken this study on the question of baptism, confirmation and the Eucharist in *SH*, pp. 240–354, and on the priesthood in *Theologisch Woordenboek*, Roermond en Maaseik (1958), vol. 3, cols. 3959–4003. (English translation, *Encyclopedic Dictionary of the Bible*, McGraw-Hill Book Co., New York [1963].) On the sacrament of penance, cf. B. Poschmann, *Paenitentia Secunda*, Bonn (1940); C. Vogel, *La Discipline pénitentielle en Gaule des origines à la fin du VIIIme siècle*, Paris (1952). On matrimony: K. Ritzer, *Eheschlieszung. Formen, Riten und religiöses Brauchtum der Eheschlieszung in den christlichen Kirchen des ersten Jahrtausends*, (Munich 1951-2), 3 parts in 2 vols. On the last anointing: A. Chavasse, *Etude sur l'onction des infirmes dans l'Eglise latine du IIIme au XIme siècle*, Lyons (1942), vol. 1; A. Janssens, *Het H. Oliesel*, Antwerp-Nijmegen (1939); P. de Meester, *Studi sui sacramenti amministrati secondo il rito byzantino*, Rome (1947), pp. 149–240; J. C. Didier and H. R. Philippeau, "Extrême-Onction," in *Catholicisme hier, aujourd'hui, demain*, fasc. 15, cols. 987–1014.

visible tongues of fire.[44] From heaven the *Kyrios* sends his Spirit in some kind of earthly visible shape. And then the Apostles take up their commission. The Church itself now begins to bestow on other men the Spirit it has received directly from Christ. That is what confirmation is. The Church does not do this through a a kind of miracle, as in "fiery tongues," but through a visible act; this is the commission entrusted to it by Christ. The Apostles, who were pious Jews first of all and well acquainted with the religious customs of their people, and who were now enlightened by the Holy Spirit, knew that the laying on of hands was often used to confer divine blessings and for other similar purposes; indeed from time immemorial among the People of God the laying on of hands was connected with the gift of the *pneuma* (the spirit). So they imposed hands upon those who had been baptized, precisely with the purpose of bestowing on them the outpouring of the Spirit. Everything suggests that it was not Christ himself who instituted, either explicitly or implicitly, the rite of the laying on of hands for giving of confirmation. It seems rather to have been the Apostles' spontaneous choice; a choice, however, in which they were imitating a way in which Christ used to act.

For Christ during his earthly life had laid his hands upon various people for various purposes; for blessing children, for healing, for the working of miracles of all kinds. And is it not significantly in character that the sacramental outward sign of the imposition of hands was employed in the Apostolic Church for several different purposes; for conferring authority for special commissions, for the rite of initiation, for healings and the rest? This was an undifferentiated, readily available and obvious rite which could be employed to many ends. Especially in the conferring of authority of office the apostolic use of the laying on of hands for the outward rite is simply the Christian prolongation of a Jewish religious custom. Quite naturally it presented itself as the rite with which the Apostolic Church was to connect a variety of meanings in the directions

[44] "Tongues as it were of fire." (Acts 2.3.)

determined by Christ (the conferring of Christian office, the bestowal of the Spirit, etc.). The relevant facts do indeed indicate that the Apostles turned spontaneously to Jewish rites, and that the theory of the so-called "generic determination" is the correct one, at least as far as some of the sacraments are concerned. This suppleness is already evidenced in the fact that whereas Christ gave the Spirit of forgiveness of sins to the Apostles while "breathing on them,"[45] the Church later on never considered itself committed to this outward sign of "breathing upon" in its penitential practice (although on the other hand, it plays a role in baptism and in exorcism).

In this we are not saying that Christ did not determine the actual shape of the outward rite in some way for certain sacraments. He said explicitly "baptize all men," and "baptize" means "immerse in something"; in other words, a (symbolic) washing.[46] That was therefore explicitly instituted by Christ himself; at the same time it is one of the common "archetypes" of the human creativity of religious symbolism. Any further determinations, fixing more precisely the actual nature of the washing with water, fall within the province of the Church. Furthermore, Christ himself celebrated the Eucharist with bread and wine, which in his day played a prominent part in the meal of the Jewish passover. The Church, then, understands his words "Do this in commemoration of me" as an obligation to retain the use of bread and wine, and has always strenuously rejected any attempts to diverge from the rule in this matter (e.g., the Aquarians). These are indications that Christ himself laid down that baptism should be with water and the Eucharist with bread and wine, although that he did so is not dogmatically defined.

This does not solve the problem entirely. For what lay within the power of the Apostolic Church does not necessarily lie within

---

[45] John 20.22.

[46] Both in the Greek (*baptô*) and in the Hebrew (*tâbal*) "baptize" means "immerse," "dip" (for example, to dip a piece of bread in wine). When it concerns washing, it means "dip into the water," "bathe in water," though there are also other words that may be used in the same sense.

the power of the post-Apostolic Church as well, since the Apostolic Church belonged to the constitutive phase of revelation. The Apostles' spontaneous selection of a particular rite in which the Christian signification is sacramentalized can therefore be normative, perpetually binding on the Church of later times. Thus the outward rite as determined by the Apostles may be something which the Church receives as unalterable. This unalterability does not mean that the Church in later times could not bring about a broader development in the ritual as a whole; for it is an historical fact that the Church has done this. But it does mean that within the entirety of the richly developed ritual the apostolic core must be retained, and must remain the truly essential factor in that ritual.

This at the very least is a real possibility, and often one to which insufficient attention is given. A confirmation of its likelihood is the fact that the Church at present tends to reach back to the most ancient ritual, if possible to the apostolic essence of the ritual (consider, for example, the *Constitutio Apostolica* "Sacramentum Ordinis," also the renewed appreciation of the imposition of hands which, in confirmation, was in earlier times relegated to a secondary place and even gave way altogether to anointing). If the theory of apostolic determination of the rite is correct, it must be granted that such a determination was in any event undifferentiated and rudimentary. Consequently the apostolic determination of the sacramental ritual, although *ne varietur,* was undifferentiated though specific: a bathing with water together with a word; an anointing of the sick together with a prayer; a laying on of hands with a prayer, and so on. It follows, then, that any subsequent and more precise determinations imposed by the post-Apostolic Church may come and go.

It seems to me, however, that it is still not proved that this apostolic selection or determination of the rite is absolutely normative for the post-Apostolic Church. We must in any case grant that in most if not all the sacraments the essential rite of apostolic times has been preserved through the centuries in the ecclesial ritual right up to the present day, in spite of the fact that an appreciation of the actual apostolic ritual has been, at times, at a very low ebb. (Consider again the priority of importance, if not the exclusive importance, the Middle Ages attached to the anointing in confirmation, despite the apostolic custom of the imposition of hands.) The fact that the apostolic use has actually endured may be an indication of its normative value. One difficulty remains, however: the apostolic rite of the laying on of hands in the sacrament of confirmation (after having been retained in rudimentary form in the actual manner of anointing) was entirely omitted from the rite, both temporarily in the West[47] and to a much greater extent in the East.[48]

---

[47] The author has traced the historical variations in *SH*, pp. 290–301; the imposition of hands as seen in Gallican literature, especially of the fifth century, is only a rudimentary remainder. Terms such as "cum chrismate et benedictione," "cum chrismatis benedictione consignare," "cum chrismate et manus impositione" have an identical meaning (cf. Council of Orange, can. 1 [*MC*, vol. 6, col. 435]; Council of Arles II, can. 16 and 26 [*MC*, vol. 7, cols. 880–81]; also D. van den Eynde, "Le Deuxième Canon du concile d'Orange de 441 sur la chrismation," in *RTAM*, 11 [1939], pp. 97–109). The wide diffusion of the *Sacramentaria Gelasianum* and *Gregorianum* furthered the development in this direction in the eighth century. Imposition of hands, in so far as it remains, is here clearly the gesture of blessing only, and has no proper sacramental significance. (Cf. *Sacramentarium Gregorianum* [*PL*, 78, col. 90].) In the Carolingian period there are clear traces of a reaction against the omission of the imposition of hands from the rite, in the "concordist" theory of writers of the time: ". . . cum impositione manus . . . unctione signetur" (Bede [?], *In Cantic.* [*PL*, 91, col. 1098]); . . . "chrismatio per manus impositionem." (Rhabanus Maurus, *De Clericorum Institutione* [*PL*, 107, col. 313].) The anointing in the rite then in use was interpreted as a "minimal" imposition of hands. This theory was maintained until the twelfth century (e.g., Hugh of St. Victor, *De Sacramentia*, II, 7, 2 and 4) and was adopted in the Church's official documents (e.g., *DB*, 419, 450). In the time of the great Scholastics the anointing is no longer thought of as also an imposition of hands (even if rudimentary) but as its replacement (cf. note 49 below). From this time on the *Pontificalia* make the anointing the central factor in the rite. In 1752 Benedict XIV revived the appreciation of the imposition of hands in his *Pontificale Romanum* in an appendix (Malines ed. [1895], p. 230). Leo XIII reintroduced an obligatory imposition of hands in his Pontifical, which has remained in the *Rituale Romanum* (since 1925). (Tr.)

[48] Again from *SH*, pp. 287–90, we note the following: This is explained partially by the place of anointings in daily life on all sorts of occasions,

St. Thomas himself interprets this fact as the substitution of the anointing for the apostolic custom of laying on hands.[49] It could be alleged that the anointing in actual use was at the same time a rudimentary imposition of hands; it was actually interpreted in this way after the disappearance of a separate imposition of hands from the rite and before the Scholastics put forward their views.[50] In this sense there would have been no actual divergence from the apostolic custom of the laying on of hands, in spite of the fact that for a time theologians in their appreciation of the rite tended to regard the opposite as true.

This seems to me to be a nicety of distinction very close to the

---

whether personal or domestic or public, partially by the New Testament references to the Holy Spirit as *unctio* (e.g., Acts, 6.27; Luke 6.18; 2 Cor. 1.21, etc.) and the very meaning of the name "Christ" to the Greek ear. At first, however, the imposition of hands was retained (*Didascalia*, II, 32.3:41.2 (ed. Funk, vol. 1, pp. 115, 131); St. Irenaeus, *Adv. Haer.*, IV, 38, 2 (*PG*, 7, col. 1106). After the third century references become rarer and are often very obscure: sometimes the three "mysteries of initiation" are simply called "baptismus, chrismatio et sumptio corporis et sanguinis Domini." Many texts suggest that the anointing has replaced the imposition of hands entirely: Cyril of Jerusalem says "Petrus per impositionem manus largitur Spiritum. In te quoque qui baptizatus es, perventura est gratia. Quonam vero modo, non dico, nec enim tempus anteverto." (*Catecheses*, XVI, 26 [*PG*, 33, col. 955].) In the description of the rite of confirmation later in the same *Catecheses* (XXI, 1–2 [*PG*, 33, 1088f.]) there is mention of an anointing only. (Also see Origen, *In Levit. Hom.*, VI, 5 [*PG*, 12, col. 472]; Theophilus of Antioch, *Ad. Anatil.*, I, 12 [*PG*, 6, col. 1041].) In present-day Eastern rites confirmation is a fairly brief ceremony, and consists in anointing the forehead and other parts of the body. Only in the Chaldee and dependent Coptic and Ethiopian rites does the imposition of hands play a part (cf. Raes, *Introductio in liturgiam orientalem*, Rome [1947]). (Tr.)

[49] "Apostoli imponebant manus . . . et loco illius manus impositionis datur in Ecclesia confirmatio" ("cuius materia est chrisma"): *De Articulis Fidei et Ecclesiae Sacramentis* (*Opuscula Omnia*, Mandonnet ed., Paris [1927], vol. 3, pp. 15 and 14). The Council of Florence repeats this text word for word. (Cf. *DB*, 697.)

[50] Cf. note 47 above. Hugh of St. Victor writes: "De Sacramento confirmationis, i.e., impositionis manuum" (although there was no separate *impositio* in the rite of his day), and "unctione chrismatis per manus impositionem" ("per impositionem pollicis" would have been more literally correct). (*De Sacramentia*, II, 7, 2 and 4). Pope Innocent III writes: ". . . per frontis chrismationem manus impositio designatur." (*DB*, 419.)

borderline. Yet considering the standing enjoyed for centuries of an "anointing through the imposition of hands," it is not, after all, an impossibility. And if it should be so, then (presupposing Christ's institution of the direction of sacramental meaning and all that has been said above about the institution of the Church as the primordial sacrament) I should be inclined to prefer the theory that the material rite (in its rudimentary specific determination) is of apostolic institution, and is normative as far as the post-Apostolic Church is concerned, however much this Church may add further determinations and absorb the basic rite into various rituals, even to the extent that the Church's further determinations become necessary for the validity of the sacrament.[51] Yet though this theory is preferable, it is not wholly convincing. Probably we have still not discovered all the finer points involved in this question of the sacrament of confirmation. Although Scripture is silent on the matter, it is not impossible that anointing was already an apostolic custom in this sacrament.[52] In that case this rite at least has been at least preserved through all the Church's history.

On account of the many changes in the rite which a positive theological study has revealed, we must allow a certain possibility that the post-Apostolic Church also is free with regard to the essential material embodiment of the outward sacramental sign—although from all we have seen in the preceding investigation the possibility is in reality pretty small. It may thus be possible that the Church of later times (always in keeping with the socio-religious rules governing amendments to the symbolism of a community)[53] is itself to redetermine the embodiment of its own symbolic sacramental acts, as long as the direction of sacramental meaning instituted by

[51] We add this last qualification partly, but not exclusively, on account of the fact that the sacramental symbolic action is dependent upon the Church's jurisdictional authority as well; which authority is involved in the symbolic action itself. If, for example, the ecclesial jurisdiction gives no faculties for an absolution to be administered in deprecatory form instead of by the indicative formula, the use of a deprecatory formula would not be the Church's symbolic act and consequently would not be a sacrament.

[52] Cf. the article by D. van den Eynde cited in note 38 above.

[53] On this point see J. A. Ponsioen, *Symboliek in de samenleving. Een sociologie van de symbolen en van het symbolisch denken,* Utrecht (1952).

Christ can still be represented by and imaged in the embodiment chosen (which after all is the essence of symbolic activity). In all of this we are naturally allowing for the fact that Christ himself may have determined the outward material rite for certain sacraments, at least in general.[54]

(c) Conclusion

That which has changed in the course of time in the outward rite, that which has disappeared from it and then been reinstated, cannot have been instituted by Christ. The essence of a sacrament, explicitly or implicitly instituted by Christ, is the signification within a sevenfold orientation as it is externally manifested in a visible act of the Church, and hence in a (liturgical) action accompanied by a prayer of faith or an indicative formula of faith (in which the special direction of the signification is made manifest). Probably the undifferentiated determination of this visible act was handed on, *ne varietur,* by the Apostolic Church to the Church which it established (the post-Apostolic Church). If this was the case, then the apostolic institution must be regarded as something positively willed by Christ the Lord; then, moreover, the sacraments were instituted by Christ, though indirectly. Nevertheless it seems to me that no thoroughly convincing argument has yet been found to support the *ne varietur* selection of the rite, and conse-

[54] Priests in the East consecrate leavened bread; in the West, unleavened bread. Further, what is bread? Does maize meal make bread? Evidently Christ did not want to lay anything down in this matter; nor in the matter of the kinds of wine or the manner of its preparation, so long as it is wine. A certain relativity naturally plays a part in the appreciation of these things. Ultimately it is the popular acceptation, which can differ from one country to another, that the Church judges, and the Church lays down the concrete norms; of these norms, therefore, it seems we cannot say *ne varietur.* It is unfortunate that so many of the manuals, confusing the different levels of the issues involved, give the impression that a theologian, in order to determine the essence of a sacrament, must among other things be thoroughly conversant with all the different species of grain and know all about viniculture.

quently, with the exception of a few cases, it may be possible that the post-Apostolic Church is free with regard to the determination of the essential outward embodiment of its symbolic acts. It seems to me that at the present time a theologically enlightened awareness of the Faith can affirm nothing further.

3. Consequences

Important consequences follow from those points in the above investigation which are in no case open to doubt. Since the essence of the sacramental sign, the signification, always in fact does exist as actualized in a richly developed dialogue of actions and prayers, this rite itself is the bearer of "that which Christ himself laid down to be preserved in the [sacramental] sign" (Pius XII). It may have been the Apostolic Church or it may have been the post-Apostolic Church that determined the core of the sacramental rite; in either case the rite in actual use is the realization of the substance of the sacrament, and necessary for validity. If, however, the apostolic institution of the essential rite does not constitute a norm for the post-Apostolic Church, it follows that it may perhaps be very difficult to discover, among the many symbolic factors with which the richly developed ceremonial abounds, the essential core of the rite which the Church sees here and now as the realization of the substance of the sacrament. For in that case the ecclesial appreciation of the essential rite can shift from time to time through the centuries. Hence what was at one time essential (as the bearer of the substance) may have given way to another symbolic factor in which the Church's understanding—which actually forms the symbols—now sees the substance of the sacrament realized.

It must be noted that this is possible only if the apostolic determination of the essential rite is not an invariable norm for the Church (in which case it would be an historical fact that the essential rite has changed). But even granting the theory of the apostolic norm to which the Church is perpetually bound, there is in practice still the possibility of a distinction (in one or another sacrament) between that which is necessary for validity in virtue of Christ's institution or the Apostles' determination and that which is necessary for validity in virtue of the conditions laid down by the post-Apostolic Church (by the power of the ecclesial authority of jurisdiction). And whatever the actual facts of the former matter may be, these latter conditions can change from time to time.

As far as the sacramental word of faith (the so-called *forma*) is concerned, provided the sacramental significance is in some way formulated in it, it is clear that this word can shift from time to time within the rite as a whole. In the history of the rite of baptism this is all too evident,[55] and in many sacraments a prayer which is now introductory to the actual sacramental formula was at an earlier date the essential sacramental word of faith (or form), that which is now the essential formula not being found in the rite at all. In extreme unction, for example, during the Middle Ages there were very striking changes in the sacramental word of faith.[56] Probably the only exception in this regard is the eucharistic words of institution. For although it is evident that in former times the *epiclesis* (in this case, a prayer that God should change the bread and wine into the body and blood of the Lord) bore at least a

[55] In *SH*, pp. 253–85, the author has collected and studied the positive historical data. Thoroughly reliable witnesses to the use of our classical formula are found, confined to Syria, from the end of the fourth century; in Alexandria from the fifth century; elsewhere not before the seventh, and not generally until the eighth century. Documents concerning earlier practices show among other formulae the Creed in interrogative form; the baptizand is immersed "sub has interrogationes: Credis in Deum? etc." (*Gelasian Sacramentary*, ed. H. A. Wilson, p. 86.) Indeed, the changes in the baptismal ritual have been greatest in the form of words employed. However, there has been no change in the trinitarian character of their essential meaning. Though it is not apodictically proved, there is some evidence for the use of Christological formulae, but by the fact that the trinitarian formulae so speedily became the constant tradition it may be argued that even the Christological formulae were appreciated as implicitly trinitarian. (Tr.)

[56] Cf. A. Janssens, *Het. H. Oliesel*, Antwerp-Nijmegen (1939).

share in the consecratory significance,[57] and although there have been liturgies from which the words of institution have been entirely missing, in the Latin Church there is nevertheless a firm inclination to regard these words of institution as the eucharistic *forma* laid down by Christ himself.[58] There are even some who hold the

[57] We summarize the author's reference in *SH*, pp. 329–54, very briefly. The Greek Church has shown a strong tendency to adhere to the strictly sacramental significance of the *epiclesis*. To cite the main examples: (1) the Byzantine Liturgy of St. Basil (text dating from the sixth century) calls the offerings, after the words of institution have been pronounced, antitypes (cf. F. E. Brightman, *Liturgies Eastern and Western*, Oxford [1896], vol. 1, pp. 329ff.). In the theology of St. John Damascene "antitype" cannot refer to the consecrated species (cf. S. Salaville, *"Epiclèse Eucharistique,"* in *DTC*, vol. V–1, esp. cols. 247–52). (2) Nicholas Cabasilas (Archbishop of Thessalonika, 1361–3) says Christ consecrated when "he looked up to heaven and gave thanks," not when he said, "This is my body" (*Explanation of the Divine Liturgy*, translation of S. Salaville in *Sources Chrétiennes*, 4, Paris [1943], p. 179; also *PG*, 150–426). In the Mass, therefore, the consecration actually takes place during the *epiclesis*. (3) In the Acts of the Council of Florence, Bessarion, in the name of all the Greeks, expresses agreement with the Latin doctrine (*MC*, vol. 31B, col. 1046) but Markos Eugenikos, Archbishop of Ephesus, protests that Cabasilas's doctrine is the true one ("Quod non solum a voce Dominicorum verborum sanctificantur divina dona," in *PO*, ed. R. Graffin, F. Nau, Paris and Freiburg-im-Breisgau [1897], vol. 17, pp. 426–34). (Tr.)

[58] As witnessed in official documents (not to speak of the writings of theologians): Letter from the Sacred Congregation of Rites, approved by Benedict XIII, stating that the power of consecration is exclusively in the words of the institution (*Coll. Lacensis*, Freiburg-im-Breisgau [1867], vol. 2, col. 439); Pius X, *Epistola "Ex Quo"* in *AAS*, 3 (1911), p. 119. The Council of Florence, *Decretum pro Armenis* (cf. *DB*, 689) has "Forma huius sacramenti sunt verba Salvatoris quibus hoc confecit sacramentum." The *Decretum pro Jacobitis* refers to the above decree and adds the formula in full. (*DB*, 717.) The Council of Trent, Session XIII, cap. 3, "De Excellentia SS. Eucharistiae," says ". . . statim post consecrationem . . . ex vi verborum. . . ." (*DB*, 876.) *Consecratio*, in the acts of this Council, clearly means the words of institution. None of these documents supports a *de fide* argument that the essentially sacramental significance belongs exclusively to the words of institution. The Council of Florence refrained deliberately from a definition on this point, stating only that the Greeks were in official accord with the doctrine as held in the Latin Church. The Council of Trent was not concerned with this precise point at all, but rather with the true sacramental power of the consecration. (Cf. *DB*, 886.) Both councils reflect

opinion that this has been officially defined in a recent decree of the Holy Office (23 May 1957). This decree is concerned with con-celebration and states: "In virtue of Christ's institution, only he who pronounces the consecratory words celebrates validly."[59] In other words, whoever does not pronounce the "consecratory words" at a co-consecration is not a co-consecrator. This is quite clear and intelligible in the light of our investigation above into the role of the sacramental word of faith. Even so, one should not read into this decree more than it actually contains. Its direct intention is to say that the priest who celebrates must, in virtue of Christ's insti-tution, pronounce the "consecratory words." Now it is indeed true that in the question that was put to the Holy Office these "conse-cratory words" applied immediately to the words of institution. As things stand these are our consecration. Nevertheless the purpose of the decree is not to pronounce as a fact that precisely these words of institution, in virtue of Christ's institution, are the words of consecration.[60] In the West it is now beyond all doubt that the power of consecration lies in the words of institution which, for this reason, we call the "consecration." But still this does not mean that it has always been so, and still less that it must be so in virtue of institution by Christ. This latter problem is entirely extraneous to the purpose of the decree of the Holy Office (which probably on account of this found it opportune to use the term "consecratory words" and not "the words of consecration" taken immediately in the Western sense).

As far as this question is concerned we must therefore leave this decree out of consideration. It would be possible to find a real

---

simply the appreciation of the sacramental formula as actually accepted in the Latin Church. The *epiclesis* therefore may have its own proper power and consecratory value in liturgies where in fact this sacramental significance is attached to it. (Notes on pp. 33–335 of *SH*. [Tr.])

[59] "Ex institutione Christi, ille solus valide celebrat qui verba consecratoria pronunciat." (*AAS*, 44 [1957], p. 370.)

[60] This was forgotten by the commentator (F. V.) on this text in *Questions liturgiques et paroissiales,* 38 (1957), pp. 228–9.

argument in the fact that the use of the words of institution as the essentially sacramental word of faith seems already to have been customary in primitive and apostolic times. Unquestionably even in the scriptural account of the Last Supper these words of institution already show all the characteristics of a liturgical use. In this sense they could indeed be an apostolic norm belonging to the constitutive revelation, and be binding on the Church of later times (though it would then be necessary to find a solution to the problem posed by some ancient liturgies from which the words of institution were evidently quite absent).

A further consequence following upon what we have said about "sacrament and word" (section 1 of this chapter) is this. During an earlier phase in the Church's developing consciousness of the Faith—which conscious awareness is the determining factor in the Church's symbolic activity—it was possible for the sacramental word of faith to have been still highly undifferentiated, while today the same vague lack of differentiation would cause a sacrament to be invalid. This follows from the essence of ecclesial symbolic activity as "the sacrament of ecclesial faith."[61]

---

[61] For obviously the homogeneous development of dogma as a whole (including therefore the Church's conscious awareness of faith in the sacraments) is going to give rise to a parallel development in the manner in which the Church manifests its sacramental faith outwardly. For the sacraments, being essentially symbolic acts of the Church as Church, are intelligible only in the light of the Church's faith. Consequently the relative implicitness (during an earlier period) of the Church's faith concerning a certain sacrament would be reflected above all in the form of words used to express the sacramental signification. Hence when this faith has become more explicit the sacramental word will become more precise. At this stage if a certain local community should retain the old undifferentiated formula it could mean that a sense different from the one the Church as such intends (and intended previously even if implicitly) is now being given to it. In this case the sacrament is clearly invalid. The judgment by Leo XIII on Anglican Orders confirms this. The *forma verborum* given in the Book of Common Prayer could be interpreted in the Catholic sense, though certainly not as the explicit statement of all the elements proper to Catholic sacramental orders. Leo writes: ". . . non ea igitur forma esse apta et sufficiens sacramento potest, quae id nempe reticet quod deberet proprium significare" (*Actes de Léon XIII*, Paris (n.d.), vol. 5, p. 70.) It is clear from the history of the

On account of the different planes upon which factors can affect the validity of a sacrament, and also on account of the occasional lack of practical certainty with regard to these factors which are now necessary for validity, the Church in its practical pastoral role acts according to the principle of *tutiorism*[62]; in other words, the Church chooses the safer way when the necessities of salvation are concerned, with the result that doubtful elements are for practical reasons considered as elements necessary for validity, so that in cases of doubt the administration of a sacrament is repeated conditionally.[63]

It is clear too, from the whole of this investigation, that the sacraments are not things, but rather spiritual and religious symbolic acts of the Church—that is to say, they are "incarnation." And precisely because this is a question of an act of the Church, upon which it is not within the competence of the individual believer to decide, the believer has to adhere to the ecclesial ritual in detail as it is prescribed, but there can be no room for anxiety or scrupulosity. Any notion that an unwitting mistake in the pronunciation of the words, for instance, would destroy the power of the rite is entirely contrary to the truth. This would be making of the sacraments a hocus-pocus indeed.

Book of Common Prayer that this undifferentiated formula was a matter of deliberate choice and, taken together with the denial of the Real Presence, etc., it means a definite divergence from the universal ecclesial appreciation of the sacrament. (Summary of *SH*, pp. 447–50. [Tr.])

[62] In sacramental theology it is vitally important to distinguish between the practical decisions of the Sacred Roman Congregations and the dogmatic pronouncements of the Church. "Hinc, in investigatione circa ritum essentialem sacramenti . . . licitum est, imo satius, ad illas practicas solutiones casuum non attendere" (referring in the context explicitly to the solutions published by the Sacred Congregations: Cardinal van Rossum, *De Essentia Sacramenti Ordinis*, Rome [1914], p. 8). Cf. *SH*, pp. 441, 442. (Tr.)

[63] Cf. the condemnation of the opposite opinion, *DB*, 1151.

4

THE SACRAMENTS IN THEIR FULLNESS:
THE FRUITFUL SACRAMENT

1. MUTUAL AVAILABILITY IN THE ENCOUNTER WITH CHRIST

1. Personal Entry into Christ's Ecclesial Mystery of Worship

The interior religious intent of the recipient is not one of the factors which constitute the validity of a sacrament. For the glance of Christ's love, directed through the Church to the recipient, is prior to any human response. The sacrament remains a real pledge of love even when man does not respond to it. But there is far more to it than this. For the interior devotion with which the recipient approaches the sacrament, or rather takes part in its prayer and celebration, is more than a presacramental attitude of mind; it is an entry into the heart of the Church's mystery of worship. This calls for an explanation.

The sense and purpose of the whole sacramental event is to bring about encounter with Christ. Since such an encounter must involve both parties, the religious intent of the recipient (who in this context is the one going towards the encounter) belongs to the essence of any authentic sacrament; one, that is, which is a personal encounter with the living God. If the sacrament is not thus personally lived with religious intent the sacramentally mediated personal encounter with Christ, and therefore with God, cannot take place. In that case, at least as far as the recipient is concerned, the sacramental symbolic act is an untruthful sign, for he contradicts by his interior disposition what the sacramental rite is affirming.

This implies that the sacrament which is fully such, the fruitful sacrament, is not only the visible manifestation of Christ's redemptive act, or the visibility of the Church's sanctifying will participating in that act, but must also be the visible expression of the recipient's personal desire for grace and will to be sanctified. On the part of the religiously disposed recipient the sacrament is his desire for grace, his personal plea and prayer uttered publicly in the visible Church, and so linked to the sacramental power of the prayer of Christ and his Church. This shows us how a personal religious life is part of the mystical body, Head and members, and how, in the sacraments above all, a personal intent in striving for holiness receives its impulse from and is supported by the reality of the communion of saints. The recipient's religious intent is a witness to his positive will to unite himself more intimately to the ecclesial communion, and in it to Christ, from whom alone we can hope for salvation. This reality is expressed objectively in the ecclesial symbolic act itself. Hence if this objective ritual embodiment of worship does not also embody the recipient's own worship, it is for him a mere fiction.

A sacrament may be seen as a reaching out in faith and love to take hold of Christ's redemption (of which the Church is the earthly representation), for it is the response to his taking hold of us in it. "The passion of Christ achieves its effect in those with whom it has been brought into contact by faith and love and by the sacraments of faith."[1] From this we can also see that the sacraments are both signs of the grace of redemption and also bestow this grace in being realized for a particular person. In the same way it is clear that the sacraments were not intended as an easier path to salvation, a sort of system by which we can get grace more abundantly for less loyalty in God's service, compared with its extra-sacramental bestowal. This was never the meaning of the

[1] "Passio Christi sortitur effectum suum in illis quibus applicatur per fidem et caritatem et per fidei sacramenta." (*ST*, III, q. 49, a. 3, ad 1.)

Church's faith in the sacraments. Did not the Church, for that matter, define explicitly that the sacraments give grace only to those who "place no obstacle" in its way?[2] In this context the Church speaks technically of an *obex*. The Latin word means "an obstacle," "a blockage on the roadway," "a hindrance." It is true that the dogmatic definition is framed negatively: the sacraments give grace to those who do not hinder it. Nevertheless for an adult "not to hinder" grace means a positive personal intent, as the Council of Florence had earlier defined: the sacraments give grace to those who receive them worthily.[3] The purely negative definition is applicable only in the case of children. The Council of Trent kept to the negative definition, which by implication applies to adults as well, in order to include both them and children in a single formula.

2. Sacraments of the Living and of the Dead

In a sacrament of the living what is required for the religious intent will obviously differ in certain ways from what is required in a sacrament of the dead.

Note first of all that "sacrament of the dead" is the accepted name in the Church for a sacrament whose nature it is to give sanctifying grace (in the special direction proper to it) to those who are not yet, or no longer, in the state of grace.[4] Baptism and penance are by their nature sacraments of this kind. The name applies in a certain sense to extreme unction as well; primarily this is a sacrament of the living, but it has the essential though secondary property of being effective as a sacrament of the dead too, since it is also directed towards forgiveness of sins. A sacrament of the living, on the other hand, presupposes by its nature a state of

---

[2] *DB*, 849 with 851.

[3] *DB*, 695: ". . . gratiam . . . digne suscipientibus conferunt."

[4] Also to those who have already repented but have not yet submitted their sins to the Church's power of the keys, and are thus still not reconciled with her.

grace in the recipient (confirmation, the Eucharist, holy orders, matrimony and, in its primary characteristics, extreme unction). On account of the complexity of human psychology these sacraments can, however, in exceptional circumstances also take on the function of a sacrament of the dead. When someone forgetting in good faith that he is in a state of mortal sin sincerely receives a sacrament of the living, it will at the same time effect the forgiveness of his grave sin because in actuality grace is always the grace of redemption. For every bestowal of grace not only deifies but at the same time makes the forgiveness of sin take a more profound hold on a person. Although forgiveness can be realized instantaneously, it nevertheless allows of a subsequent process through which holiness steadily takes possession of and re-forms the whole psychological make-up of the "convert." This also indicates that the different sacraments, however much they may be formally distinct from one another, make up one organic whole through which grace gradually completes its victory and man becomes wholly redeemed.

Thus the requirements for entry through religious intent will differ for the sacraments of the living and of the dead. Since it is clear that reconciliation between an adult and God must be personal—which means God's gratuitous merciful forgiveness must become interiorized in the human person, and this can be achieved by perfect contrition alone[5]—it follows that an act of perfect con-

---

[5] The author refers to SH, pp. 561–85, where he has made a study of the subjective requirements for the reception of a sacrament of the dead. He begins with a brief summary of the biblical notion of justification; this concept is fundamental to the whole study, and provides the key to a solution of the problem. Justice is fundamentally God's redeeming love, manifested above all in Christ's; "Now . . . the justice of God is made manifest. . . ." (Rom. 3.21ff.) Complementary to justice in this sense, justification is also the immanence of redemption in humanity: "God . . . was in Christ reconciling the world to himself." (2 Cor. 5.19.) Now it is through faith (again in. the biblical sense) that I make this reconciliation mine personally: "For by grace [the free bounty of God] you are saved by faith." (Ephes. 2.8; cf. Rom. 4.16, 17.3 and passim; etc.) All is due to the Father's initiative, even the human response: ". . . justified freely by his grace through the redemption that is in Christ Jesus." (Rom. 3.24; Eph. 2.8 continues: ". . . and that

trition corresponds on the recipient's side to sacramental forgiveness.[6] This must be taken in the following sense. When a person in mortal sin wishes worthily to present himself for a sacrament of the dead, it is strictly necessary, and at the same time it is sufficient, that the penitent (or the adult to be baptized) should have an imperfect contrition. With this the sacrament of Christian reconciliation is made the expression of the recipient's personal longing for grace. Then he enters personally into the sacramental ritual worship and pleading for grace of Christ and of his Church. This ritual power to save of the sacrament effects the grace of forgiveness as it is actualized, though as it were by the second phase of its realization. But this effective reconciliation actually brings about in the

---

not of yourselves, for it is the gift of God.") But faith is essential—"he who believes and is baptized . . ." (Mark 16.16)—and as that which brings the person into contact with the redemption it necessarily includes contrition and hope and love as well. St. Thomas sees this scriptural faith as a composite act: "Liberum arbitrium in justificatione impii movetur in Deum motu fidei, caritatis et spei . . . et haec tria computantur pro uno actu completo inquantum unum includitur in alio. . . ." (*De Veritate*, q. 28, a. 4c *circa finem*.) In the actual situation there cannot be a *motus liberi arbitrii* to the redeeming God—i.e., away from sin—which does not necessarily include perfect contrition. This contrition is the necessary disposition for the faith which Scripture shows is necessary, or rather it is the converse of the love which that faith includes. (Tr.)

[6] Cf. the previous note. Since all grace comes from the Father through Christ (2 Cor. 5.19, etc.), every grace is Christian; i.e., realized visibly in history in the economy of salvation which Christ established. Every grace is "incarnation" and therefore sacramental. Thus the grace of contrition—faith-hope-love (in the actual situation a composite unity)—though its first effects might precede the sacrament, is essentially a sacramental grace of forgiveness. For conversely the grace of penance is not bare forgiveness but the principle of theologal life too; faith and hope and love. This life might be less "vital" in its initial (presacramental) stages than it becomes in the sacrament; when love hovers on the borderline of being servile, contrition is servile too: attrition. The sacrament, personally willed and entered in upon by the recipient, removes the imperfections; it turns attrition into contrition as it makes servile love grow to filial love and dead faith to living. In this sense contrition corresponds to forgiveness in the actual sacrament. The author has made a detailed study of all these points in *SH*, pp. 579–606. (Tr.)

person as such an act of perfect contrition, which on the personal plane is the converse aspect of the grace of forgiveness.

Hence when some catechisms say that "imperfect contrition is necessary and sufficient in the sacrament of penance, although perfect contrition is more desirable," this does not refer to the reception of the actual grace of forgiveness but only to the worthiness of the approach to the sacrament. They refer to the beginning of the sacrament of confession, to that minimum necessary for a personal entry into the sacramental ritual prayer, in order that this should in fact become effective and be able to carry the process of conversion to its end (i.e., to actual forgiveness with its corresponding act of perfect contrition). Imperfect contrition is therefore merely the necessary point of departure; by the power of the sacrament it is lifted up and transformed into the perfect final activity. (And hence it is clearly better to go to confession already with perfect contrition.) Thus, for example, if a confession is not also at the same time a personal prayer which integrates the penitent into the sacramental visibility of the Church and so brings him into contact with the heavenly saving act of Christ "who never ceases to intercede for us," this confession cannot bestow the grace of forgiveness. It is sufficiently evident in all this that the sacrament is not in the least a sort of magical automatic device.

The requirements for the sacraments of the living, then, are as follows.[7] An increase in grace on the personal plane is by its nature only possible through an act of love more intense than it was before the increase. For basically sanctifying grace means personal communion with God, which above all comes about in love. "Increase of grace" is nothing but a quantitative way of speaking about growth in closeness to God and so alternately about growth in love. When you say "increase of grace" and are thinking of

[7] In this place we are considering only those general requirements that are necessary for a sacrament to be fruitful rather than merely valid; in other words, we are concerned only with the fruitfulness of sacraments in general, with the increase of grace, not with what is specifically required for each sacrament in particular.

grace on the personal plane you have *ipso facto* said "growth in love."[8] Therefore it is clear that on the part of the recipient a more intense act of love must correspond with a sacramental increase of grace and so with the sacraments of the living.[9] This means that when a person wishes worthily to present himself for a sacrament of the living, its reception must come from and be supported by his own act of love. For it is indeed a matter of a love-life striving to grow. This love urging on to greater love expresses itself in the sacraments of the living, in the public sacramentalism of the visible Church, and through the Church this longing urge of love is caught up and made part of both her own public worship and Christ's life of redeeming love. Through this

---

[8] Cf. *SH*, pp. 621–3. St. Thomas says: "Hoc est quod facit Deus caritatem augendo, scilicet quod magis insit et quod perfectius similitudo Spiritus Sancti participetur in anima." (II–II, q. 24, a. 5, ad 3.) Grace, as we have seen, is close union with God; the union comes about through love—"God so loved the world. . . ." Thus the more intense our love, the more the God of grace is in us. ("*Deus . . . magis insit.*") The intensity of love is the personal "index" of grace. (Tr.)

[9] Love is not only the "index" of grace (see previous note). Since grace is an effect of God's love for me, it becomes mine only as an effect of my response in love for him (though this too is given me by God). A love grown lukewarm cannot respond with new intensity; love and therefore grace cannot grow in this state. In no sense at all does this lay an obligation on us to be free from all minor distractions to love—from all venial sinfulness—in order that the reception of the sacrament may "increase our grace." There are no grounds at all for anxiety or scrupulosity. The sacrament manifests, objectively and effectively, God's love for the recipient; he has but to respond. Like all human acts, this response is subject to the psychological ups and downs of human life: according to the traditional distinction, *devotio* (the response) can be *actualis, virtualis* or *habitualis.* When a man's fundamental attitude of life is theologal (*habitualis*) he may for any number of reasons not be able here and now to make an act of love of any intensity (*actualis*), but even so his love is there, burning in the background of his consciousness (*virtualis*). Man's response to the sacraments is human, not automatic like the sales-machine's response to the drop of a penny. When he comes to make a fully personal and intense act of love, it is the sacramental grace that he makes fully and personally his own. Before this he had really received the "new" grace, but it was psychologically out of focus, virtually but not fully and actually his own. Cf. *SH*, pp. 623–32. (Tr.)

integral contact the sacrament effects *ex opere operato* the increase of grace which the recipient takes personal possession of by a more intense act of love, itself a consequence of the sacrament in his personal life. The more intense and vital experience of love thus belongs essentially to the sacramental increase of grace.

It has been maintained that it is sufficient for a normal person in possession of all his faculties merely to be in the state of grace in order to receive worthily the sacraments of the living, and mistaken attempts have been made to justify this view by an appeal to Pius X's decrees on Holy Communion.[10] But besides the state of grace which these decrees require, they also speak of the necessity of a "right and devoted state of mind." If all the elements of a human act are considered, this ultimately means the act of love which, as we pointed out, is required for the worthy reception of a sacrament of the living. So if Communion, for example, or entry into the sacrament of matrimony, is not also a personal prayer expressed in the ecclesial symbolic act, then the sacrament cannot possibly give an increase of grace; then the actual encounter with Christ does not take place.

3. The Sacramental Bestowal of Grace upon Infants

Needless to say, no religious intent is expected of infants in sacraments which they are capable of receiving. The recipient is simply not able to form an intention; on the other hand, he does not put any hindrance in the way of grace. But it would be wrong to consider that the state of grace acquired, or the increase in grace

---

[10] *DB*, 1981–90. Cf. *SH*, pp. 625–6. These decrees teach that besides the state of grace, Communion must be inspired by a longing (a willing: *velit*) to satisfy God's commands, to be united more closely with him in love, and to seek in this sacrament a remedy for human weakness and failing. It may not become a matter of pure routine, or be received for vain or human considerations. (Cf. the complete text of the *Decretum Sacrae Congregationis Concilii, approbatum a Pio X: Acta Sanctae Sedis*, 38 [1905–6], pp. 401ff.)

(say in infant baptism or in the confirmation of a child), is exactly the same as in adults. For the difference is not merely that while both possess sanctifying grace only the adult has the "use" of it. The difference is more profound, and lies in the manner in which each possesses the grace. The infantile and the personal manner of the possession make their difference felt in sanctifying grace itself; it is possessed in the full sense of the term only by a person. He alone can enter fully into relationship with God, personal grace freely accepted and assented to. It is certainly not this in the baby just baptized or in the child just confirmed.

St. Thomas teaches that in children the faith of the Church makes up for the absence of their own religious intention.[11] This means that when a sacrament is administered by the Church to a child the communion of saints, in heaven as well as on earth, gathers itself around him in union with Christ to beg God, through the ritual prayer of the sacrament, to bestow grace on him. Hence the one sacrament, as it were in the second phase of its realization, actually gives the child the grace which was prayed for. This clearly brings out once again the dogmatic and liturgical meaningfulness of an active and prayerful participation of the whole parish community in the administration of baptism.

It also makes clear the special nature of the sacramental bestowal of grace upon a person who for the time being is unconscious. Unconsciousness—as we know from infant baptism—is no hindrance to God's merciful gift of grace. But we must take into account that an adult who receives a sacrament in this condition had a particular attitude of life before he lost consciousness. If he was in a state of grave sin he must first have aroused in himself some longing for grace, whether implicitly or explicitly, if the sacrament he receives while unconscious is to be really fruitful. With an insight into the personal character of human acts and the nature of the sacramental

[11] Cf. *ST*, III, q. 68, a. 9c, ad 1 and ad 2; q. 68, a. 10, ad 3; a. 1; a. 12, ad 1; q. 69, a. 6, ad 3; q. 34, a. 3. (The above is not a direct citation but the composite sense of the texts. [Tr.]) For children who die without baptism, see below in the section on sacraments of desire.

bestowal of grace such cases, which are in fact rather exceptional, can easily be solved.

2. SACRAMENTS OF DESIRE AND THE REVIVAL OF THE SACRAMENTS

We have seen that there are two sides to sacramentality which closely influence each other; validity and fruitfulness. They may be described more precisely and less legalistically as follows. There is an objective side to sacramentality, the ecclesial expression of Christ's will to encounter, directed to a particular individual; and there is a corresponding subjective side, the personal acceptance of Christ's grace-giving will. Precisely because a sacrament presupposes a will for grace already evoked in the (adult) recipient, which it carries by the power of Christ to full fruitfulness, sacramentality of its nature includes both the extra-sacramental and the sacramental bestowal of grace. The incipient religious intent which manifests itself in the worthy reception of a sacrament is indeed already an effect of the grace of Christ. An adult approaches a sacrament in virtue of a certain spiritual life (which can be of different kinds, tending towards a sacrament either of the living or the dead) in order to grow more deeply into it. All this is due to the working of grace.

The problem, however, goes deeper still. Since this personal spiritual life (apart from the intention) is not one of the constitutive elements of a valid sacrament, a certain separation is possible between the two planes, the objective ecclesial celebration in mystery (validity) and the personal life of grace (fruitfulness). And thus it can happen that the forgiveness of sins, for example, precedes the actual reception of a sacrament of the dead, or that the actual reception of a sacrament such as adult baptism precedes the required religious dispositions. There is a special terminology to cover these instances: the former is called a "sacrament of desire" (an explicit or implicit longing to receive the sacrament), the latter the "revival" of a sacrament already received.

1. *Sacraments of Desire*

The question here is this: Is the effect of a sacrament of desire really an anticipation of the effect of the desired sacrament and thus a sacramental grace in the strict sense, or is it merely a bestowal of grace outside the sacraments? Note first of all that not all of the sacraments can have a corresponding sacrament of desire. The exceptions are matrimony and orders; in their case it is impossible. This arises from the social significance proper to them in the Church; longing in grace for the married state or for the priesthood cannot make a person wedded or ordained. In the case of the other five sacraments, desire for them can produce an effect. Baptism of desire does cleanse from original sin and remit all personal sins; it does not, however, give the character nor (connected immediately with this) does it bring about visible incorporation into the Church; nor, in consequence, the ability to receive the other sacraments. It leaves the person only imperfectly a member of the ecclesial community. From this it is evident that a sacrament of desire does not simply have the same effect in an extraordinary way that normally a sacrament would have, though sometimes the vital personal experience and appropriation of grace may be more intense than in the reception of the actual sacrament (compare, for example, a baptism of desire with a normal baptism).

Since the Church according to Christ's plan is the means of grace, such a presacramental bestowal of grace is not possible unless there is at least an implicit desire for the sacrament.[12] In this sense the so-called presacramental bestowal of grace is actually sacramental.[13] Then does this mean a true anticipated effect of the future ecclesial symbolic act? Not at all.[14] For Christ does not ob-

[12] St. Thomas, *ST,* III, q. 79, a. 1, ad 1.

[13] "Si consideratur [contritio] in quantum habet virtutem clavium in voto, sic sacramentaliter operatur in virtute sacramenti poenitentiae, sicut et in virtute baptismi, ut patet in adulto qui habet sacramentum baptismi in voto tantum." (St. Thomas, *De Veritate,* q. 28, a. 8, ad 2.)

[14] "Nihil . . . prohibet id quod posterius tempore, antequam sit, movere secundum quod praecedit in actu animae. . . . Sed illud quod nondum est in

tain grace for us from the sacrament, but makes his own grace present to us in it. Were this not so there would have to be some kind of anticipated efficacy of the sacrament, in whatever way this came about. It is, however, quite impossible for a sacrament to have a retroactive effect of this kind. What in fact takes place is this: Within the totality of the risen Christ's eternal act of salvation, the bestowal of grace before the reception of the sacrament begins the historical realization of something that is brought to completion by the same eternal saving act, and that achieves the fullness of its historical manifestation in actual reception. Thus it is a process in more or less the same mode as the progressive revelation of the Old and the New Testaments, the gradual historical manifestation of the eternal God, our salvation; a historical manifestation that arrived at the fullness of its reality in Christ alone. The intrinsic purpose of the preliminary elements lies in those for which they prepare. There is no question at all of elements later in time having a causal effect upon those which preceded them. The Creator and Redeemer whose omnipotence is timeless and present in all time gives each element its full share in the whole, whatever the point in time to which it may belong. This does not mean that he confers an historical retroactivity on later elements. Depending as both do upon God's eternal saving act, the extra-sacramental and sacramental life of grace form one meaningful whole in such a way that the first effects of a sacrament of desire grow from within towards the essentially sacramental encounter with Christ in which the mature perfection of the life of grace is achieved. Whether we think of a baptism of desire, a spiritual communion, or a longing for the sacrament of the sick, all of this applies with equal truth. These are not, therefore, an extraordinary way to grace but an initial stage—something which of its nature requires to grow to com-

---

rerum natura, non movet secundum usum exteriorum rerum [viz., the ecclesial symbolic act itself which does not yet exist cannot have an effect]. Unde causa efficiens non potest esse posterior in esse, ordine durationis, sicut causa finalis." (*ST*, III, q. 62, a. 6c.)

pletion—of the ordinary and universal mode of the bestowal of grace.

This brings out the fundamental meaning of a sacrament as a living contact with the visible Church, in which dwells the fullness of Christ. The first and immediate effect of every sacrament is the (initial or more intense) establishment of man's contact with the visible communion in grace as a member of that communion. This clearly shows that every grace is given in and through the man Christ, and that the explicit encounter with this man can take place within the sacramental Church alone; outside the Church the encounter remains implicit or incipient (cf. the encyclical *Mystici Corporis*). Thus for those who have been baptized the moments of sacramental contact with the visible Church of Christ are the decisive points of their Christian living.

The possibility of a presacramental bestowal of grace throws some light on the question of salvation for children who die without baptism. The Church teaches that whoever dies in original sin cannot inherit heaven. But this is quite different from saying that whoever dies without baptism is *eo ipso* excluded from heaven. As far as adults are concerned, that is denied by the fact that baptism of desire is possible. Now baptism of desire is certainly not a case of human activity preceding the grace of God and grasping for itself the opportunity of a heavenly reward. This is quite clear from what we have seen above. God's grace takes the initiative and the man of good will responds to it; this response is necessary in adults by reason of the psychological character of personality. Without question, therefore, God can just as easily bestow grace upon little children before the reception of a sacrament as upon adults. Whether in actual fact he does we do not know. The rejection of the very possibility by some theologians is due to a misunderstanding of the relation between sacramental grace and the bestowal of grace before the reception of a sacrament. They fear that if we agree to the possibility of heaven for children who die without baptism, we shall be making the need for sacraments merely relative. They forget, however, that even when an adult receives baptism of desire in faith and love, and has a real chance of heaven though still un-baptized, the actual reception of the sacrament remains necessary and is not rendered meaningless. In the same way baptism would still be meaningful and indeed necessary in the case of a child, even granted that grace may be bestowed beforehand.

Pius XII's address to nurses and midwives (29 October 1951) has been appealed to in recent discussions of this question. The Pope did not in any sense say that apart from the sacrament of baptism there was no possibility of salvation for children. In that address his teaching is based upon the principle of a nurse's practical and immediate responsibility; his intention was to convey the truth that in fact human beings can help these children effectively only by baptizing them. He did not speak at all of what God in his mercy is able to do, since in the case in point that cannot affect the nurse's responsibility in any way. At the same time it may have been the Pope's intention (although this is not brought out in the actual text) to suggest, as it were between the lines, that theology at the moment cannot find an answer to the problem whether "baptism of desire" is possible where the human conscience is not active. The fate of children who die without baptism is therefore still an open question.

In this matter there are three principal truths to be kept in mind. First: Man is born in the state of original sin; this is a concrete fact. Second: In principle the sacrifice of Christ has overcome human sinfulness. The complete application of this redemption from the state of sin can take place only by the actual reception of the sacrament of baptism. Finally: Presacramental or extra-sacramental grace is a universal possibility, for children as well as adults, since grace is absolutely prior to any human co-operation, and can therefore be given before it. Such presacramental bestowal of grace does not in any way affect the necessity of baptism. All of which allows us to hope that for a child to die without baptism is not necessarily at all the same thing as dying in the state of original sin. Are there then children who die in original sin? We cannot answer either Yes or No with any firm assurance. All that the Church expresses in her doctrine is the meaning of original sin and its special punishment. She is silent about the fate of individuals and leaves the judgment to Christ alone.

2. The Revival of Sacraments

This too is something which rests upon the possibility of a separation between the objective and subjective sides of sacramentality. Here, however, the order is different. In the previous section we considered the subjective desire as preceding the objective sacrament. Now the valid reception of the sacrament is already an accomplished fact, but only later on are the dispositions necessary for the sacrament to be fruitful elicited. In a situation of this kind, since a valid sacrament is genuinely a ritual pleading and prayer of Christ and his Church on behalf of the recipient, all that is necessary on its side for it to confer grace infallibly (i.e., *ex opere operato*) has been accomplished. The sacrament would in fact confer the grace that is prayed for were it not for lack of the recipient's religious intent. It follows that only the removal of this hindrance is required for the sacrament to take immediate effect. For the visible Church is a sign of grace really filled with the reality it signifies. Voluntary contact with the holy and sanctifying Church means *eo ipso* an acquisition of grace, unless some positive opposition to it is offered. (In legal terms: A valid sacrament gives a right to grace.) The break between validity and fruitfulness in a sacrament is essentially a distortion, an abnormality; by reason of human freedom it remains a real possibility.

Now the fact that a sacrament achieves its full effect as soon as the hindrance is removed is metaphorically, though not very happily, termed the "revival" of the sacrament. It is clear from what we have said that nothing actually revives. Although the act by which it took place is in the past, the authentic (or valid) incorporation of a person into the sacramental prayer of Christ in his Church is an enduring reality which bestows grace infallibly as soon as the hindrance to it is removed.[15] Medieval theologians understood the matter rightly when they spoke of a sacrament "remaining." Because baptism links us to the visible communion in grace, every sacramental contact with the Church is of its nature life-giving as long as there is no personal obstacle in the way.[16] The first effect of each of the sacraments is contact (within a sevenfold orientation) with the visible communion in grace.[17] This effect is always achieved if the sacrament is valid, whatever the interior dispositions may have been. On the other hand, this effect can never be achieved by a pure sacrament of desire. The character (see the next chapter) gives a clear indication of this. A person bears the character really and ineradicably from the moment that the ecclesial rite is validly performed upon him, even when the sacrament bears no fruit in grace. Conversely the character can be conferred only by the sacrament, not even by a baptism of desire. The enduring sacrament, the personal link established by proper intention with the sacramental prayer of Christ in his Church, is therefore the foundation of the "revival" of sacraments.

Up to the present it has not been defined dogmatically that a sacrament can work its effect some time after its actual reception, but it has been taught ever since the days of the early Fathers and is universally accepted in the Church. If sacraments could not "revive" in this way, impossible consequences would follow. For there are sacraments which confer a character and may be received only once, and if somebody received one of these validly but fruitlessly he would be forever excluded from the full benefit of the sacrament, even though later on he should come to a religiously more proper state of mind. The same is true of matrimony and

[15] The permanence of a sacramental contact with the visible Church cannot of course be measured by the criteria of physical permanence.

[16] This has sometimes been interpreted (by Marin-Sola and others) as though every sacrament were an ontological amendment to the baptismal character; this permanent amendment would then provide the principle of revival in sacraments. This, however, reduces the true facts to the level of the physical.

[17] The scholastic term for this is *res et sacramentum*. See below.

extreme unction, which are relatively unrepeatable (while both partners are living, or during the same illness). Theologians are divided about the possibility of the Eucharist or confession "reviving."

It is generally said of confession that if it is unfruitful it is also invalid. Some hold that a confession is valid so long as the penitent is repentant, but that if the repentance is too minimal to constitute a worthy reception of the sacrament it remains unfruitful and could therefore revive. Almost always, however, in this dispute the ecclesial character of confession is forgotten. The sacrament of penance is a reconciliation with the Church, and hence with Christ and in him with God. The remission of sin which it brings about is essentially ecclesial. In the same way Karl Rahner rightly says that "binding on earth" means the ecclesial manifestation of an interior state of sin. The Church there dissociates itself from the sinner,[18] and by her act makes public the segregation which the sin itself brings about.[19] Since the Church frees the penitent from that which is ecclesially "bound"—i.e., revokes its dissociation from him—he enters fully again the ecclesial communion in grace. In this way the Church's "loosing on earth" becomes the sacrament of the "loosing in heaven," the divine forgiveness of sins. It was, for that matter, the practice in former times to give sacramental absolution only when the ecclesial penance had been performed.

Hence if the requirements for reconciliation with the Church were less than, not identical with, the requirements for a fruitful reception of sacramental forgiveness, then a confession could be valid without at the same time being fruitful, and so "revival" would be possible. For if this were the case, the sacrament would truly be a ritual prayer of Christ through his Church even when not fruitful. The question is therefore whether there is a sacrament in this sense

[18] "Vergessene Wahrheiten über das Buss-Sakrament," in Schriften zur Theologie, 2, pp. 143–84.

[19] The Church brings it into sacramental visibility, which although not identical with the *forum externum,* is something more than the *forum internum:* sins are really confessed to the Church through the accusation made to her priest.

when the penitent, really having the intention to receive it, does all that the Church asks him on the socio-sacramental plane, submitting and acknowledging all his sins and agreeing to perform the penance imposed. That, it seems to me, would be a valid sacrament. However, if all this were not at the same time an expression of an (at least incipient) genuine will to repentance, the sacramental sign would be a fraud. Hence it would be fruitless and so sacrilegious. And then it could "revive" just as baptism can.

The fact that there are still many contrary and apparently irreconcilable theological views on this issue inclines us to beware of apodictic assertions. For it may indeed be asked whether reconciliation with the Church is possible without some inward repentance, however minimal. May ecclesial reconciliation, the sacrament of reconciliation with God, be purely juridical, as the minimum required for a valid sign? To point this question more sharply: In order to be valid, does confession, the outward sign of reconciliation, require nothing more than the free acknowledgment of sins and the readiness to accept a penance from the Church? Or is it perhaps a special characteristic of confession, setting it apart from the other sacraments, that the intention freely to accept the outward sign is not sufficient for validity? To this we might answer that since confession is a sign of reconciliation it must correspond to an inward *metanoia,* an inward spirit of repentance. If on the contrary the answer to the previous question were in the affirmative, a confession could be valid without being fruitful. This savours of juridical fraudulence. There are grounds for the reproach, which touches every valid but unfruitful sacrament: In the nature of things these are untruthful. God, of course, cannot be outwitted by fraudulent signs, but the Church can be deceived and, acting upon the outward gesture, can really will to be reconciled with the sinner. In agreement with the Thomist view of confession, we prefer to say that the outward sign of reconciliation with the Church must be real if it is to be the sacrament of reconciliation with God; there is no true reconciliation when only one party, the Church which absolves, fulfils the requirements. So confession appears to be a special case, since the recipient's intention does not suffice to make it valid; a minimum of repentance for the wrong done to the Church must, in its visible manifestation, be necessary to the constitutive and valid sign of reconciliation.

This is St. Thomas's opinion, while the Scotist view is the contrary. An argument confirming the Thomist position could be drawn from the fact that the Church requires a fresh submission to the ecclesial authority of sins confessed in a "bad" confession, even one in which the accusations were in order and the penitent intended to perform his penance; this would not be necessary at all if a confession which remained fruitless merely on account of the lack of an inwardly repentant spirit could really be valid. Still it may be asked whether this canonical ruling rests upon the law of tutiorism,[20] in which case it has no dogmatic value and clarifies nothing —or if it rests upon the nature of the sacrament of penance. In this latter case all theories must give way to the norm of faith in the practice of the Church; in other words a confession which is unfruitful would also be invalid. In virtue of all this it appears to me that "revival" remains an unsolved problem with regard to the sacrament of confession, though the weight of evidence is against it.

A second matter of dispute concerns the revival of the Eucharist, although the answers are generally negative. In this question it is always the reception of Communion alone that is considered, even though authentic participation in the sacrifice of the Mass (even without communicating) calls just as much for investigation. The problem is whether it is possible to receive the sacrament of Communion validly, or participate in the Mass authentically, without thereby sharing in the fruits of the sacrament. It is generally agreed that this sacrament cannot "revive." For in the nature of the case it is impossible for a sacrilegious Communion to be a sacramental nourishing. And a free but purely physical presence at Sunday Mass, for example, without the slightest religious attention, has no sacramental significance at all (quite apart from the fulfilment of the Sunday obligation, which to some extent is another question).

[20] See above, Ch. 3, note 62.

The reason why the Eucharist is excepted in this way is that "a sacramentally valid Communion" is meaningless. The intention of the person who participates in the celebration of Mass and receives Communion contributes nothing to the validity of the Eucharist, which under this aspect depends only on the priest who consecrates.

A confirmation of the view that confession and the Eucharist, in contrast to the other sacraments, cannot "revive," is found in the fact that there is no need for them to. These sacraments can simply be repeated. They may be received as often as desired, and so in their case another reception of the sacrament with the right religious disposition can effect that which in other instances must come about through "revival."

Partial "Revival"

Partial revival is possible in all sacraments. For if a sacrament is not only validly but also worthily received it really causes grace. But if a sacrament is administered to someone, for example, who is unconscious, presupposing his religious intent, grace or its increase is given in the manner of the bestowal of grace on infants, and only later in the next vital Christian act does the grace given become a personal possession.[21]

[21] Actually this is not "revival" in the strict sense. For the sacrament received during unconsciousness gives grace immediately, though it remains potential with regard to personality; in the recipient's next conscious moral act, which is an *actus gratiae sacramentalis,* it is made actual and personally appropriated. More in keeping with "revival" in the strict sense is the example of a sacrament received while the mind is (not deliberately) distracted. Distractions exclude the actual loving intent necessary for a sacrament to be fruitful to the full. Though venially sinful, they are not a hindrance to grace, since they do not affect the basic will, but obviously they leave room for improvement in the application of the mind and will to the sacrament, and thus in the personal acceptance of grace. There is a certain parallel between distraction and unconsciousness and infancy as far as *res sacramenti,* the encounter with Christ in grace, is concerned. The author rightly remarks that "In all questions of this sort we must see the sacramental economy of salvation as a favour God grants us, as the visible manifestation and incarnation of his love, and most certainly not as a narrowing down—making a sort of obstacle course—of the way to salvation." (Cf. *SH*, pp. 616–19. [Tr.])

5

ENCOUNTER WITH CHRIST
IN THE CHURCH AS SACRAMENT
OF THE ENCOUNTER WITH GOD:
THE EFFECTS OF A SACRAMENT

This investigation of the essence of a sacrament has shown us that it can be realized to the full only if there is a positive response on the part of the recipient to the sacramental encounter with Christ in his Church; a response that manifests the recipient's desire for grace in the visibility of the ecclesial symbolic act itself. When the recipient responds in this way the sacramental encounter with Christ infallibly takes place in the way indicated by the sevenfold symbolism of the sacraments. Since every sacrament means an encounter with Christ in his Church, each has a double effect: the one in relation to the visible Church (the ecclesial effect), the other in relation to Christ and God (the religious effect, grace). Moreover these two effects are related in such a way that the former—as signified in the external rite—is the sacrament of the latter.[1]

1. THE ECCLESIAL EFFECT AS SACRAMENT OF THE
GRACE EFFECT

Medieval theologians used to speak of this as the character or, in the case of sacraments which do not confer a character, as a certain

[1] Hence medieval theologians named the first effect the *res et sacramentum*, meaning that it was both the effect of the external rite and sign of the more profound effect, grace, which was in its turn called the *res tantum*. The outward rite was the *sacramentum tantum*, sign alone.

loosely defined "adornment of the soul."[2] The theory grew from the speculations of Christian antiquity concerning the "permanent sacrament," which remains a reality even when it is not fruitful in grace in spite of the fact that its actual administration and reception is past. Undoubtedly these ideas reflect a basic truth; it is only, however, in the last few decades that we have realized more clearly that the reality perceived is fundamentally an ecclesial effect which is always present provided that the sacrament was administered validly.

We said above that the core of the outward sacramental sign consisted in voluntary entry into contact with the visible Church. The sacrament incorporates into the Church, in the case of baptism, or gives her members a new and special concern in one of her constitutive elements or specific commissions, in that of the other six. Thus with these six the sacrament deepens the inward link with the visible Church, sacrament of the grace of the Kingdom of God, or gives a more precise qualification to our incorporation into her.

1. The Character as the Ecclesial Effect of Three Sacraments

(a) Historical Sketch[3]

In the course of the Church's history a particular sacramental reality came to be known by a name borrowed from the cultural world of antiquity: "character." In the secular culture of former times, "seal" meant a sign of recognition, a sign of distinction, or indicated the idea of property or possession. The soldier or the slave

[2] *Ornatus animae.* Cf. D. Löcher, *Die Theorie vom sakramentalen Seelenschmuck, I. In der Hochscholastik,* Düsseldorf (1913).

[3] Cf. *SH,* pp. 487–555. Among the more recent works dealing with this matter, cf. especially N. M. Häring, "St. Augustine's Use of the Word 'Character,' " in *MST,* 14 (1952), pp. 79–97; "Character, Signum und Signaculum," in *SK,* 30 (1955), pp. 481–512; see too the bibliography in the article "Merkteken," in *Theologisch Woordenboek,* vol. 2, Roermond en Maaseik (1957).

was branded and sealed with the initials of the Emperor or the owner; this seal enabled the soldier to be recognized and distinguished from one who was not in the army. When the recruit was marked off with the seal it signified that he was entering into the service of the Emperor, from whom he received his orders and commissions. By this seal he entered into the line of authority, so that he fulfilled his commission in virtue of his office. For when the seal was imposed on a person, and was not merely the branding of cattle, it was at the same time a sign that the person was entering the service of someone who held authority in the community; the *paterfamilias* (the father in the home, in the Roman sense of the word), or the Emperor, or the god of a religious community. To be marked with the seal was therefore a sign of entry into a community. The obligations arising from the mark of the seal were not purely onesided; the Emperor or the father or the owner for his part took the person marked in this way under his protection. Thus the mark was also a sign of protection and a shield. A man bearing that mark might not be molested by others without their incurring the owner's revenge.

It was against this cultural background that, chiefly in Latin Africa and especially with Tertullian and St. Augustine, men gradually became aware of a special dimension in ecclesial sacramentality; a dimension which before this time had rather been lived out in practice than defined in a reflective understanding of it. Some of the sacraments were, quite simply, not repeated; the Church's practice in this matter then caused people to reflect. St. Augustine developed his explanation with explicit reference to the custom of marking soldiers with a seal. His terminology, however, differed from that which is customary nowadays. What we call the "character" he commonly called the "sacrament," and vice versa. For St. Augustine the outward sacramental rite itself is the seal which characterizes us, a sign by which one can mark that a person has been baptized and so belongs to the Catholic Church, in distinction from those who do not. Even if a person falls away or becomes a heretic, the mark, the seal of baptism, remains indelible and invulnerable. In secular thought the deep scarring or branding of the seal was also proverbially ineradicable. Nevertheless, St. Augustine held that besides the outward rite that imposed the mark there was a deeper, more permanent, reality which he called the "sacrament"; a permanent effect which is, however, distinct from sanctifying grace and independent of personal merit. This effect is present purely by reason of the valid administration of the sacrament.

Developing this Augustinian doctrine, the early scholastics kept the name of "seal" or "character" for the outward rite. But after Peter Lombard a change took place; in three sacraments the permanent inward "mysterious" effect distinct from grace, formerly called the "permanent sacrament," came to be called the "character." All the properties of the outward mark or seal were attributed to this inward reality: it was called a distinctive mark. This, however, gave rise to many difficulties. How can inward reality be a sign? What is the purpose of this sign? Who can perceive it?

As the doctrine developed, the intrinsic connection between the outward rite and the inward spiritual reality was restored. In this way there grew an understanding that the inward reality which some sacraments confer can be called a "character" only in connection with the outward sign which effects and signifies it. The sacrament consists of the outward sign together with the inward reality, and this duality-in-unity is the sign of grace.

It was St. Thomas who finally brought order into this confusion of ideas. He refers back to the use of the seal in ancient culture, and calls the outward sacramental rite itself a marking with the seal. But, he says, in this signing with the seal attention should be drawn not so much to the outward mark, to the sign itself, as to what is signified and thus to the purpose for which it is used. In human society the purpose of a seal is to signify that the one upon whom it is conferred is incorporated into an association under competent authority, so that within the association he receives an office in virtue of which he is to exercise a certain competence and carry out certain commissions. St. Thomas applies this to the sacramental character. As a sign it is the sacramental rite itself. But as that which is signified and conferred by the sign it is a competence, a commission within the community of the Church. Hence the basic idea of the Thomist theory of the sacramental character is a relationship to the Church as visible community: the outward rite of three sacraments signifies and confers a special competence and commission within the visibility of the Church. In this St. Thomas sees the community of the Church under the formal aspect of a community of worship, differentiated according to three sacraments. This competence is conferred, outwardly sealed and declared authentic by the reception of the external sign. The competence or the commission itself is thus not a sign or character, but by metaphorical transference the name of the outward rite, the signing or sealing, is applied to the ecclesial competence actually conferred by it. Thus the competence is conferred through a visible act of the Church and also relates to the performance of such visible acts in the Church.

An authorization of this kind to participate in the characteristic acts of a community normally takes the form of "jurisdiction," a socio-juridical reality. In virtue of the specific nature of ecclesial ritual activity and worship, however, a purely juridical authorization is insufficient. For the public worship of the Church is carried out personally by Christ in sacramental form. Hence a purely juridical authorization is clearly not enough. The person who receives the commission, who is deputed by Christ in his Church actively to participate in and carry out acts of a specifically ecclesial ritual, must receive a real "ordination" for this purpose, making it possible for his acts to be really the acts of the risen Christ. Because of the essentially Christian nature of these public ecclesial acts the outward sign and seal confers an inward spiritual reality in the soul. To this we must add the qualification: At least in so far as the commission given by the seal concerns ritual acts. It was for this reason that St. Thomas called the inward character or competence a participation in the high priesthood of Christ—a participation in different and subordinated degrees, depending on its deviation from the characters of baptism, confirmation or the priesthood.

This Thomistic doctrine was not universally accepted by later theologians, and up to the present day it remains a purely theological view upon which the Church has made no dogmatic pronouncement. Scotus followed a quite different line, in conscious opposition to St. Thomas. According to him, the character is a spiritual reality "imprinted" on the soul as a material seal is imprinted on the body. In what the spiritual imprint actually consists remains rather vague. But it is perhaps typical that Scotus too seeks an explanation in terms of a relationship to the visibility of the Church. He calls a character an "extrinsic relation to Christ and his Church."

If we leave aside the interpretations developed by the different schools of theology, we may conclude that from the time of St. Augustine through the Middle Ages up to the present, and in spite of the differences of theological system, one factor in this discussion has always remained constant: A person who bears a character or mark bears a certain relation to the visible ecclesial community. This, it seems to me, is fundamental.

Very little has been dogmatically defined concerning character. The Council of Florence[4] and of Trent[5] composed the following dogmatic definitions. Three sacraments, baptism, confirmation and order, confer a character that is indelible here on earth so that they may not be received more than once. Nothing is said about what this character actually is. It is described in terms that are not too precise, with which the theologians of the different schools could agree; the character is "a spiritual mark on the soul." The formulation of this description is Scotist rather than Thomist, but the Thomists too, as we have seen, could accept it in their own quite different sense. To this dogmatic definition we can add the fact of a constant tradition (which as such is of greater value than a mere theological view): The character relates one to the visible community of the Church.

[4] *DB*, 695.   [5] *DB*, 852.

(b) The Character as the Ecclesial Effect of
Baptism, Confirmation and Order

When we consider character within the context of the whole synthesis of sacramental theology set out in the preceding chapters, its inner meaning is more readily understood, for then we see the full force of its relationship to the visible Church. Just as character itself is threefold, so it relates us to the visible Church in three different ways. In order to clarify this we must return for a moment to what we saw in our first chapter.

(1) The Character as a Commission to Carry
Out a Visible Activity in the Church

(a) The Characters of Baptism and
Confirmation

The mystery of Christ, as we have seen, embraces two essential factors: the worship of the "Servant of Yahweh," the Son made man, which the Father accepts in the resurrection, and the establishment in power of God the Son in his humanity, by which he becomes perfectly filled with the Holy Spirit and so, as man, becomes the source of the Holy Spirit for us. The mystery of Christ is the incarnation completed in the mystery of Easter and Pentecost. Of this mystery of worship of the High Priest, the Church is the manifestation in history; filled with its saving reality, the Church itself is a mystery of worship which sanctifies through bestowal of the Spirit.[6] The Church is the earthly prolongation or, better, visibility of, Christ's high priesthood in heaven. On the one hand the worship

[6] Cf. what has been said about the mystery of worship (in the man Jesus: ch. 1, section 2; prolonged in the Church: ch. 2, section 2). In the full sense of the term this includes religion both as cult and as apostolate. The ritual worship of the community therefore means the service and the praise of God, and this finds its realization in acts of praise as well as in acts of the apostolate.

of the Church, as child of the Father, is the worship of perpetual praise; a community of worship with which the Father is always well pleased. In this way the Church is the visible sign on earth of the eternal mystery of passover or resurrection from the dead. On the other hand the Church is the one who is "established in power" at Pentecost, and therefore the earthly sign of Christ as possessing the fullness of the Spirit and as sender of the Spirit. Therefore the Church herself is filled with the messianic Spirit whom she continues to bestow ever more fully upon the world of men.

Now at least in the primitive Church baptism and confirmation together formed the rite of Christening; initiation into the mystery of the Church and thus incorporation into the mystery of Christ. In this initiation confirmation was seen as perfecting the incorporation.[7] From the earliest times baptism was thought of in association with Christ's death and resurrection, confirmation in association with the mystery of Pentecost.[8] Thus the two elements of the one Christian initiation are clearly related to the two fundamental mysteries of Christ's life: his passover or religious sacrifice for brotherly love, with which the Father is well pleased, and his establishment in power as *Kyrios* whereby, as man, he becomes the sender of the Spirit. This means that our incorporation into the Church, the sacramental communion in the mysteries of Easter and Pentecost, is perfected in two stages: through the celebration-in-

[7] In keeping with the purpose of this work, we shall not go into the positive theological and liturgical basis for this. A comprehensive view that will help to understand the facts is enough. A more thorough investigation has been made in the article "Vormsel," in *Theologisch Woordenboek,* 3, cols. 4840–70.

[8] We cannot agree with Karl Rahner, who connects baptism with Christ's death, confirmation with his resurrection ("Kirche und Sakramente. Zur theologische Grundlegung einer Kirchenund Sakramentenfrömmigkeit," in *GL,* 28 [1955], pp. 434–53). We have said above that Christ's resurrection from the dead is, on trinitarian grounds, formally distinct from his exaltation and enthronement as *Kyrios* and sender of the Spirit. This distinction holds quite apart from the problem of whether these two mysteries are simply two aspects of one and the same event or two different events, one following the other. Death and resurrection belong together.

mystery of baptism and through that of confirmation. Hence these two sacraments are clearly distinct, in the same way as the two mysteries which they represent among us sacramentally. But together they form the sacramental representation of the one redeeming mystery of Christ perfected to the full. Hence both sacraments form an organic and living whole: one rite of initiation made up of two essential sacramental elements (which may therefore be separated in time). The liturgical rite of initiation was originally one and undivided, but gradually, after reflection, men came to recognize the obvious distinction between its two elements.

We must also remember that the mystery of sanctifying worship becomes present in the Church's sacraments only as directed towards the recipient. This implies that a person receiving baptism is incorporated into the Easter mystery of the visible Church and thus into the eternal passover of Christ. On the other hand, when a person is confirmed he begins to participate in that fullness of the Holy Spirit which the visible Church possesses, and in her activity of sending the Spirit; thus he is incorporated into the eternal Pentecost mystery of the glorified Lord. Consequently baptism makes us members of the ecclesial People of God, the "child of the Father"; we become children of the Father, *filii in Filio,* in the power of the Spirit of sonship which baptism gives us. Then in confirmation, as members of the Church and so as children of God, we are "established in power"; within the visible Church, we receive a share in her fullness and bestowal of the Spirit, and thus in the Pentecost mystery of Christ himself. Therefore confirmation makes us adult members of the Church, incorporates us into the fullness of its mystery *filii Dei in virtute.* The *robur* or strength of which theological tradition has spoken since the Middle Ages undoubtedly reflects an essential aspect of confirmation.

If we do not grasp that the whole essence of the redemption is the historical revelation of the mystery of the Trinity, it is impossible to understand why it takes two sacraments to complete the initiation into the Christian community. For this initiation is something that is fully achieved only by incorporation into Christ both as Son of the Father and as co-principle of the Spirit. Both these trinitarian relations acquire an historical, saving significance in the man Jesus; in his service as Son of the Father and in his human establishment in power as sender of the Spirit.

The fact that baptism makes us children of the Father through the Spirit of sonship, and that the Spirit is already given to us by baptism on its own, always proved a hindrance to the understanding of confirmation as a gift of the Spirit. Now the difficulty can be resolved. As we said above, even before Christ was "established in power" he lived his life of service to the full, even to death, in the power of the Holy Spirit. Baptism, by the same power of the Spirit, gives us a participation in the service which the Son of God rendered to the Father through the *invisible* mission of the Spirit. In baptism and in the person baptized, that which becomes visible, though in the power of the Spirit of Christ, is the mystery of passover; death to sin and life unto God in Christ Jesus. But in confirmation and in the person confirmed it is the mystery of Pentecost that receives a visible manifestation, a visible witness to the fact that we are "established in power" by the Spirit of Christ. For we must not forget that the characters of both baptism and confirmation relate us to the visible Church, and thus to her inner mystery. This means that through these characters the commission given us by baptism and confirmation is, of its nature, a commission to carry out visible ecclesial acts. If this were not so, the whole sense of the mystery of the Church would be weakened.

Therefore we cannot possibly consider baptism merely as related to an inward spiritual life, and confirmation as that which makes the power of this inward life public in the visibility of the Church. As sacraments they are both a sanctification of the person. But as sacraments which give a commission and consequently a character they give us, of their nature, an order or relationship to the visibility and public life of the Church. The special nature of the commissions to public activity given by baptism and by confirmation cannot be defined arbitrarily according to our personal preferences. It is only from their significance in the saving history which constitutes them that we can learn their inner meaning. We understand the commission of baptism from the baptismal incorporation into Christ's passover mystery in its ecclesial visibility; and the commission of confirmation from the incorporation, effected by this sacrament, into the Pentecost mystery of Christ in the historical tangibility of his earthly Church. Hence a baptized member of the Church receives the commission and therefore the competence, duty and right to take an active part in the ecclesial mystery of Easter. This activity is primarily the sacramental activity of the Church, above all in the Eucharist, in which the mystery of Easter is realized in the fullest sense.

There seem to me to be no dogmatic or liturgical grounds, therefore, for considering a baptized person "liturgically unsuitable" for communicating or for taking part in the celebration of the eucharistic sacrifice.[9] For a person who is baptized is truly incorporated into Christ's resurrection from the dead, through the character-given commission to make this ecclesial Easter mystery visible. Furthermore, the baptismal character also gives the commission to carry out other specific activities of the Church community, except those activities assigned to the commissions of confirmation and order. A person who is only baptized, however, fulfils these commissions as one who is not yet "established in power." It is for this reason that establishment of the baptismal commission in full power is a primary characteristic of the seal of confirmation. Thus the

[9] This, to my mind, is a point on which B. Luykx has erred by exaggeration (cf. "Théologie et pastorale de la confirmation," in *Paroisse et liturgie,* 39 [1957], pp. 180–201, 263–278). From what we have seen the normal time for first Communion would be after confirmation; until then our membership of the ecclesial eucharistic community is not complete. Yet the administration of confirmation after the reception of Communion is not a *contresens liturgique.* To maintain that it is to devalue the significance of baptism, which, however closely it may be connected with confirmation, is nevertheless an independent phase of the initiation. Moreover, a custom preserved for centuries in the Church—even in a particular Church—even if it is a relatively recent custom in comparison with the ancient usage, can never be meaningless, as St. Thomas quite rightly points out, although it may indeed represent a change of emphasis.

character of confirmation is also ordered to an active participation in the sacramental life of the Church; in particular to the celebration of the Eucharist. Not until his initiation hás been completed by confirmation can a person take part in the celebration of the Eucharist as a child of the Father established in power; not until then does his share in the offering of the Eucharist begin to function fully as a share in the work of propagating and strengthening the Church. But this function derives from the special significance of the commission received in confirmation, which must be clarified before we go any further.

We saw that confirmation confers upon us the commission to take part, within the visibility of the Church, in her divine sonship established in power; to take part, in other words, in her visible activity of bestowing the Spirit. It is in this sense that the Acts understand the great sending of the Spirit on the day of Pentecost: "Being exalted therefore by the right hand of God, and having received of the Father the promise of the Holy Ghost, he hath poured forth this which you see and hear."[10] It is because he is filled with the Holy Spirit that the Christian who is confirmed, who is established in power, takes his place in the public life and work of the Church, actively and visibly sharing in Christ's work of sending the Spirit. This is not his first investiture with the apostolate. The grace of baptism, as life-out-of-death, and the commission given in baptism are of their nature also apostolic realities. It is not possible to conceive of a Christian grace or a Christian task in the Church which, while being a service of God, would not at the same time be an apostolic work. Yet the fullness of the messianic power is lacking in Christians who are not confirmed; the situation is more or less parallel to that of the earthly Christ who, though he was the Messiah, could not visibly unfold the full force of his messianic purpose among us through the sending of his Spirit until he had entered into his heavenly Pentecost mystery.

In confirmation the Church's charismatic activity in the Spirit

[10] Acts 2.33.

is visibly extended in the life of the person who has now become wholly initiated. Whatever form this charismatic activity may take —and it may be assumed that its outlet will take on new and different shapes as time goes on—it is all a manifestation of the Church developing her participation in Christ's sending of the Holy Spirit through her confirmed members, her bearing witness to Christ as visible reality of the witness borne by the Spirit himself. For it is evident both from Scripture and from the whole of subsequent tradition that witness to Christ is the typical outward result and manifestation of "being established in power" in the *pneuma*. "But when the Paraclete [the Helper] comes, whom I will send you from the Father . . . he shall give testimony of me."[11] Moreover, Christ had said: "And you shall be brought before governors and before kings for my sake, for a testimony to them and to the Gentiles. But , . . take no thought how or what to speak: for it shall be given you in that hour what to speak. For it is not you that speak, but the Spirit of your Father that speaketh in you."[12]

We find an echo of this in the first Christian community, in which bearing witness was repeatedly connected with the promptings of the Spirit. In the primitive Christian community the charismatic activity of the Spirit was everywhere palpably evident. And this was seen in connection with the event in the Cenacle and with other related bestowals of the Spirit. The *pneuma* or the Spirit, as the fullness of power in the messianic mission, becomes visible in the acts of those who have been confirmed. This remains the profound meaning of confirmation, no matter what actual expression the Spirit gives to his activity in those who are confirmed. Thus if confirmation is called the sacrament of Christian maturity, we must understand this not so much in the sense of human, biological or even psychological maturity, but rather as an aspect of saving history; just as Christ became Messiah to the full through his resurrection and exaltation by the Father's side and through his establishment as human sender of the Spirit, so too the baptized child

[11] John 15.26. [12] Matt. 10.18–20.

of the Father becomes an adult Christian with his establishment in power through confirmation. From this it is clear that there can be no objection to giving the sacrament to infants and young children. For they will have within themselves the principle enabling them to act as children of God established in power when they develop psychologically. This is an empowering in function of redemption; and in this sense confirmation is the sacrament of the apostolate which overcomes the world, since it is the work of the Spirit of Christ through the visible action of adult children of God. It is a Spirit of testimony.

Now Christ by his sanctifying service, his worship of the Father, is the High Priest. Therefore the Church, as the earthly representation of this sanctifying mystery of worship, is of its nature a priestly People of God.[13] Thus initiation into the Church through the sacraments of baptism and confirmation is an initiation into the ecclesial priesthood of the faithful. And since the mystery of Easter is itself a priestly event, the idea that confirmation alone, not baptism, initiates us into the kingly priesthood is seen once more as a failure to recognize the special worth of baptism. Baptism invests us with the priesthood of the Church, and confirmation establishes this in power. Both these sacraments give a commission. Baptism gives the priestly commission visibly to live in the Church as children of the Father, participating in the worship and apostolate of Christ's service. In the liturgical rite of baptism, the prayer that accompanies an imposition of hands is that the recipient may "serve the Father in the Church with joy."[14] The commission given by confirmation is the priestly one visibly to live as children of God established in power. Thus under the aspect of priesthood baptism lays the foundation which confirmation brings to fulfilment. In this way we come to see that the characters of baptism and confirmation are really a participation in the priesthood of the visible Church, and therefore in Christ's priesthood as St. Thomas, the first to work out

[13] 1 Pet. 2.2–10; Apoc. 1.6:5.9:20.6.
[14] ". . . Ut laetus tibi in Ecclesia tua deserviat"; the prayer is addressed to "God, the Father of our Lord, Jesus Christ."

this problem, has shown. Through initiation into the priestly People of God, these characters give the faithful a share in the messianic mission of the humiliated and exalted High Priest.

Being a participation in the priesthood of the Church, and so of the High Priest, the characters of baptism and confirmation are also an ordination. Since baptism incorporates a person into the community of the Church, even if he lacks grace—union with the Father in the power of the Spirit of sonship—a baptized person is irrevocably a child of the Father, even though a "lost son."[15] Similarly, even if a person who is confirmed is no longer filled with the Spirit, he is nevertheless irrevocably a son established in power. Hence the character gives us a permanent status and ordination, which can become divorced from personal communion with the three divine persons in Christ Jesus even though on God's side, and ecclesiologically, it is essentially connected with being united in grace to the Father and with the personal possession of the fullness of the Spirit. Without grace this status and ordination is abnormal and distorted, but on account of our sinfulness that is a real possibility. This indicates that the two characters—or more precisely the ordination and commission bestowed by the rites which give us them—are not merely a juridical reality, but by reason of their ecclesial nature are also a Christological reality "imprinted upon our soul," as the Council of Trent suggests.

Theologians have with good reason repeatedly warned against a "mystification" of character. Still, there are others who constantly tend to see in it no more than a juridical reality. But a baptized person really does remain a child of the Father even though he acts

[15] St. Augustine compares the permanent character in an initiate who has fallen from grace with the mark and sign of his commission which the deserter bears indelible on his body even though he has broken service. (*In Evangelium Johannis*, tract. 6, 15 [*PL*, 35, col. 1432].) At the same time this means that any personal act which the baptized and confirmed perform in virtue of their character is really the "administration of a sacrament," an official ecclesial act. These acts are not new sacraments, over and above the seven, but are the actual exercise of the commissions of baptism and confirmation.

contrary to his baptismal promises, and this fact can hardly be called a purely juridical reality. For here we are confronted with the inherent paradox of a child of God having no relationship of love with the Father. On the other side we must not separate the inward ordination of baptism and confirmation from its relationship to the visible Church. This relationship remains an essential and constitutive property of the character and ordination. Precisely because persons who are baptized and confirmed are incorporated into the visible Church they irrevocably bear a relationship to Christ as Son and to Christ as co-principle of the Spirit, since the Church is the earthly visibility of his whole mystery. The indelible inward ordination therefore can neither be opposed to nor considered as adding anything to the irrevocable initiation into the visible Church. St. Thomas and Scotus have both uncovered true aspects of character.

We may sum up the commission of the characters of baptism and confirmation as follows. These characters, since they initiate us into the Church, the *laos* or the People of God, give us the status of laymen.[16] Thus for the baptized and the confirmed the lay state gives ecclesial status, and therefore their Christian mission as laymen is truly an ecclesial commission. Baptism together with confirmation gives us the commission to lay activity in the Church, and this is a priestly activity. At the Lay Congress held in Rome in 1957 Pope Pius XII broke, very rightly, with the mystique of the canonical "mandate" to lay activity in the Church, through which the dogmatic sense of the mandate given by baptism and confirmation had been entirely lost. There has now been a return to the realization that by the fact of a person's bearing a character he possesses a

---

[16] The word *laos,* people, in the Septuagint translation of Scripture, is used exclusively of the People of God, in contrast to *ethne,* which is used of heathen, non-Jewish peoples. Against this background, then, *laos* in Scripture means the People of God as distinct from its leaders (cf. I. de la Potterie, "L'Origine et le sens primitif du mot 'laic,'" in *NRT,* 80 [1958], pp. 840–53). Theologically, therefore, we may say: *laikos, laicus* or layman is a member of the People of God as formally distinct from the hierarchy of the Church; a member of the People of God with his own proper lay commission in the Church.

commission to the lay apostolate in the Church. A juridical mandate given after the character has been received cannot confer this commission, nor can its absence nullify the commission possessed by anyone who has received a character. Such a mandate, if given, relates to no more than the practical needs of organization. Hence to be a layman means, in an unqualified sense, to be a member of the messianic and priestly People of God in virtue of baptism and confirmation. And although baptism alone makes one a layman-in-the-Church, confirmation is the actual establishment in power of this Christian lay status, and is thus the full initiation into the Church's apostolic laity.

(b) The Character of the Priestly Apostolic Office

In contrast with lay priesthood, which is bestowed upon us by baptism and confirmation, the character of priestly orders initiates us into the *clerus* of the ecclesial People of God; i.e., into the priesthood of the apostolic office or the episcopate.

The priestly nature of Christ[17] and of the People of God as a whole[18] was historically the first to be recognized and was expressed in Scripture itself as an article of faith. Starting from this twofold fundamental conviction of faith and because of it, Christians gradually became aware of the specially sacerdotal function of the apostolic office in the Church. The raison d'être of the apostolic office and of the Church's episcopate derives from the very thing which constitutes the community of the faithful as the Church: the revelation in reality and the revelation in word, sacrament and word. The People of God is built upon sacrament and word; it is founded, that is to say, upon the historical manifestation of the divine saving reality which the word manifests as a reality given to us. Christ entrusted the guidance of this People of God to

---

[17] Heb. 3.1:8.4:10.21; ch. 7, and throughout the epistle.
[18] Cf. the texts cited in note 13 of this chapter.

the apostolic office, which therefore holds authority in the Church. Consequently the competence of this leadership relates, in the first instance, to those factors which fundamentally constitute the Church; to sacrament and to word. The administration of sacraments and the service of the word properly belong to this office with the fullness of authority. The priestly function of the People of God, which is present in all who are baptized and confirmed, is present in the episcopate in the mode of a guiding authority, and hence as the immediate representatives of Christ in his role as Head of the Church. Hence this priesthood as manifested in the mode of ecclesiastical authority, in which quality it is distinct from and constituted above the *laikoi* or the members of the priestly People of God. Authority as such implies jurisdiction and the power of government, and therefore in a religious context is called pastoral authority or office. But in virtue of the character of the ecclesial community this authority is also the principle of the administration of the sacraments and of the preaching of the Gospel (teaching authority). The various divisions of authority in the Church, the hierarchy, are derived from her authority over sacrament and word; they are merely the systematic organization of the one underlying reality: the apostolic office or the episcopal priesthood. Thus in contrast to baptism and confirmation this is a priesthood of authority: priestly, kingly and prophetic activity having the function of authority in the Church. Therefore the Apostle or the bishop is fundamentally the liturgical minister of the community of the faithful, the teacher and preacher, and the prince of the Church, or more precisely the "good shepherd" who watches over the People of God in the name of Christ. The character of the priesthood gives to already initiated members of the community a commission and an ordination to act in the person of Christ as Head of the Church. To the priesthood of authority, the episcopate, Christ has entrusted the sacramental expression of the heavenly mystery of worship in the earthly form of the Church, as well as jurisdiction and the authentic preaching of the Faith (though the episcopate may admit others to a share in this). Christ carries out his activity as High

Priest in the acts of this priesthood; priestly acts are the personal acts of Christ himself made visible in sacramental form.

The character of the priesthood, like the characters of baptism and confirmation, empowers us to perform visible ecclesial acts. In giving to others a participation in the divine realities of salvation the priest (bishop) must act through the visible sacrament; only in sacramental signs may he bestow grace on others and only in his audible preaching of the word can others hear the word of God within them.

If we compare the priestly character of baptism and confirmation with that of the priesthood in authority, it becomes clear that the first two are most certainly not a participation in the hierarchical priesthood. All three are a participation in the fullness of the priesthood of the Church; the first two share it in a lay manner, while the priesthood of authority possesses it fully, that is, in the manner of the *clerus*. For example, when a priest celebrates the eucharistic sacrifice it is he alone who consummates the sacrifice in the name of Christ and his Church. But the sacrifice is offered in virtue of the general priesthood of all the faithful. Yet it is precisely because the priest does not merely act in the name of the faithful but in the name of Christ himself that he does after all act in the name of the faithful; for Christ, whose place he takes in the visibility of the Church, is personally the representative of the whole People of God. On the plane of the ecclesial manifestation of the heavenly mystery of Christ as the Way to the Father, the priest is the "sacramental Christ," *alter Christus,* here present for the faithful.

From this we can also understand why a person must be baptized and confirmed before he can be ordained. Only a person who is fully incorporated in Christ both as Son of the Father and as sender of the Spirit can exercise, charismatically, an official priesthood of authority in a Church which is the earthly representation of these mysteries of Easter and Pentecost. Although he is a priest in the very acts of this priestly function, he is a member of the Church, with all the obligations that this membership entails.

The presbyterate[19] is a participation in the priesthood of authority. The bishop, in virtue of his office, gives the ordinary priest a partial share in that which he possesses to the full. The ordinary priests are a body of sacerdotal assistants to the episcopal or apostolic college. By reason of his ordination to the priesthood, the ordinary priest is able to perform whatever he is commissioned to perform by the episcopal college or by the Pope. The presbyterate is a participation in the priesthood of authority or the apostolic office. In the nature of the case the priest acts in the name of the bishop and as his vicar.

(2) *The Three Characters as Sacraments of the Bestowal of Grace*

A character gives us a relationship to the visible Church; an office and a commission in the Church's historical visibility. As the ecclesial effect of three sacraments the character (as one with the outward rite) is the sacrament of the bestowal of grace. For—we repeat—the Church is a sign of grace filled with the saving reality it signifies. Commission to an ecclesial office, clerical or lay, of its nature includes the conferring of a corresponding messianic sanctity, unless the initiate personally and positively opposes it.[20] Those who belong to the Church exist in a context of sanctifying grace which infallibly takes a hold on them as long as they do not op-

---

[19] "Presbyters" are those who are customarily called priests. Strictly speaking the bishop alone is "the priest"; the presbyter is priest by participation only. This is not the place to examine closely the relationship between presbyterate and episcopate; it has been analysed historically and speculatively in the article "Priesterschap," in *Theologisch Woordenboek*, 3 (published separately in translation: *Sintesis teologica del sacerdotio*, Salamanca [1959]). Cf. also "Het apostolische ambt van de kerklijke Hiërarchie," in *SC*, 32 (1957), pp. 258–90, which is a summary of the above article.

[20] *Non ponentibus obicem;* cf. the analysis above in ch. 5, ss. 1, 1. In the twelfth and thirteenth centuries it was already generally accepted in theology that the character was a "disposition to grace." Modern scholasticism speaks in more legalistic terms of a "right or title to grace."

pose it. As a community with a mission, the Church is at the same time a community in grace. The Church is holy. A lay or clerical initiation into this holy Church, when it is all that it should be according to the nature of the Church, is necessarily a sanctification, an initiation into holiness. A rupture between office and holiness, although a real possibility, is ecclesiologically a distortion and an abnormality. As long as the person who possesses a character places no obstacles in the way, i.e., as long as he is open to receive grace, his commission of its very nature gives it to him. Therefore St. Thomas could call a character "the root of the spiritual life."[21]

Thus the character of baptism is the sacrament of all the further graces flowing from baptism. Incorporation into the visible Church as the manifestation of the mystery of Easter is of itself incorporation into the Church's inward mystery, into the mystical body of Christ. It is, in other words, forgiveness of original sin and all personal sins, the sealing with Christian faith, and union in grace with the heavenly Father, with all the other consequences of being a child of God. From the moment a man is baptized, throughout the rest of his life, the character of baptism keeps exercising its infallible function, although other sacraments are needed to remove fresh obstacles that may arise and so to reconcile man with God again. Confession itself is an ecclesial act of a baptized person.

The character of confirmation gives us a commission in the visible Church to take part in her divine sonship established in power; to take part in her activity of bestowing the Holy Spirit upon men. The commission to this office is also a personal sanctification and grace, by which our personal initiation into the mystery of Christ is brought to completion. Confirmation gives us an inner union in grace with Christ as sender of the Spirit, based upon baptism by which we are united in grace to Christ as Son of God. For this reason confirmation also brings our personal life of grace to its full development.

The character of order, the commission in the Church to the

---

[21] "Radix vitae spiritualis" (*IV Sent.*, d. 22, q. 2, a. 1, sol. 1).

priesthood of authority, by the fact that it confers an official status also sanctifies the person, provided the recipient does not oppose the sanctity bestowed upon him. This character gives a priest an intimate union in grace with Christ as Head of the Church, in such a way that his priestly ministration shows forth the holiness of the leader of God's people, Christ Jesus.

Thus confirmation and order make man's relationship with God (which faith and baptism have brought about) inwardly more profound, precisely because they contain a special grace. This is the general effect which is included in the particular effects of these sacraments of the living, which we examined in a previous chapter.

Now if we consider the character and the corresponding grace together, we must say that office and holiness together form the charism of an ecclesial commission. Office and charismatic sanctity are not as widely separate as they were once thought to be. Their separation arose from a tendency to regard the charism as in some way opposed to mere office. On the contrary the mission and mandate of Christ in his Church, and the holiness of those who have been given a commission in this Church, together forming one reality, are the foundation of the many charismatic and unusual, even miraculous, things that happen when saints carry out the Church's commissions in the world.

2. The Ecclesial Effect of the Other
   Sacraments

Although in a certain sense all the sacraments may be called sacraments of commission, it is better to restrict this terminology to those sacraments which confer a character. Nevertheless we do find that the first effect of the other sacraments, like the first effect of the three sacraments of commission, is an ecclesial reality which becomes the sacrament of the bestowal of grace. The immediate effect of each sacrament is the establishment of a special relationship to the visible Church. Here we need only indicate this very briefly.

The ecclesial effect of the sacrament of penance is reconciliation with the Church as the sacrament of our reconciliation with God in Christ. The Church is the earthly manifestation of God's redeeming mercy, and confession is visible contact with the Church precisely under this aspect. It establishes us in the ecclesial status of penitents who, by the performance of the penance required by the Church and through the mercy of her absolution, become reconciled with God himself.

The Eucharist too brings about, in the first place, a deepening of the inner belonging to the eucharistic People of God: it is the sacrament of the unity of the Church, the bond of which is love. Now Christ is present in the Church's Eucharist precisely as the bond of her unity, for it is his real presence under the covenant of the consecration.[22] The individual becomes personally united with Christ in his sacrifice of the cross to the extent that, by taking part in the Eucharist and especially in receiving Communion, he enters into the sacrificial community of the Church. For the Church, the People of God, is the community of the eucharistic covenant, entry into which is the sacrament of personal communion with the Christ who sacrifices, of communion in that sacrifice with which the Father is well pleased.

Again in the anointing of the sick, it is clear that the sacrament bestows the gift of grace by making visible connections with the Church. For the Church is the earthly representation of Christ's redemption which, overcoming sin, overcomes death. Now in the sacrament of anointing, the Church, precisely as conqueror of death, is acting for the Christian who is grievously ill. And her act is filled with the reality which it shows forth. Therefore this sacrament, as specific contact with the Church victorious, effects either a recovery of health or the future life-out-of-death. Thus the ec-

[22] "Calix sanguinis mei . . . Novi Testamenti. . . ." See Karl Rahner, "Kirche und Sakramente." (There is a play upon words here which is lost in translation. *Verbond* suggests the idea of "tied together," "unity," much more forcefully and immediately than its English equivalent, "covenant," while "bond" is the same in both languages. [Tr.])

clesial effect of the anointing of the sick is a specific incorporation into the Church having the eschatological power to overcome death. The ecclesial act of anointing gives the Christian in mortal suffering a participation in the suffering of the Church which, in principle, has already passed over into glory. In this way the anointed enter into a special ecclesial status which is the object of the Church's special care and prayer.

Finally, matrimony has an ecclesial effect which is also the sacrament of the bestowal of grace. In her visible life and activity the Church manifests herself as the bride of Christ. Matrimony thus unites the marriage bond of man and woman with the bridal relationship of the Church to Christ. And because the visibility of the Church is filled with the reality it signifies, the union of two people in matrimony becomes through its objective ecclesial character a sign of corresponding inner grace.[23]

In this first effect of the sacraments (character, and the other four specific relationships to the visible Church) it is clear that the sacraments unite us in grace with Christ because they bring us into contact with the mystery of the visible Church. From this we can come to understand why there are in fact seven sacraments.

3. Explanation of the Sacraments from the Nature of the Church

It is the nature of the Church which accounts for the fact that there are seven ritual sacraments. We cannot, of course, overlook

[23] Recently, closer attention has been paid to the ecclesiological effect of the sacraments. The following essays are examples of this: M. Schmauss, *Katholische Dogmatik,* Munich (1952), vol. 4, pt. 1, "Die Lehre von den Sakramenten"; K. Rahner, "Kirche und Sakramente," in *GL,* 28 (1955), pp. 434–53; O. Semmelroth, *Die Kirche als Ursakrament,* Frankfurt-am-Main (1953); P. Smulders, "Sacramenten en kerk. Kerkelijk recht, kultus, pneuma," in *BJ,* 17 (1956), pp. 391–418; J. Tyciak, *Der siebenfältige Strom aus der Gnadenwelt der Sakramente,* Freiburg (1954). F. Taymans d'Eypernon has sought, more in the perspective of mysticism, for the link between the outward sacrament and the inner gift of grace in *La Sainte Trinité et les sacraments,* Brussels-Paris (1949).

the human factors which play a part in fixing this number and which make it fitting. Birth, growth to maturity, the daily need for nourishment, moral disablement, marriage, the events of illness and death, the awareness of the *tremendum,* the majesty of God before whom one does not dare to appear except through the advocacy of a human intermediary or priest—the religious man knows all these as turning-points in the course of life on earth. He is aware in a way he cannot express that in all these factors something above himself, something vitally important, is at stake. These are problems of life affecting the whole of life; faced with them man spontaneously experiences that life and its supreme moments are not in his control. Spontaneously, too, he seeks to surround such moments with sacred symbols; man's puny cry to the higher Power of Life which will take pity on him and assure him all will be well. At one time man may have thought that in these symbols he could control the life force as if by magic; they can also be used with religious intent. Religious mankind, in the primordial elements of human life, is here living out, though unconsciously, an awareness of its fallen state and of its need for redemption. Unquestionably there is a psychological basis for the manifold ritual confession of man's vital needs and his quest for contact with a power of life above this earth. This is part of the reason why there are seven sacraments. (It is not, of course, an *a priori* proof that there must be exactly seven. It merely shows that the fact of there being seven is psychologically meaningful.)

Now we have already seen that this natural dimension is lifted up and made an intrinsic part of the Church's sacraments. The powerless cry of man is caught up by the all-powerful answer of God who, in Christ, responds to it in a way that goes far beyond all human expectation. In the impotent *materia* offered by man (for example, in the pouring of water on the head of a baby), God in Christ, by the power of his saving word believed by the Church and expressed in the sacramental *forma,* brings about a deeper and divine mystery. The seven chief elements of human life thus become *kairoi;* that is, they become saving moments in which God, through

Christ, makes himself manifest in a form that belongs to our earthly reality. The sacraments become the visible sign of the saving fact that God personally concerns himself with the success of human life.

Connected with this and following immediately upon it is the ecclesial necessity of the seven sacraments, which makes clear why there are this number. This necessity is in no sense intended as an *a priori* deduction from the essence of the Church, but merely relates the fact that there are seven sacraments in an intelligible way to constitutive properties of the Church.[24]

If the Church is the historical manifestation of Christ's work of redemption, it is itself in the fullest sense when it is acting as such; when it administers sacraments, celebrates the sacrifice of the Mass; when it is teaching, governing, shepherding. The Church in its visibility expresses itself by bringing others to a share in itself. In this action it is constituting itself in those who encounter it; first of all in baptism, and progressively to a greater depth in the other sacraments. Consequently the Church is itself to the full wherever in actual fact it comes to be salvation to individual persons; in the saving encounter with a person it is the sanctifying community, manifesting its effective presence of grace. The salvation of an individual is at the same time a communal and ecclesiological event; it is a moment in the process by which the Church, in this world continually coming into being in its subjects, brings about its own realization.

Now it was seen in our brief analysis of the ecclesial effect of the seven sacraments that each brings us into vital contact with some essential property of the Church as earthly presence of the messianic salvation of the humiliated and glorified Christ. These characteristics coincide exactly with the sevenfold response to man's need of the Church in the decisive moments of life. It is precisely in the seven sacraments that the essence of the Church expresses itself by giving men a share in itself; bringing them to a participation in

[24] This, it seems to me, is the true value and sense of Karl Rahner's article "Kirche und Sakramente."

itself as "child of the Father" established in power (baptism and confirmation) who, in union with Christ's sacrifice of the Cross which the Father accepts (Eucharist), through her priests (order), brings man to an eschatological salvation victorious over death (anointing) and the mercy of Christ the Redeemer (penance), and makes human life in the marriage bond a participation in her own bridal relationship with Christ (matrimony). In these sacraments the essential properties of the Church are truly made visible, since they place human situations and the needs of human life in a divine perspective.

In the sacraments, therefore, the primary aspect is not the response to a sevenfold human need but rather a sevenfold Christian grace and commission, which is of course related to this need. The primary significance of the "seven" is a manifold messianic bestowal of grace and a commission of the ecclesial People of God as the earthly sacrament of him "who for us men and our salvation came down from heaven."

2. THE GRACE EFFECT OF THE SACRAMENTS: SACRAMENTAL GRACE AS THE ENCOUNTER WITH GOD

At the heart of all ecclesial sacramentality is obviously the encounter itself with God in and through the sacramental encounter with Christ in his Church: sacramental grace. We must now briefly draw together the many aspects of this problem.

In general "sacramental grace" means that grace which is bestowed through the sacrament. In the nature of the case this means grace that comes visibly. This ecclesial visibility of the bestowal of grace is the general but fundamental meaning of what is called "sacramental grace." By this the problem of the anonymity of extra-sacramental grace is resolved. The gift of grace is made real for us while it is showing clearly the demands it makes on us.

Moreover sacramental grace is the grace of redemption itself, since the deepest meaning of the Church's sacraments lies in

Christ's act of redemption. This remains a permanent actuality in which we become involved through the sacraments. All turns upon a participation in the grace of Christ. This Christological aspect of sacramental grace brings us to a personal communion with the Trinity. For in the sacraments we are taken up into the eternal Easter and Pentecost mystery of the *Kyrios,* in which the three persons in their unity and distinctness play an active part. The effect of the mystery of the man Jesus' sanctifying worship is that in the power of the Spirit of sonship the Father becomes our Father. (See Chapter 1.) To encounter Christ is, as we have said, to encounter God. Sacramental grace is this personal communion with God. It is an immediate encounter with him, not an indirect meeting through creation. But an encounter with God is essentially an encounter with the Trinity, since there can be no participation in the divine nature[25] which is not a communion with the three persons who alone are the Divinity. Therefore sanctifying grace, as immediate relationship with God, is essentially a divine relationship with the three persons in their distinctness and their unity, for this is what God is. Sacramental grace is incorporation into the mystical body or into communion in grace with Christ, and is thus the identification of the goal of our life with the death and resurrection of the Lord; in this way it brings about our own personal communion with the Trinity. The indwelling of God, of the redeeming Trinity, which inwardly re-creates us in Christ and makes us *filii in Filio,* children of the same Father, is the overwhelming effect of a fruitful sacrament, and it is faith that gives us a conscious and living awareness of this.

Furthermore, since the sacraments are the embodiment, in a sevenfold perspective, of Christ's eternal act of redemption, sacramental grace is the grace of redemption itself in its direction and application to the seven possible situations of a Christian in the Church, according to the special symbolism and telling significance of each sacrament. Therefore sacramental grace is the grace of re-

---

[25] ". . . made partakers of the divine nature." (2 Pet. 1.4.)

demption having a particular function with reference to a particular ecclesial and Christian situation of life, and to a particular human need.

In this way we bridge the gap between the diverging Eastern and Western stresses in sacramentality. The East lays emphasis on the grace of divinization; upon the fact that in the sacramental encounter with Christ we become children of the Father or become his children more perfectly. The communion of existence and of life with the glorified "Servant of God" given us through the sacraments means that God shows himself to us as *our* Father in the power of Christ's Spirit of sonship. Through the sacramental encounter with Christ, the sanctifying and divinizing personal communion with God comes progressively to a deeper and more inward realization.

The West, on the other hand, lays emphasis on the grace of healing and sees the sacraments above all as a process of gradual restoration; through the Church of Christ fallen mankind is carried back to the unspoiled integrity of nature.[26] This aspect cannot, however, be separated from the former. On this point there is an interesting development in St. Thomas's work. In the *Summa,* influenced by pseudo-Dionysius, he has synthesized the Eastern view with that of the West which was shaped chiefly by St. Augustine and the school of St. Victor.[27] For the sacraments are indeed a divinization which takes the form of restoration and redemption; they are the grace of *vita ex morte,* life out of death, after the pattern of the sacrifice of life on the cross brought to glory in the resurrection. Of their nature the sacraments place us in the situation of, and make ours the destiny of, the humiliated and exalted Christ, and draw us in him

[26] "Diversi sacramentorum effectus sunt ut diversae medicinae peccati et participationes virtutis dominicae passionis." (*De Veritate,* q. 27, a. 5, ad 12. This theme is recurrent.)

[27] "Gratia sacramentalis ad duo ordinatur: ad tollendos defectus praeteritorum peccatorum et ad perficiendam animam in his quae pertinent ad cultum Dei secundum religionem christianae vitae." (*ST,* III, q. 62, a. 5; q. 63, a. 1; a. 5; q. 65, a. 1.) The mystery of worship gets greater emphasis, and the *necessitas vitae christianae* is expressed in more positive terms. The negative "remedy for sin" gives way to the positive notion of "sanctification." (Cf. *ST,* III, q. 60, a. 5; q. 61, a. 2: q. 63, a. 3, ad 2.)

into the divine life. This means—to express the same thing in another way—that self-expropriation and self-sacrifice are the basis of our communion with God and that only through the humiliation of life do we come to share in the exaltation of Christ. Through this very fact the "wounds of nature" are healed. Suffering is not eliminated from the Christian situation, but it can be made an integral part of our living experience of God and may become the supreme factor in manifesting our attachment to the Father. Thus sacramental life gives birth to the new, integrated man; the Christian with his Christlike integrity.

Hence sacramental grace is sanctifying grace itself; sanctifying grace which comes to us visibly in the Church, in the fullness of its power, specifically aimed and ordered to the particular ecclesial needs of life and to the particular commissions of a Christian. A certain grace can be present apart from the sacraments, but this is an incipient grace which reaches its full development only in them, for there communion in grace with God is achieved in the sanctifying context of the Church as the fullness of Christ, in the visible Mystical Body.

The personal communion with God finds its expression in the theologal activity of faith, hope and love, the essence of life in union with God. Part of the fruitfulness of every sacrament, therefore, is the intensification of such activity in its Christological and ecclesial bearing. Faith in Christ, hope in Christ, love for Christ, with the echoes these call forth in human relations, drawing men together as into a family, with Christ the bond—all this, the true riches of a life lived for God, finds its inward meaning in the sacraments. For here we really experience Christ as the sacrament of our encounter with God, because this theologal activity is our only immediate connection with God himself.[28] The God-centred activity

---

[28] This very brief sketch of the theologal life of the sacrament may be filled out with the aid of several articles written for *Tijdschrift voor Geestelijk Leven*. For faith, "Ik geloof in de levende God," 6 (1950), pp. 454–67; hope, "Het hoopvolle Christusmysterie," 7 (1951), pp. 3–24; the love of God, "Het mysterie van onze Godsliefde," 7 (1951), pp. 609–26; and love of our neighbour, "De broederlijke liefde als Heilswerkelijkheid," 8 (1952), pp. 600–19. We shall return to this point in the last chapter.

of the life of the sacraments is the encounter with Christ as sacrament of the encounter with God, the culminating point of the whole
sacramental economy of salvation.

Theologal activity in grace, a life lived for God, is expressed in
moral behaviour. We look upon our human existence in this world
together with our fellow men from the vantage-point of our relationship with God. The moral norm, formally speaking, is no longer
the created human value of personality, but this human value taken
up into the relationship of child to Father. Hence moral virtue
comes to depend on personal communion with God; it becomes the
embodiment of our divine communion on every plane of human
living, and so serves and promotes the life of grace. Therefore the
sacramental encounter with Christ affects the whole of the Christian moral life. Through the God-centred grace which they give,
and through our fidelity to this grace, the sacraments heal the
"wounds of nature" and build up in us the "new man" in the image
of Christ.

Finally, grace is not something which, once given to us, we are
expected to assimilate by ourselves. In our friendship God and I
are both continually active. This implies something that is generally
called actual grace. Because the sacraments, each in its own special
way, give positive commissions which remain valid for the whole
of life, they themselves are the basis of the subsequent actual graces
which we need if the commissions are to be fulfilled. The permanent
ecclesial effect of the sacrament (different in each case) is the permanent foundation of this subsequent bestowal of grace within the
limits of the sacramental contact with the Church, which may be
absolutely unrepeatable, relatively unrepeatable, or repeatable.
Therefore it is sometimes said legalistically that the sacraments also
give the right to actual grace; this means that man living by the
sacraments is never alone, but that, united with the God who is ever
active, he is carrying out his commissions as a Christian.

The fruitfulness of a sacrament in grace, then, includes all the
richness of Christian life in communion with the Church, the visible
sign of grace in which the fullness of Christ is present. The Church,
the *pleroma* of Christ, fills us with the fullness of him who is filled

with the fullness of God. And this is man's encounter with God in full mutual availability.[29]

3. THE RELIGIOUS VALUE OF THE SACRAMENTS IN THE SEPARATED CHRISTIAN CHURCHES

In connection with the questions we have been treating, "sacraments of desire" and the way in which the ecclesial sacraments confer grace, something must be said about the religious worth of the sacraments in those Christian Churches which have become separated from Rome. In order to deal with this point in its proper context we must begin by briefly considering the meaning of the sacraments for the Reformation.[30]

Quite apart from the complication that Protestants differ among themselves in their interpretation of the sacraments, it is difficult for a Catholic to present a Protestant view fairly and correctly, for we are too readily inclined, thinking as we do in terms of Catholic dogma and theology, to uproot the Protestant terms and try to explain them outside their proper context. Consider, for example, the doctrine of *sola fides,* justification by faith alone. Catholic theology has given us an ordered analysis of justification and the disposition towards justification and we judge the Protestant belief along the lines of this scheme, not realizing that by so doing we fail from the start to appreciate its special character. The Protestant view of the sacraments derives from two basic doctrines: on the one hand, from the view of grace as purely and entirely the generosity of

[29] There is another special effect of sacramental grace which we shall deal with separately in the seventh chapter.

[30] A selection of Protestant literature on the sacraments: D. H. Asmussèn, *Das Sakrament,* Stuggart (1948); W. Aalders, *Kultuur en sacrament,* Nijkerk (1948); G. C. Berkouwer, *De Sacramenten. Dogmatische studiën,* Kampen (1954); W. F. Dankbaar, *De sacramentsleer van Calvijn,* Amsterdam (1941); G. van der Leeuw, *Sacramentstheologie,* Nijkerk (1949), *Les Sacrements* (Collection "Protestantisme"), Paris (1942). See too, W. H. van de Pol, *Karakteristiek van het reformatorisch Christendom,* Rœrmond-Maasiek (1952).

God and in this sense onesided (though in modern Protestant writings it appears that this onesidedness is not exclusive and does call for some reciprocity); on the other hand, from the concept of the Church as no more than the community of true believers who, keeping the body of Christ in being, constantly reform it. The genuine administration of the sacraments is possible and their meaning can be grasped only within the community of true believers conducting itself according to the word of God; only there do the sacraments have any religious significance, and only in these circumstances do they have the character of a divine institution (cf. the *Netherlands Confession,* art. 29). Upon this principle the existence, number, meaning and manner of administration of the sacraments in the Catholic Church are subjected to criticism.

The Protestant notion of the sacraments can be understood only in the light of the peculiarly Protestant theology of the Covenant, for though much of their terminology is superficially similar to our own, it embodies a spirituality that is entirely different. Calvin could speak of sacraments containing and really giving grace; nevertheless there is a world of difference between their Calvinist and Catholic interpretations.

God's promise, his grace, comes to us through the announcing of the word. The word of God calls upon man and places him in a new relationship to God. The revealing word makes known to us this new relationship in which God places us; this relation is salvation, grace, reconciliation. Now the revealing word comes to us in two ways; through preaching and through the Church's sacraments. Through both of these, and through the act of faith, man receives a share in that salvation. The reality which the sacraments mediate is, therefore, the objective fact that God has graciously spoken to man. Preaching remains primary; the sacraments underscore what the preaching has told me, that what Christ did once and for all on the Cross concerns me, the recipient of the sacrament, personally; and so the sacraments bring about and strengthen the act of faith in the grace-giving word of God. Therefore the reality received in the sacraments is the same that came to us through the preaching in which we believe. The sacraments only emphasize the fact that God's word is something which is valid for me personally.

Justification through faith, or rather, through the word of God in which he takes hold of me by way of faith, is the basis of the whole Protestant interpretation of the sacraments. "The sacraments are holy visible signs and seals, instituted by God, in order that by the use thereof he may the more fully declare and seal to us the promise of the Gospel, namely: that he of grace grants us forgiveness of sin and life eternal, for the sake of that one sacrifice of Christ, finished on the Cross."[31]

Therefore the sacraments presuppose God's promise, without which they would be meaningless. They are an addition to this promise, of which the word assures us. The addition of the sacraments to the preaching does not imply any insufficiency in God's spoken revelation, a gap which the sacraments would fill. The word alone is enough. The sacraments are a strengthening, not of God's own word, but of our faith in the word. They are necessary not because the word of God might lack complete assurance but because the human heart, hardened and insensitive, obscures it. (Calvin, *Institutions*, 4, 14, 3.) Hence they are signs and divine seals of God's promise, meant to strengthen our faith (4, 14, 9), witnesses of God's grace (4, 14, 7). In the sacraments it is therefore not possible to separate sign from God's activity in the sign. Only through the Spirit of God who convinces you, by sacramental confirmation of the word, of the truth and reality of the divine promise, is it possible to grasp by faith the trustworthy and unfailing word of God, and in faith to give yourself over to it. Therefore, it would be incorrect to call the Protestant sacraments "mere signs," *signa nuda*. It is true that Zwingli considered them to be such, but Calvin and Protestants in general have always reacted against this view. Calvin teaches explicitly that the sacraments have a divine and saving power beyond the psychological force of their value as

---

[31] The *Heidelberg Catechism*, Q. 66 (this translation is taken from *The Doctrinal Standards and Liturgy of the Reformed Dutch Church*, Cape Town [1876], p. 20).

signs: they are really "filled with much power" (4, 14, 9). The sacramental sign has a significance in the hand of God who acts through it, and in virtue of its divine institution it is "full of power for the faith." "So God effects everything in us that he shows us through these holy signs." (*Netherlands Confession,* art. 35.) This is a radical denial of any possible distinction between validity and fruitfulness. A sacrament administered on God's command (apart from which it cannot exist) can never lapse into pretence or fiction. To the Protestant mind it is simply unthinkable that an act in the power of grace (and a sacrament is the divine sealing of such an act) should not penetrate into the human heart, or should be hindered by the lack of right dispositions in the recipient. In Catholic terminology, a valid but unfruitful sacrament is impossible. A sacrament, as God's institution and act, always has a saving worth; if it did not then God's promise (the genuineness of which is guaranteed by the sacrament) would be untruthful and untrustworthy.

It is clear that the background of this interpretation of the sacraments is the correlation between faith and God's promise. Sacrament and faith belong together; they are constituted by the divine promise precisely in their relation to one other. The conjunction of sign and what is signified enters into the definition of the sacrament. A sacrament, therefore, is not only a pledge of the divine mercy and generosity, but as a pledge it is also the outward sealing of the genuineness of my own inward submission to God's action in me. God's pledge and my submission are inseparable, and this shows that faith is essentially a divine act in me, an act which has nothing whatever to do with my merit or good dispositions. Grace, the Protestants say, is irresistible; its movement cannot be checked by the free will of man. G. C. Berkouwer has expressed this view clearly and concisely: "[A sacrament] has meaning only in relation to the word of promise, and so it can enter the personal sphere of God's addressing us in promise which at the same time makes room for a relationship in which subjectivity is not opposed to objectivity, but in which the subjectivity of faith rests in the Word of God." (*De Sacramenten,* 91.)

From this the Protestants also determine the number of the sacraments, and the same principles explain their attitude to the Catholic teaching of the minister's intention. Because the sacraments are divine seals of the divine promise through the instrumentality of earthly elements, these elements cannot contain this meaning of themselves, but only by the power of God's institution. Therefore the visible sign must have been instituted clearly by Christ and on the principle of *sola scriptura* the institution must be clear and evident in Scripture.

Although a definitive decision on the number of the sacraments was arrived at only gradually—absolution offered the longest resistance to innovation in this respect—it was eventually agreed that there are only two sacraments, baptism and the Lord's Supper, since Scripture attests clearly to these two alone, and these alone are intelligible on the principle that the sacraments are essentially the sealing or confirmation of God's promise.

Because the power of the sacraments comes from God's promise which we take hold of by faith, and because on the other hand the Church is not a saving institution but purely the community of all true believers, the intention of the minister does not enter into the sacramental event in any way. The sacraments are God's confirmation of his own promise. It makes no difference whether the minister enters into this event with religious intent or whether he merely pretends to do so, or even ridicules it.

When Protestants say that the power of the sacraments comes from faith, they do not mean that the sacramental economy of salvation is something purely subjective. They mean that the power of the sacraments derives from God's promise which takes a hold on us by faith. In this there is no denial of the objective reality of the sacraments, but rather an outlook on grace and faith totally different from ours. In the Protestant view it is impossible to speak of an objectivity in grace and sacraments which would be extrinsic to faith. "Faith" here means not "the faith of the Church" in the Catholic sense, into which a believer enters personally (for without *this* faith we too can acknowledge no saving reality: "un au-delà de la pensée est impensable"; otherwise we should be agnostics), but *fides subjecti* or the faith of the individual. Without this contact in faith with God everything would be meaningless; the sacraments would signify nothing.

Up to now we have been looking chiefly into the Calvinist interpretation of the sacraments. The Lutheran view is closer to the Catholic. Luther held determinedly to the objective power of the sacraments to save. This comes out very clearly in his *De Captivitate Babylonica* where, writing on infant baptism, he says: "by the prayer of the Church which believes and offers [sacrifice], and for which all is possible, even a little child is changed, purified and renewed by the faith infused into it."[32] Faith which alone can save performs its miracle of grace in the very act of baptism itself. Luther affirms the objective realism of the sacraments much more strongly than Calvin. This is very clear in the Lutheran doctrine of the Eucharist, which comes close to the realism of the Catholic doctrine. It would probably be correct to say that Luther believed quite simply in earthly signs which signify and bestow supernatural realities, but that this Catholic notion becomes distorted in his thinking because of his denial of the Church as a saving institute and of the office of the priesthood.

We may now ask whether these sacraments have any religious value. Needless to say baptism, as it is usually administered by Protestants, is recognized as valid by the Catholic Church. Where the sacrament is valid there is no special problem in the strict sense of the word. A problem does arise, however, about sacraments which may be administered only by a priest who is validly ordained, but which are administered among Protestants by persons who are not ordained. In practice the problem is confined to the sacrament of the Lord's Supper, the Protestant Eucharist or Holy Communion service. The Catholic faith does not allow us to consider this a valid sacrament. For some theologians this seems to settle the question; at most they would agree that there may be a certain purely sub-

[32] Cf. *Opera Omnia*, Frankfurt ed., vol. 3, p. 87.

jective religious value in this Protestant sacramental rite. But the
matter is not quite as simple as that. Hans Asmussen, an Evangelical theologian in Germany, has put the problem to Catholics in
clear and striking terms.[33] He accepts the fact that according to
Catholic doctrine the celebration of the Lord's Supper, presided
over by the Evangelical minister, cannot be a valid sacrament. We
Evangelicals, he says, must try to understand this attitude. He himself is deeply disturbed by it. And he asks Catholics whether they
would prefer the Evangelicals not to celebrate this sacrament because it is heretical, or whether they are glad that Evangelicals do
live a sacramental life. In other words, he is asking Catholic theologians to answer clearly whether or not the Protestant sacrament
has any value at all. The question, as I see it, is genuine and in
earnest, arising from a profound reverence for the real will of Christ
and a sincere love of the gospel.

What is our answer to be? Obviously in posing this problem we
have in mind those individuals and religious communities who are,
to use the Catholic terminology, Protestant or Evangelical in "good
faith." In order not to discuss the question in the void, I would like
first to describe briefly the liturgical rite of the Communion Service
followed at present in several Reformed Churches in the Netherlands.

The ceremony begins with an introductory text from Scripture:
Ps. 34 (the psalms vary; I am taking the example of a service which
I have been able to attend). Then the congregation sings a psalm
(Ps. 24). Next the presiding minister greets those present: "The
grace and peace of God our Father and of our Lord Jesus Christ
be with you." The people respond: "And with your spirit." Then
comes a confession of guilt, followed by a psalm (Ps. 51). After
the minister has proclaimed God's grace, the congregation sings a
hymn. The minister then prays, "Lord, open my lips," and the
people reply, "And my mouth shall announce thy praise." The
minister invites the congregation: "Come, let us adore the Lord

---

[33] "Fünf Fragen an die Katholische Kirche," in *Una Sancta,* 2 (1956), pp.
127ff.

who made us," and all sing Ps. 150, concluding with: "Glory be to the Father and to the Son and to the Holy Spirit, as it was in the beginning is now and ever shall be, world without end. Amen."

Next there are readings from Scripture: on this particular day they were Isa. 55.1–7; Apoc. 19.6–9; Luke 5.27–32, followed by a hymn. At this point the Creed (Nicene) is read solemnly by the minister, the people answering: Amen. Prayers follow: a morning prayer, some prayers special to the occasion, a Communion prayer, and the *Our Father* (together). After this, the actual celebration of the Communion Service begins. The minister goes to prepare the Communion table—a long table in a central position, covered with a cloth and with seats around it. The minister takes a loaf and breaks it into as many portions as are necessary; he pours wine into a chalice. The congregation meanwhile sings a hymn. When all is ready, the minister reads solemnly the words of institution. There is a general invitation to partake of the meal, and those present move to their places at the table. The minister gives each a particle of bread, which is taken in the hand and then consumed. Then he passes the chalice (two chalices if there are many communicants) around; all sip from it. While those present remain seated with bowed heads, the minister says a prayer of praise and thanksgiving (a *communio*). Then all return to their places, and the congregation begins a hymn. The ceremony closes with a blessing by the minister: "The grace of our Lord Jesus Christ, and the love of God, and the fellowship of the Holy Spirit, be with you all." (2 Cor. 13.13.) Having answered "Amen," the congregation leaves the church.

This is approximately the structure of the ceremony of the Lord's Supper in its modern form (the result of various, perhaps even of some "romanizing," liturgical reforms brought about in our own day). It would be superfluous to say anything about the value of this ceremony as prayer; we are clearly considering a community prayerfully confessing its faith in Christ. But that is not all. Since we hold with St. Thomas that even the pagan "sacraments of nature" possess a religious value, and again with St. Thomas find an implicit reference to the mystery of Christ in them, *a fortiori* it is clear that the sacraments in the separated Christian Churches have a certain "sacramental" value, more so even than the Jewish sacraments, and that to the same extent they contain grace. This is not merely the engracing quality of human sacramentality in general; it is explicitly a part of Christianity. Christians of the Reformed Churches really mean to return to the Eucharist as it was instituted by Christ. True enough, this does not make the Communion Service even partially a valid or genuinely ecclesial sacrament of the Church of Christ. In this sense there is no sacrament here, for according to Catholic faith (which for us is an absolute principle) the true ideal of the sacrament committed to us by Christ has been seriously misrepresented. This, however, does not conclude the matter, for we must take other aspects into account; aspects in which this ceremony has really, though invalidly, a positive and Christian significance. I want to examine this delicate question closely, in the light of Thomistic principles.

St. Thomas, it is true, did not deal with this question. He speaks only of priests who, though validly ordained, have broken with the Church, or of priests who are validly ordained in schismatic Churches.[34] Naturally he did not know of the Reformation. Nevertheless we find in his works the fundamental principles which will enable us to estimate the true value of this new situation. First of all, whoever is validly baptized (and baptism is valid in most of the Protestant confessions) possesses an inner orientation to the Catholic sacrament of the Eucharist.[35] Furthermore, valid baptism is implicitly a "Eucharist of desire."[36] Therefore in virtue of their baptism Christians of the Reformation have an inner orientation to the Catholic Eucharist. For the baptism is truly a Catholic sacrament which in consequence incorporates them not into the separated community but into the Catholic Church (presupposing their "good faith," which is normally verifiable in the present situa-

---

[34] *ST*, III, q. 82, a. 7 and a. 8.
[35] *ST*, III, q. 65, a. 3; q. 73, a. 3; *In ad Joh.*, 6, lect. 6.
[36] *ST*, III, q. 80, a. 9, ad 3, with the quotation from St. Augustine.

tion).[37] Objectively, valid baptism is a *votum eucharistiae* or a "Eucharist of desire"; no single grace comes to us, says St. Thomas, except through a desire, at least implicit, for the Eucharist.[38] For the *res sacramenti,* the essential effect of the sacrament of the Eucharist, the "unity of the Mystical Body," is absolutely necessary for salvation.[39] Yet it is not absolutely necessary that we achieve this effect through the real sacramental reception of the Eucharist. A "Eucharist of desire" suffices, and is necessary for salvation. Celebrating the Communion Service, and being firmly convinced that he is following Christ's will by so doing, an Evangelical Christian undoubtedly possesses a "Eucharist of desire"; therefore in this liturgical celebration he really participates in the *res sacramenti* or in the effect of the sacrament (though not to the full; see below).

Up to now we have remained to some extent in the subjective aspects of grace. But we may go further. According to St. Thomas a "Eucharist of desire" is possible in two ways: Through conscious longing for the fruit of the Eucharist (for example, through a so-called "spiritual communion") and through the objective orientation in a particular sacramental rite which *in figura* (as a foreshadowing) points towards the Catholic sacrament; in this way the fathers in the desert, eating the manna, really communicated "in a spiritual manner."[40] This is more than a mere "spiritual communion." It is the spiritual reception of the sacrament itself: "This is not only to eat Christ spiritually but also to partake spiritually of the [true Catholic] sacrament."[41] Such a statement has many and far-reaching consequences. For it is impossible to deny that the Protestant rite of the Lord's Supper is truly a *figura Eucharistiae,*

---

[37] "Quamvis haereticus per fidem rectam non sit membrum Ecclesiae, tamen in quantum servat morem Ecclesiae in baptizando, baptismum Ecclesiae tradit; unde regnerat filios Christo et Ecclesiae, non sibi vel haeresi suae" (*IV Sent.,* d. 6, q. 1, a. 3, sol. 2, ad 2); their entry into the separated Church takes place only in the conscious act of choice which they may elicit later.

[38] *ST,* III, q. 79, a. 1, ad 1.

[39] *ST,* III, q. 79, a. 1, ad 1; q. 73, a. 3; q. 80, a. 11.

[40] *ST,* III, q. 80, a. 1, ad 3.   [41] *Loc. cit.*

more so than the manna, more so even than the Jewish Passover meal. It is not merely a foreshadowing, it is a direct commemoration of the Last Supper, even if not in the full ecclesial sense of the word. Some of the fundamental aspects of the Catholic Eucharist are lacking in the Protestant Communion Service, but others are retained in it. And this is sufficient to enable us to apply with even greater right the ancient patristic and scholastic view of non-Catholic sacraments as *vestigia Ecclesiae,* traces of the true Church of Christ, to the Protestant sacraments. The objection is made that this application is not valid precisely because we are dealing with schismatic sacraments, by which the true sacrament is excluded and in which, therefore, the relation to Christ disappears. But this objection holds only in a formal sense; that is, when the heresy is a formal one, not a divergence in good faith. Given good faith in any particular case the objection does not hold, because there is no formal rejection of that which Christ willed.

Consider, then, these three facts: The orientation of a valid baptism to the Catholic Eucharist; the genuine and honest desire to establish contact with Christ's sacrifice through the celebration of the Lord's Supper, and the objective Catholic traces which, we consider, are still discernible in the celebration of the Lord's Supper. As far as we can see these are sufficient reasons for holding that in the ceremony of the Lord's Supper there is more than merely a subjective religious value—we say this with reservation, for the teaching authority of the Church may possibly decide differently. The rite of the Communion Service (though it is not even partly a valid sacrament) is therefore a quasi-sacramental manifestation of an explicit eucharistic desire which, moreover, implicitly looks forward to the true fruits of the Catholic Eucharist. Thus in the Protestant Lord's Supper there is an intrinsic tendency towards integration into the Catholic Eucharist. Its objective religious value lies in this tendency, and therefore this value derives in the ultimate analysis from the Catholic Eucharist itself. In all this the force of the general Catholic teaching is maintained: only the true reception of the real sacrament can bestow the fullness of eucharistic grace (and this holds true of both "spiritual communion" and the reception of a *figura sacramenti*).

The conclusion, then, is obvious. Though we as Catholics have the apostolic duty to desire the return of all separated Christians to the true Eucharist, until that comes about it can only be a joy to us that Evangelical believers lead, in good faith, an intense and frequent sacramental life, and that through their celebration of the Lord's Supper they really grow in unity with Christ and with men. However paradoxical it may seem, this celebration is implicitly a sincere prayer *ut omnes unum sint*. When the World Council of Churches gathers to strive for greater unity in the Church through theological discussion, the Lord's Supper which they celebrate in common will do far more to achieve this unity than all discussions—though these are necessary too.

6

SACRAMENTAL ENCOUNTERS WITH CHRIST: CULMINATING MOMENTS IN THE ECCLESIAL CHARACTER OF CHRISTIAN LIFE

1. SACRAMENTAL AND EXTRA-SACRAMENTAL GRACE

A question often arises concerning the purpose of the sacraments: Are they needed for our approach to Christ? Those who put this question make a distinction between the normal and the unusual ways in which grace is given. They then argue that when the sacramentality of the Church is disregarded inculpably through ignorance, the grace of Christ, though coming in an unusual manner, can produce the same wonders of holiness as when it comes through the sacraments. But this we cannot grant.

We must remember that the essential factor in ecclesial sacramentality is Christ's eternally actual redemptive act, made to concern each one of us personally. This comes about through Christ's Church, the earthly manifestation of his will to redeem us. Now this heavenly act can affect and influence men outside the sacraments, although it will not then be *visibly* present among them. This may indeed be called an extra-sacramental bestowal of grace, but nevertheless the Church will always be involved in it even if only through the daily sacrifice of the Eucharist for the good of all men. When we too receive grace apart from the sacraments it comes through Christ the Mediator in and through his Church, primordial sacrament.

It is from these facts that we must begin to investigate the relationship between the sacramental and the extra-sacramental bestowal of grace. We should first notice that in the natural order, alongside the decisive and central acts of life, there are everyday actions which call for a personal involvement of a lesser kind.[1] In the same way there are decisive Christian acts and everyday ones. There is moreover another psychological aspect which must not be neglected. The human body and its contacts with the world around are the realities through which and in which the soul grows to personality, just as they are the realities through which the soul expresses its personal development. In human activity a person's own bodiliness is an aspect of the active subject. The bodily expression is not merely the manifestation of a free spiritual act after it has already been fully achieved in pure interiority; the spiritual act can only be achieved in incarnation. Because it is only an imperfect revelation of the inward personal act, the outward element is only a sign of that act. Every personal act is one and undivided; in it the interior element is made visible at the same time as it is given its fully personal and human character by its opposite pole, the bodily element.[2]

There is a similar relationship between a religious act which is sacramental and one which is not. That which is lived out in an everyday manner outside the sacraments grows to its full maturity in them (this, at least, is the purpose of the sacramental system of salvation). Seen from Christ's point of view, the sacraments are the express taking-hold of the man who receives them, because they are the earthly manifestation of the heavenly act of redemption. But the response to Christ's willing availability in encounter must therefore grow in the recipient to a culminating point which is personal and decisive. It is partly on human grounds that this response

[1] This distinction has been investigated by continental philosophers. Cf., among other works, G. Gusdorf, *La Découverte de soi*, Paris (1948), pp. 504ff.

[2] Cf. Karl Rahner, "Personale und sakramentale Frömmigkeit," *Schriften zur Theologie*, 2, pp. 115–41—although we cannot entirely agree with the many passages in which the author makes the constitution of a personal act —and not merely its human character—depend on the bodily element.

is possible, since the recipient humanly realizes his desire for grace in the visibility of the Church which is full of grace. This desire for grace is made manifest in a definite and tangible form in which the human person is entirely involved in concentrated action, taken hold of as he is by a tangible action of Christ. The anonymity of everyday Christian living is removed by the telling power of Christ's symbolic action in and through his Church.

The fact that the sacraments are (or should be) culminating moments in a personal Christian life is something that rests on more than merely human grounds (on these alone the sacraments would only be of relative importance). The supremely important character of the sacraments derives from the fact that they bring a person's desire for grace to ecclesial manifestation (this fact does of course include psychological elements). So through the sacraments the individual's desire for grace is linked with the redemptive power of that mystical body which is one with Christ. Again they are culminating moments because they are a special divine contact with a person in a situation which, for the Christian view of life, is decisive. The sacraments bring about the encounter with Christ in exactly those seven instances in which, on account of the demands of a special situation of Christian life, a man experiences a special and urgent need of communion with him. They are the divine act of redemption itself, manifest in the sacred environment of the living Church, making a concrete appeal to man and taking hold of him in a living way, as really as does the embrace of a mother for her child. And it is not enough for the child merely to know that its mother loves it; it needs the actual embrace to perfect the experience of love.

On the other hand these special moments are prepared for, depend upon, and can be intensified by growing maturity of soul in the everyday acts of life, just as they may be weakened by everyday acts in which all fervour is lacking. Therefore, the sacraments cannot be isolated from the organic unity of a whole persevering Christian life. Thus it may also happen that experiences of God may be more intense outside the sacraments than during their actual reception. The sacraments determine the objective importance of certain moments in life, to which we personally and in a religious spirit must give full value. But besides these moments which are decisive objectively, in the life of a religious person, there can be others which are of vital importance subjectively. These extra-sacramental bestowals of grace can in fact raise the Christian to greater heights than the grace received in the sacraments them-selves. The sacraments are necessary as markers, milestones on the way, so that by living the Christian life *as a whole* we may become more and more one with Christ.

Again we should not forget that every grace coming to a baptized person bears, in the last analysis, a relation to his sacramental status as baptized. Baptism is a blessing on the whole of life. In the same way in marriage the strength to face all the moments of difficulty and decision in life comes from the sacramental grace of mat-rimony. The practice of religion in the Church—the regular recep-tion of the sacraments—is therefore a vital and necessary condition for a living awareness of communion with God.

2. THE CHRISTIAN LIFE ITSELF AS SACRAMENT OF THE ENCOUNTER WITH GOD

Besides the duty frequently to receive the sacraments, the official acts of the Church as means of salvation, the faithful have the further duty to practise their religion in a broader sense, though still in close connection with the mystery of the primordial sacra-ment, the Church.

The problem of ecclesial living has been presented very clearly in books such as those of Fr. I. Rosier[3] and Fr. J. Loew.[4] Rosier wishes a distinction to be made between "churchlessness," a

---

[3] *Ik Zocht Gods afwezigheid,* The Hague, vol. 1 (1956), vol. 2 (1957); *I Looked for God's Absence: France,* New York, Sheed and Ward (1960). See too, I. Gadourek, *Cultuuraanvaarding en Cultuurontwikkeling,* Gron-ingen (1958), and P. Smits, *Op zoek naar nihilisme,* Assen (1959).

[4] *Journal d'une mission ouvrière,* Paris (1959).

state of withdrawal from the reception of ritual sacraments, and "dechristianization." Among the several causes of churchlessness, he finds, the most important is the lack of a true familiarity in the Church's approach to us in its liturgy, in its sacraments, in the whole form in which it manifests itself on earth. Many describe the condition of the workers as dechristianized, but Rosier writes: "The world of the worker still belongs to the Church as the community of all who have been redeemed by Christ, though it remains outside the Church's historically developed forms."[5] There is a grain of truth in this, and we should do well to dwell upon the problem for a moment, to bring it out. It will moreover help us to avoid the error of limiting the meaning of religious practice (and thus of ecclesial existence) to "regular attendance at Mass and frequent confession."

We have already said that the Church, as the visible presence of grace among us, is made up of both clergy and laity, the priestly hierarchy and the faithful People of God together. It is this whole community of the faithful which is the "sign raised up among the nations." The ecclesial (i.e., the sacramentally visible) presence of grace is not something which merely proceeds from the ecclesiastical hierarchy and from the characters of baptism and confirmation in the faithful; it is something which also arises, and proceeds visibly, from the inward communion of the faithful in grace with Christ the Lord. In this connection, many of the faithful have a kind of totalitarian notion of the Church, and confuse the absolute claims of a Church in which the hierarchy does hold the office of administration of Christ's visible grace with a sort of secular dictatorial power arrogated to itself by the Church, and making of the laity nothing more than a group of subjects who can carry out only what the hierarchy decides they must do. This notion is not only incorrect; it is completely alien to the true character of the Church and in fact heretical.

The Spirit of Christ, the active principle of the entire Church,

[5] *Ik Zocht,* etc., vol. 1, p. 218.

leads and guides her not only through the hierarchy, from above, but also through the faithful, from below. Both office and charism are essential to the whole of the Church, and both come under the guidance of Christ the Lord. Both are ecclesial. When we look for the way in which the Church is a sign raised up among the nations to show to all the victorious Christ, we must look not only to the teaching authority of the Church and to its pastoral government but also, and as essentially, to the Christian lives of the faithful: to their constancy, as to their unselfish love and goodness, to the humility and faith and resignation with which they bear life's difficulties, to the living Christian example and the responsibility of a father and a mother, to the courage and purity of heart which is visible in their actions, to the virginity of those who consecrate themselves wholly to Christ, to the "old maids" who, though they may not have wanted to remain unmarried, nevertheless do not become soured by their lot but know how to give it the meaningfulness of a new vocation.

All of these are true manifestations of the Church, the visible presence of grace among us. So are the various forms of desire for grace: the appearance among the laity of a variety of Christian movements, of hopes and trends towards new forms of Christian life and activity—in all this the Spirit of Christ is guiding and governing the Church. The works that Christian artists and thinkers achieve through the strength of their life in the eucharistic communion in grace, the forces they release in the context and in the mind of all Christendom—all this is a true part of the reality of the Church, all this is the visible activity of grace among us, a sacrament of God's love for men. In some periods of the Church's history the movements created by Christian writers and thinkers and the results they have produced have done far more to manifest the presence of grace than has the hierarchical government of the Church. These various, constantly renewed and often surprising activities, all having their source in the charisms of the ecclesial communion in grace, should in our own times be getting much more attention than they are. To live as a member of the Church means much more than simply to practise one's religion in the narrow sense of the word "practise." Beside regular reception of the sacraments, and no less essentially than this, it means giving a visible reality in our everyday life to our faith, our hope and our love; to our holiness itself.

The Spirit of Christ breathes where he will, not only on the Pope and among the ranks of the bishops, but also among the people and their priests. The assistance of the Spirit which Christ has granted to his Church is not only for the exercise of the hierarchical office in the Church, but for the life of the Church in every other aspect too. It is granted to the whole community of believers. True, the whole life of the Church remains under the control of the Church's authority, which is supreme and from which there is no possible appeal. But it is of the essence of the ecclesial character of the hierarchy that it allow the true ecclesial character of the laity its proper scope. All sorts of tension can arise from this double aspect of ecclesial character. We do not want to examine them now. We want simply to point out that what we believe in is this Church as it is in the concrete, the living Church of Christ, and not an abstract ideal. We believe in the visible presence of grace among us, a communion in which nevertheless we still find sin. This is the Church that is the object of our faith.

Throughout its history there have been individuals who have allowed themselves to be so scandalized by its weakness that they became blind to its strength and grace, visible and untarnished, constantly living and spreading. Again and again men have fallen into the heresy of regarding the Church as merely the invisible communion of those who truly live in the union of grace with Christ. They deny the Church its incarnation. They take away not only its weakness and sinfulness but also the visibility of its grace, which means that they take away grace itself. We must be able to achieve that strength of faith which will enable us to believe in the Church as it is; that is to believe in it as manifestation of Christ's redeeming grace, and by the same faith to accept that in head and in members all is not yet wholly what is proper to it as Church; there is still some human weakness, lack of understanding, impersonal mechanical routine, and especially in past times—why should we be shy of historical fact?—earthly lust for power and crass covetousness. Let us say again, the Church as such is holy. That belongs to its essence. In this sense St. John says, "Whosoever is born of God commits no sin . . . he cannot sin because he is born of God,"[6] and he says this because the Church is a reality, not something ethereal, divorced from the facts of experience. "We know that whosoever is born of God does not sin."[7] And yet, when the same St. John is speaking of Christians, he says, "If we say that we have no sin, we deceive ourselves."[8] If this does not involve a contradiction, what does it mean? It means that in the Church all is not yet wholly what should belong to it as such.

The Church is the visible shape of salvation, the sign filled with the reality it signifies. Its members can therefore sin only to the extent to which they positively withdraw themselves from its sanctifying influence. To the extent that a man sins, he is outside the Church; in himself, and thus in his place in the Church, he brings about a rupture between the sign and the reality it signifies. All of this implies that the Church has not yet reached its final state. For we cannot hold that it will cease to exist at the end of time, and make place for a purely spiritual communion of the saints in grace. In virtue of Christ's incarnation the bodily visibility of grace is not a provisional and temporary measure but the definitive reality. Only in heaven will the Church reach its full maturity, still as a visible saving society. The resurrection of all flesh establishes and perpetuates in glory the earthly history of the Church, just as the personal holiness which the saints have fought for and won in this life will be visible in their bodies when they rise again. All that is weak and sad and troublesome will have disappeared from the Church in heaven, but it will continue to show us the face of its holiness in the visibility that comes of incarnation. Indeed, only in heaven shall we see this to the full.

[6] 1 John 3.9.   [7] 1 John 5.18.
[8] 1 John 1.8.

The Church, as the earthly sign of the triumph of Christ's grace, still remains in a state of weakness, needing to purge itself of all that is sinful. This fact shows us two things; first that the glory of the Church on earth is a veiled glory, for around it there is still a broad margin of weakness and shortcoming; and second, and more especially, that the power of God is fulfilled in and through the weakness and poverty of the Church. The Church is great and glorious, but not on account of its earthly strength and achievements; in it Christ's redeeming grace always triumphs in spite of human weakness. It is in this weakness that the divine power comes into its own and becomes visible as divine. The Church is therefore not only the object of our faith; it is also the test of our faith. It can become an obstacle and a danger to faith. For belief is not a conviction to which a person is forced by the glory of the Church manifest in his experience of her. We always believe in the midst of darkness. And if we look at it in this way, the weakness of the Church is a *felix culpa*, for it makes us realize that our only boast is in the power of God. Just as Christ was a scandal to the Jews because to the Jewish mind he set himself up in opposition to Yahweh, so too the Church must pass through its pilgrimage, poor and despised, for the power of redeeming grace alone will bring the victory. This is the real strength of our faith in the Church.

The Church is not only the ecclesial community in which we believe; at the same time it provides the motive for a morally and rationally justified faith. The First Vatican Council valued this motive highly and emphasized it: "The Church is the sign raised up among the nations, inviting all who do not yet believe." The Church (once again, not only the hierarchical Church, but also the charismatic activity of the whole People of God) allows us to experience, as St. Paul says, that "God is among you indeed."[9] We must go more closely into this matter.

[9] 1 Cor. 14.25. In this passage St. Paul is writing of the charismata characteristic of the primitive Church, especially of the gifts of tongues and of prophecy. He makes rules to preserve the harmony of the whole community in the exercise of these gifts. St. Paul himself says that it is the visible charism of the whole community that proves such an effective sign

In the genesis and in the exercise of supernatural faith, there are always two elements present, two kinds of witness: (1) The inward invitation to faith coming from the power of God's grace which draws us, and (2) the historical realization of this grace, its "outward conferring." This latter is tangible reality, part of our human experience, which, united with God's inward appeal, embodies it in our actual situation. For God has given outward reality to the interior call to personal communion with himself. Naturally (and quite rightly) this immediately recalls the saving history of Israel and of the life of the man Jesus. But historically speaking, all this is long past. To people who live today the meaning of saving history and of the Church is found in encounter with present-day Christians and their priests. Our Christian life must therefore be the outward embodiment of God's interior call to grace in the hearts of our fellow men. Christian living, the experience of encounter with saints living among us, is the true apologetic for our faith. All that is good in a man already responds to the call of grace within him, but it is the personal holiness of us Christians and of our priests that must make others consciously aware of the call within themselves. For all men, encounters with their fellow men are the sacrament of encounter with God.

If a certain heresy is not confined to just one period of the Church's history, but taking on new forms recurs again and again, this heresy must contain a grain of truth. Such, for example, is the error of those who become scandalized at the unholiness of Christians and consequently deny the visibility of the Church. This shows that men are led to belief by the Church only when they can discover a genuine holiness truly incarnate in the Christians they meet. Incarnate love, the love of God transposed into brotherly love for our fellow men, is the irresistible motive of credibility for the Christian faith. It is this that confronts men with the reality of salvation in the midst of daily life. In the course of their life men can

---

of the presence of grace in the Church: "But if all prophesy, and there come in one that believeth not . . . he will adore God, affirming that God is among you indeed." (1. Cor. 14.24–5.) (Tr.)

encounter grace visibly present in such a way that they cannot avoid it, but must decide for or against.

But if this is the case, then it is necessary for the Church's holiness to become truly visible to all men. In this, it seems to me, we find the main crisis facing its present-day apostolate. Very many indeed have wearied of the Church precisely because its outward appearance is so disappointing. We find signs of this at a very early stage in its history. St. Augustine himself complained ". . . those who had already come close to me on the way to believing . . . are frightened away far too often by the bad lives of evil and false Christians. How many, my brothers, do you think there are who want to become Christians, but are put off by the evil ways of Christians?"[10] It is symptomatic that in the Western world, in which the Church has been rooted for centuries, the mass of the people no longer see or hear its witness. It is so easy simply to pass Christianity by. Hence in one way or another the witness, the telling visibility of the grace of Christ, is kept hidden. Yet it cannot be said that the level of the Church's holiness has fallen. There are, therefore, only two possible explanations: Either human encounter is no longer made use of as the effective sacrament of our love of God, and Christians sanctify themselves in their own little corner without having any contact with the rest of the world, or where new methods of approach in apostolic work have re-established a living contact with men, this human encounter is not sufficiently an interpretation of an inward encounter with God, a sacrament of divine love, but merely a new kind of convert propaganda.

It seems to me that both explanations are valid. To develop an awareness and an appreciation of the fact that the power of appeal in Christianity lies in the visible presence of grace, in the sense just explained, is not simply another tactic, a new method of apostolate, but demands a real and unfeigned love of neighbour. To use this order of things as a technical method of religious efficiency would be to degrade holiness to the level of a means of propaganda. This

[10] *Ennarrationes in Psalmos,* ps. 30, sermo 2, 6. (*PL,* 36, col. 243.)

would destroy genuine holiness and therefore the power of attraction in the visible presence of grace. In our times we cannot recommend higher values to people by making speeches about them. People—to put it very bluntly—have had their bellyfull of our sermonizing. They are seeking a source of strength for their lives; they want a sense and a meaning that will give them this strength. The higher values and vital strength can be recommended to others only by making them actively present in ourselves. Contact with Christians must be an experience which proves to men that Christianity is a power transforming the whole of life. Through Amos his prophet God makes a reproach that could very often be laid at our door: "If you offer me holocausts and your gifts, I will not receive them. . . . Take away from me the tumult of your songs: and I will not hear the canticles of your harp. But let judgment flow as water, and justice as a mighty torrent."[11] Our existence and activity as Christians in the world is very often a dilution of the true visibility of a life redeemed in Christ. And in this, the very thing we minimize, we should recognize the rightful position of the laity, indeed of all believers, in the Church. We may go to Church on Sunday and abstain from meat on Friday—well and good—but we are still a long way from having made holiness a reality in the midst of this world. And until we do, we are obscuring the sign that the Church should be to all the world.

We must show a real love for our fellow men, and this love must truly be the sacrament of our love for God. But this sacramentality in its turn has an effect upon our human love for our fellow men, for however much we as believers can and should share the problems of unbelievers in order to retain side by side with them a solidarity in human experience, we cannot share their lack of redemption. A Christian's *présence au monde*, which is the great motive of credibility for the Christian faith, is always motivated by redemption. The Christian lives in the world because he lives in and with the living God; his is a redeeming presence.

[11] Amos 5.22–5.

For this reason not only may we not, in our human solidarity with unbelievers, go so far as to share with them those situations of life which are sinful (as the "priests of the poor" in Coccioli's unfortunate novel, *Le Ciel et la Terre*), but even in those situations, the common lot of all men, in which the disturbing results of the Fall are most clearly felt, our experience is essentially different from theirs. The tension and the suffering are not lessened for the Christian, but he knows that God "who gives joy to his youth" is with him. All this gives to the visible Church its persuasive power of drawing men. The miracles which, with fairly regular irregularity, occur in the life of the Church are after all a quasi-normal phenomenon accompanying the presence of truly holy people in this world. They are a motive of credibility not so much of themselves, but insofar as they point to the visible presence of grace in the midst of the world. Miracles spring from grace incarnate as normally as do sparks from a fire.

There have been some who have looked for the whole of salvation in human encounter (even though their actual approach to such encounter made it far too little of a sacrament). That they did so came from their acute awareness that Christianity possessed true doctrine and redemption, yet like treasure in a chest to which the key had been lost. The key is indeed a real approach to men, but it must be the expression of our love for God. We do not merely toss out dogmas to men who are crying out in dire need. We begin to teach Christian truth successfully by ourselves beginning to live for our fellow men. Our life must itself be the incarnation of what we believe, for only when dogmas are lived do they have any attractive power. Why in the main does Western man pass Christianity unnoticingly by? Surely because the visible presence of grace in Christians as a whole, apart from a few individuals, is no longer evident.

If Christianity is to be offered to men as something really worthy of their serious attention, this collective witness is once again urgently required. It is only then that the Church, the visible mystery, will come to occupy a central position in the ordinary everyday lives of men, and the others who are without faith will not be able to escape the challenge of Christianity, which will then be irresistible. There are so many people who are swept along by the world's current and who have never encountered, in their own particular environment, anyone whose life has suddenly brought them up against the idea that it is really possible to transform life into something more beautiful. People do discover their potential depths in the eyes of other men. The murderer was converted when he looked into the eyes of Christ on the Cross, and learned from them the depths of which his own heart too was capable. It is up to us as Christians to make the Church appear as visibly present to those people who are carried along by the current in this world, by providing the simple direct evidence of our Christian behaviour and way of life. We can thus give them a real desire for salvation, and make it possible for them to come to believe. This belongs essentially to our Christianity not only as apostles but in our total life in the Church.

It often seems, in this world, that people only want to make things difficult for each other, and consequently everyone is deeply impressed whenever he comes across truly disinterested generous love—charity, like a bright ray of light breaking through from another, higher world into our own. The result often is that a man is disarmed, and compelled to admit defeat. It is in cases like this that the essence of the Church, as the visible presence of grace in this world, is to be found, and that the Christian faith is seen, in concrete terms, to be worthy of man's acceptance. Whenever saints and sanctity are no longer visible in the world, we begin to live in darkness. Nonetheless, however painful this may be, we should not forget that even though there may be an insufficiency of visible grace peresent in and through the whole of Christian society, grace is all the same present and is able, as we have already said, to exert power in circumstances of impotence and misery. In this way the Church can be seen to be the lowly and submissive sacramental sign of the triumphant Christ. It is possible by means of this continual challenge to our faith to direct attention to the fact that the Church is not the work of man, but was instituted by God for man's salvation, and this can even act as a motive for becoming a member of the Church.

Let us express our answer to the problem we have posed in the the following way. There are only seven official sacraments, but there are numerous forms of sacramental expression within the life of the Church. It would be wrong to identify the life of the Church with that life which is confined within the bounds of the priesthood and the official sacraments. It is not exclusively from the sacraments that we derive grace—it also comes, for example, from fraternal contact between Christians and their treatment of each other and their fellow men; all this is included in practising the Church's pattern of life, and even "receiving a sacrament." Such contacts are certainly able to develop into a true conversion—a "confession." The seven sacraments are there precisely so that the sacramentalism of the Church, in its more extended sense, can be fully realized in everyday life. The truly Christian life in the midst of this world is— for other Christians—an external and meaningful supply of grace, dogma and preaching. Similarly, when non-Christians come into contact with those whose life is truly Christian, they are in fact coming up against the Church, as the visible and effective presence of grace in the world. It is through this kind of contact that they can be led to the full sacramental practice of Christianity, in which the Eucharist stands out as the point of centrality. It is true to say that, in one respect, there is a greater and more pressing need today for grace to be present and embodied in Christian life in this way— visibly present among men—than there is for a new and more modern form to be given to the Liturgy, in order to narrow the gap existing between it and the people. I feel sure that the first will lead to the second—that the visible presence of grace, embodied in the Christian way of life, will create a positive and dynamic force which will result in liturgical reform. After all, liturgies are not constructed—they develop organically from a renewed spirit. When this point has been reached, the sacraments will be able to exercise once again their true influence, which is of central importance in the life of the Church.

Since we have deliberately emphasized an aspect of the Church's pattern of life which is not usually stressed, it is important to bear in mind that the sacramental experience of Christian life, and thus the practice of Christianity in the more narrow sense of the word, occupies a central position in this way of life; the sacraments are at the very heart of Christianity. They are the centre from which the Christian life stands out in relief. It is by these central sacraments too that the level of Christian experience which has already been reached is raised. It is also vital for day-to-day Christian activity to keep in close touch with the sacraments, if it is to be prevented from becoming grey, featureless and quite anonymous. Once the sacramental way of life is abandoned, Christianity itself and, in the long run, any kind of "ecclesiality" whatever will be lost. Thus an element of truth can be found, deep down, in the rather colourless phrase so often used when referring to a Christian—"a man who still practises his faith." The sacramental experience is potentially the culminating point of all Christian experience. It is the apex of man's contact with God, in the shape of a contact with man—in this case, a priest—for it should not be forgotten that no one administers a sacrament to himself, but that a sacrament is always administered by and to another person, a fellow man. The sacrament thus forms the culminating point of the Church's appeal to us and bestowal of grace upon us, through the heavenly Christ who is present within her. Our stand as Christians in the world, our encounter with living Christianity through our contact with our fellow men, in other words our way of life as practising Catholics in the wider (but no less essential) sense of the word—all this has the effect of increasing our desire for the fullness and perfection of sacramental contact with the Church. What we must infer from this is, then, that it is the Christian way of life followed by the layfolk and priests within the Church—insofar as they also act as believers in their contact with each other and with their fellow men—which in fact leads to the hierarchical and liturgical way of life of the sacraments.

None of us has any right to complain about the slackness of our fellow Christians in following a sacramental way of life (in the latter sense). We are, after all, to blame for the fact that our way of life within the Church (in the wider sense) does not strike them as acceptable and its sacramental aspect is not recognized by most men in their day-to-day life. All this is quite simply due to the fact that the Church is much more than a hierarchy and that all Christians have the task of visibly representing the Church by what they do and indeed in their own persons. In this way, they will form a corporate part of the "*signum levatum in nationes*." Many baptized Catholics who lapse from the Faith do in fact retain a genuine religious outlook and a true spirit of charity, which they have in the first place derived from the Church. In this respect, then, they can not only be regarded as being truly religious, and indeed specifically Christian, but they are also, in a certain sense, still following the Church's way of life.[12] This also holds good for those who have never been baptized and who have thus, from the very beginning, always lived outside the Church. Such people, in fact, never live entirely outside the influence of the "Church" if, in this instance, the Church is seen as a reality which is present throughout the whole world. They practise Christianity in part, and the extent to which they live according to the Church's pattern depends upon the extent to which the ecclesial mode of life is present in them. They are, however, cut off—or they cut themselves off—from the full and bountiful self-revelation of the Church, and because they are deprived of full contact with the Church, there is always a danger that this relative share which they still have in the Church's way of life will be entirely smothered. But, so long as this relative share in the Church's life remains, the possibility that it will serve as a positive impulse towards full true membership of the Church

[12] What I am attempting to do here is to amplify to some extent what I have in fact already suggested by implication in my article "Op zoek naar Gods afwezigheid," which appeared in *Kultuurleven*, 24 (1957), pp. 276–91.

herself will also remain. And this is most likely to happen through vital contact with living, practising Christians.

What emerges from all this is that the sacramental Liturgy is certainly a culminating point of the Church's life, but that we ought not to identify the whole of the Church's life and the way it is lived out with the mystery of liturgical worship or with hierarchical activity. The sacraments are flashes of light within the whole of Christian life, which has a wider sphere of influence. To seek refuge in the Liturgy would be the result of a failure to appreciate the full value of the Church's role in society. To seek a solution outside the Liturgy, on the other hand, would also be the result of a failure to understand her eschatological character and the fact that she is involved in the profane life of the world—one might almost say the fact of her complicity with the profane world. It is possible to think of Christian life as an oscillation between two points— between the Church as an office and an institution (the official face the Church shows to the world) and her other aspect, equally a manifestation of her holiness—her world apostolate, carried out by her members, the faithful, in their different vocations, in their life as a family and in every contact between Christians and non-Christians.

It is precisely because the Church is a sign of grace and, as such, points particularly in an eschatological direction, calling men home, that she is constantly showing us a vision which goes beyond this world and indicates rather what is to come. But this eschatological orientation of the Church serves at the same time to remind us that we are, here and now, in this world, and are to live in it as Christians. By pointing out to us what is to come, the Church is also warning us that what is to come is certainly not yet here and that we ought not to stand, like the Apostles, gazing up at the cloud into which Christ has vanished and in which he will come again, but that our task is to go out to meet the world and bear visible witness there of Christian holiness.

What must emerge from our contact with our fellow men, at whatever level this contact takes place, is the fact that we are redeemed. This surely is the best sign of the Church's presence in the world. The Church is a visible invitation to men to accept charity, and it is precisely in this way that brotherly love can be understood to be the sacrament of contact with God—humanity and the love of God our redeemer for us are made visibly manifest in and through Christians themselves. This contact between men—acting as a visible manifestation of God's contact with man—is most meaningfully expressed in the office of the Church, that is, in the administration of the sacraments and in the Church's preaching of the word.

3. EVERYTHING IS "GRACE MADE VISIBLE"

Christ's visible and efficacious presence in the Church calls to mind the image of a stone thrown into a pond, making ripples spread out in continuous concentric circles. The ripples flow in all directions from this one central point. This point is the Church, the visible presence of Christ's grace on earth, and from it all movement can be seen to flow. The sacrament of the Eucharist is situated at the heart of this central point—the Eucharist is the focal point of Christ's real presence among us. Around this focal point can be seen the first radiant lights—the other six sacraments. This central mystery is, however, revealed to us only through the medium of the Church's preaching. Instructed and enlightened by this sacrament of the word, our vision is extended, and we can see the whole wide, continuous sphere of the Church's sacramental life. Grace is made visible for us in the Christian life itself of the faithful members of the Church and comes forward to meet us, within this life, offering itself to us. These sacramental ripples, however, continue to spread still further, though they gradually become less and less clearly defined—at this stage they are the sacramentals. Still further away from the centre they merge into the reality of the material and historical world of man, but this too is still under the influence of the triumphant *Kyrios*. In Christ, God ensures that everything will ultimately be for the good of those who love him. The sacraments, the word, all human conduct which proceeds from grace, the entire world of man—all these are, in their various ways, visible realities in this world of which the Lord avails himself, using his rich fund of inspiration in the most diverse means, to orientate man existentially towards God in Jesus Christ.

The result of this, then, is that the grace of Christ does not make itself felt in us only in an inward manner; it comes to us also in a visible form. This is the abiding consequence of the incarnation of the Son of God, the mystery of God made man. The veil which conceals this mystery is drawn aside in the Martyrology at Christmastime—*voluit consecrare mundum*. The Son's incarnation admits the world into a personal relationship between God and man and man and God. A close unity exists between "inward" and "outward" grace, but the whole created world becomes, through Christ's incarnation and the God-man relationship which is consequent upon it, an outward grace, an offer of grace in sacramental form. As a result of Christ's visible manifestation of himself in the world—a manifestation which embraces the whole world—the preaching and the sacraments of the Church can be regarded simply as the burning focal points within the entire concentration of this visible presence of grace which is the Church, for thanks to the Eucharist Christ is really *somatikos—physically*—present in her, and because of this physical presence also personally present.

7

THE MYSTICAL QUALITY OF THE
SACRAMENTS

In the previous chapter we have seen that the sacraments are culminating points in the more general sacramental way of life of
Christianity. This, however, raises an important problem. If we are
to sound the most profound depths of the tragedy which afflicts the
life of faith, we are bound to come sharply up against the experience that, however basically sincere our desire for grace and however genuine our trust in God may be, the resultant effects in our
active Christian life do not, despite frequent good moments, really
measure up completely to our desire for grace or our trust in God.
It is a common human experience that the frequent reception of the
sacraments does not always result in a mature Christian life. But
this is of course just what we hoped to gain from our frequentation
of the sacraments. We expected the strength of their grace, which is
much more powerful than our own disposition, to break through
into our lives and have an effect upon all our actions. This problem
brings us face to face with the mystical quality of the seven sacraments.

We must stress that contact with God is itself the sacrament
which ultimately bears fruit. It is within this sacrament of contact
with God that God's dispensation of grace and man's response to it
are intimately woven together. We should, however, be careful not
to infer from this that it is our own personal sacramental act which
sets the tone for this gift of grace. What in fact our sacramental act
does do is to set the tone for God's gift of grace insofar as we have

personally assimilated it. Let us consider this problem a little more closely.[1]

The Council of Trent laid down that grace is given to us "according to the measure which the Holy Ghost deems necessary for the justification of each separate individual, and also according to the disposition of the individual and the degree of his co-operation."[2] It is therefore certainly not possible for us to make the sort of statement which sometimes occurs in that type of theology which is based on almost mathematically precise reasoning, that given an identical disposition in two different subjects the same sacrament will produce exactly the same degree of grace in each recipient and that the rest is more or less dependent upon human intention and endeavour. A conclusion of this kind virtually ignores the *personal* quality of God's love and the fact that he loves each individual human being *separately,* and further that it is this utterly personal love directed separately to each individual person receiving the sacrament which forms the basis of the Church's sacramental system. God thus distributes the gift of his love as he deems fit.

On the other hand, however, the part played by the attitude of the person receiving the sacrament is clearly restrictive and limiting, for the perfectly simple reason that sanctifying grace is a personal communion with God, an intimate relationship fully shared by God who is infinite and man who is finite. It is therefore not possible for our religious disposition or personal effort to determine the measure of grace which is given to us. Our own effort certainly plays a part, but God's love is always greater than ours, and his grace always transcends our personal religious attitude. God's grace is so profuse and abundant that it constantly exceeds the measure of it which we are personally able to assimilate or to incorporate into the actions of our lives. This, then, is where the mystical quality of the sacramental life begins to become apparent. Weakness or infirmity means that though we may well have a sincere longing for grace and a genuine religious attitude, we are inconsistent in em-

---

[1] See *SH,* 1, pp. 575–7.   [2] *DB,* 799.

bodying these in our lives. Sacramental grace is, as we have already seen, a "curative" grace—one which restores us to health—and as such has the additional effect of actually *compensating* for any lack or impotence on our part, so long as our disposition remains sincerely religious. This effect is brought about by the spirit of Christ —the spirit which "helpeth our infirmity."[3] Sacramental grace has a corrective function, and makes up for our defects—the defects which continue to exist despite our sincere efforts.

The sanctifying effect of sacramental grace penetrates too deeply for its operation ever to be fully apparent in our active lives. It is in this gratuitous quality, this absolute generosity, that the mystical aspect of the redemption reaches its highest point. We certainly have no intention, in this connection, of making a kind of quietistic division between the theological and the moral ways of life, although there is always a tension between the two. It is, for example, a common experience to meet people whose lives are firmly based on a deep theological knowledge and yet whose moral conduct is often blatantly inconsistent. In the same way one comes across countless others whose lives are perfectly sound from the moral point of view, but in whom there is hardly any evidence of supernatural Christianity, stemming from a life informed by theology. But grace is always effective in the case of anyone who sincerely tries to do his best, and it is given so copiously that it far exceeds his power to assimilate it all. The practice of the sacramental life involves a certain risk, in the religious sense, for the Christian, in terms of the power of God's grace in him. He can, so to speak, go a long way with grace and he is able by virtue of its all-embracing power to assimilate it and transmute it into Christian action in his life. Yet, however sincere his disposition may be, he cannot keep up with this grace which constantly goes ahead of him and corrects the frailty and immaturity that still remain in him. This aspect of grace is traditionally known as *gratia praeveniens*—a wonderful phrase which implies the grace which not only *prevents* our folly,

[3] Rom. 8.26.

but which is also always a few steps *ahead* of us, with the result that we are constantly learning *now,* at this present moment, that God's grace was closer to us *then,* at that moment in the past, than we ever suspected it to be.

The objection may be made here that too little emphasis is still being placed on the personal character of grace. It would seem that, according to my reasoning, grace sanctifies us, at least partially, but without regard to the person in whom grace is operative as a person. This is, however, not the case. True, a certain element is sacrificed in the subject's personal appropriation of God's grace—this is the element of risk to which we have already alluded. But this element is not lost in the subject's personal submission to God's prevenient grace. In our faithful submission to grace, we permit God alone to put right what is still faulty in us, and in this way the seed of grace, which transcends our own ability to use it without sacrifice of any part, is still assimilated into our own personal spiritual life. Everything that we know of the spiritual life more than adequately confirms this view. The fact that we, as human beings, are inconsistent does cause a gulf to occur between God's grace and the use we make of it, but whenever our spiritual effort, however defective it may be, is sincerely made—this of course rules out a purely routine reception of the sacraments—this gulf is bridged by our faithful and trusting commitment of ourselves to the sanctifying and corrective influence of the spirit of Christ which is operative in the sacraments.

Thus it is possible for us to say that our personal spiritual experience is in fact the measure of grace that is suggested to us, and this must be thought of in terms of our submission to grace. This submission must in turn be seen in terms, not of our active use of the grace given to us, but of our readiness to be informed by its divine operation in us, that is to say, by the act by which God shows his confidence in us at the moment of its inception, when he seizes upon the spirit and calls upon it to submit to him. The maturity which accompanies the sacramental way of life based on sincerity of intention is thus, at the same time, first and foremost a mature attitude of submission to Christ as redeemer. The moral assimilation of grace always tends to lag behind. The sacramental relationship with God which is established in the case of those Christians who communicate frequently, but whose reception of the sacrament is not simply a matter of routine, may not necessarily result in a particularly striking or tangible improvement as far as their lives are concerned. We can, however, safely maintain that this relationship does bring about a *more profound interior growth* in their spiritual lives. It is possible for the lives of such people to achieve an astonishing degree of religious depth, and this spiritual growth in turn enables them to see with increasing clarity how inconsistent man's reaction to the limitless abundance of God's grace is.

This spiritual depth and Christian awareness is, of course, particularly noticeable among older people, despite the fact that they too continue to be visibly inconsistent. But lifelong practice of the sacramental way of life also visibly bears fruit in them. It cannot be denied that a certain degree of spiritual risk is involved in the sacramental life, whereby man tends to lose some of the grace given to him. But this is really due to God's boundless generosity—grace is gratuitously and liberally showered on man and is always ahead of him, so that he can do no more than murmur: *"Non nobis, Domine, non nobis, sed nomini tuo da gloriam!"* Grace, proceeding from this mystical depth of the soul, is able to bring about an imperceptible transformation in the Christian's moral attitude and in his whole life. It is then that the man whose life is based on sacramental grace begins to realize how grace surrounds him and guides all his actions, and to see his most deeply personal spiritual intentions appear before him in an entirely new and surprising light—as something that he can no longer understand simply on the basis of his own personality or explain in terms of human psychology. He gradually learns to realize that there is someone else at work within him—"So is every one that is born of the Spirit"[4] and, in the words of St. Paul, "And I live, now not I; but Christ liveth in me."[5]

[4] John 3.5–8.   [5] Gal. 2.20.

CONCLUSION

In considering the seven sacraments against the broad backcloth of the Church's sacramental system, we have managed to enter step by step into their essence. But all this amounts to a definition of the sacrament, of which the *signum efficax gratiae*—the effective sign of grace—provides us with no more than a pale, though not inaccurate, outline. The form, appearing as sacramental activity veiled in the symbols of the sacraments, is in every case objectively identical. It is the mystery of Christ's sanctification in and through his Church, and is expressed in God's *agape,* his condescending and generous love in Jesus Christ, in the love of his Church as the bride of Christ, and in man who as a believer emerges from himself and transcends his own limitations. All the foregoing come together in the sacrifice of the Mass and, at this point of contact, the final consummation is reached in the glory of the Lord himself. "You have shown yourself to me, Christ, face to face," says St. Ambrose: "It is in your sacraments that I meet you."[6] It is by the sacraments that we journey toward our final goal—the sacramental way is our hidden road to Emmaus, on which we are accompanied by our Lord. And even though we are not yet able to see him, we are conscious of his concealed presence near us, for when he addresses us through his sacraments, our hearts, intent upon his word, burn with longing and we turn at once to Christian action—in the words of the Evangelist, "Was not our heart burning within us whilst he spoke in the way?"[7]

[6] "Facie ad faciem te mihi, Christe, demonstrasti, in tuis te invenio sacramentis." (St. Ambrose, *Apologia Prophetae David,* 12, p. 58 [*PL,* 14, col. 875].)

[7] Luke 24.32.